Handbook of Adult Religious Education

Handbook of Adult Religious Education

edited by

NANCY T. FOLTZ

Religious Education Press
Birmingham, Alabama

Library of Congress Cataloging-in-Publication Data
Main entry under title:

Handbook of adult religious education.

   Includes bibliographies and index.
   Contents: The purpose and scope of adult religious
education / Leon McKenzie—Basic principles of adult
religious education / Nancy T. Foltz—Working with
young adults / Sharan B. Merriam and Trenton R. Ferro
—[etc]
   1. Christian education of adults—Addresses, essays,
lectures.   I. Foltz, Nancy T.
BV1488.H36   1986   268'.434   85-25754
ISBN 0-89135-052-7

Religious Education Press, Inc.
5316 Meadow Brook Road
Birmingham, Alabama 35242
10 9 8 7 6

Religious Education Press publishes books exclusively in religious education
and in areas closely related to religious education. It is committed to enhancing
and professionalizing religious education through the publication of serious,
significant, and scholarly works.

To my husband Robert Scott Foltz

Contents

Introduction

A sandcastle sits on the corner of my office desk. I put it there to remind me to dream. A card came in the box with the castle that said dreams are plentiful and the castle is a fortress for my dreams. Time, so the card said, would not destroy the sandcastle. Weekly schedules and routine tasks are important, but I need to remind myself to take time to dream. Over the years I have learned that often my planning and dreaming time at the castle becomes my realistic plans for tomorrow.

The most exciting adult religious education I do begins with someone else's needs, visions, and dreams. For example, a minister came to talk about reconstructing the faith of his church's leaders after a fire burned the church to the ground.

A lay leader was standing with the pastor and together they cried as the church building burned. The pastor noticed writing on the burning church wall and asked what it was. The lay leader explained that the young people requested permission to write faith slogans on the outside wall before the new siding was put on. So . . . through the flames the pastor and lay leader read the slogan: "Shout faith!"

We began to list what people had done to reconstruct the faith of others, to rebuild the confidence of leaders. After a couple of hours, he looked at the planning board where we had listed the work done, and the dreams of what could be, and said "I didn't know we had done so much. When I came I wasn't sure where to begin."

Adult religious education opportunities such as this present themselves in ways and times we least expect. For a pastor of a burning church there was a message of hope, "Shout faith!" So, out of the hot embers came the possibility for new dreams.

Adult religious education is more than classes, seminars, workshops, denominations, religious organizations, and buildings. It is about people. Adult religious education is about adulthood—how adults learn, what transitions occur in adulthood, and how religious educators can assist people to find meaning in life, to contribute, and to share their faith. Adults are capable of doing more and being more than filling an office, or carrying out a specific responsibility. The challenge of adult religious education is in the lifestyle lived.

It is impossible for religious educators to work without knowledge of adult education. This handbook is designed to be a resource tool for the adult professional as he or she does ministry. The handbook is to inform, affirm, and encourage the religious educator. Adults are complex beings with intense needs to learn and to find meaning in life. Adult religious educators are in a critical position to aid the adult in this search to find meaning, to contribute, and to produce. The handbook is to stimulate ideas about adult religious education and to be a launching pad for new dreams of ministry. This handbook is intended to do just that!

The handbook is to encourage professionals who observe that the majority of adults are not interested in present ongoing adult educational efforts. There is a profile of the adult throughout the book.

The handbook is to bridge a gap between the field of adult education and adult religious education. The contributors were selected for their contribution in both fields.

The first two chapters provide the foundations for adult religious education. The foundational work of Leon McKenzie in *The Religious Education of Adults* is expanded in chapter 1, "The Purpose and Scope of Adult Religious Education." McKenzie challenges educators to ask the pragmatic question "What is adult religious education?" McKenzie provides illumination on the old but complicated discussion of defining how theory and practice relate to one another. He challenges educators to encourage and to engage learners in critical reflection and evaluation of their faith. Ultimately, he suggests, adult religious educators are facilitating learners to recognize their mission as bringers of meaning to the world. This chapter is not only foundational to the handbook, but to an understanding of adult religious education.

In the second chapter on "Basic Principles of Adult Religious Education," I take a look at research on the adult as learner. Biological, intellectual, and social changes that occur through adulthood are examined. The intent of the chapter is to present current research in light of the task of ministry. A profile of the adult learner and ten principles to apply in adult religious education are discussed.

The next seven chapters focus on periods in adult life. Some are age-related and others are related to circumstances. Sharan Merriam and Trenton Ferro combine their efforts to write chapter 3, "Working With Young Adults." Six vignettes open the chapter, each representing young adulthood with its commonalities and diversities. The chapter is informative, descriptive, and challenging, with program suggestions for the adult religious educators. Three basic issues for young adults are outlined; an evaluation matrix is presented. The chapter offers a clear description of young adulthood.

"Working with Middle-Aged Adults" is the subject of chapter 4, written by R. E. Y. Wickett. Wickett integrates the mid-life years and the spiritual, religious, and psycho-social needs of the adult learner. The role and function of the adult religious educator is clearly delineated. Wickett is the author of the only study to date to examine adult learning projects on religious development. Wickett was a student of Allen Tough from the Ontario Institute for Studies in Education. Wickett's research on Adult Learning Projects and Religious Education with middle-aged adults will be a significant contribution to adult religious educators.

Chapter 5, "Working With Older Adults," asks, "How can older adults, looking back over their life and their world and facing the knowledge of their mortality, affirm life with joy and hope?" With the American population aging, adult professionals must address this critical question. Linda Jane Vogel offers a model and strategies for developing ministries with older adults. The author's experience and study combine to bring both theoretical and practical ideas to this chapter. The author's intent is to realistically assist the older adult to accept limitations while expanding visions.

R. Michael Harton speaks in chapter 6 about "Working with Educators of Adults." He challenges the professional to be "more than a promoter of denominational programs for adults or an 'activities director for adults.'" The educator described by Harton establishes philosophy, cooperates in setting objectives, assesses needs, and facilitates adult learning. His historical tracing of the profession sheds light on the past as well as the future.

Chapter 7, "Working with Single Parents," by Richard Hunt, discusses ministries by, to, for, and on behalf of single parents. He suggests options for a general program, a cooperative community effort or special groups to serve the needs of single parents. A community survey instrument is included in the chapter as well as specific questions for personal reflection. Hunt's perception of the single parent possibilities for ministry adds vision and insight to adult religious education.

Often the church is last to know about the separation or divorce of persons within the church. Neil Paylor writes about the pain and needs of persons who are separated or divorced. Chapter 8, "Working with Adults in Separation and Divorce," begins with a counseling session with members of the Anderson family. Adult religious educators can benefit by understanding the historical "Augustinian connection" which affects our present perceptions of marriage, parenthood, and divorce. Although divorce is an issue and experience that, as Paylor suggests, affects us all, few are equipped to handle the pain and circumstances which surround this complicated issue. Resources and a perspective are offered as a way to inform educators on the subject. The historical tracing from the time of Saint Augustine offers a refreshing reminder that present perceptions are shaped and molded from our reflection on historical experiences.

Mary Louise Mueller's chapter 9, "Working with Adults in Death-Related Circumstances," draws our attention, not to death which she suggests we can only assimilate, but rather to the process of dying which the adult religious educator can enhance. Bereavement, grief, and mourning are discussed. The role of the adult religious educator is written in a creative format, using "mutual pretense dialogue," between the dying patient and four successive "visitors." Each of the four visitors offers a different awareness content.

Dreaming about the future and what adult religious education might look like is the purpose of chapter 10, "The Future of Adult Religious Education." In this chapter I outline a trend schematic with five trends for the future. Each trend is discussed with suggestions for the role of the adult religious educator.

The chapter begins by examining what presently is and suggests using a trend schematic to envision what might be. Dreaming is a realistic way to project what could possibly occur, and to be futuristic as well as practical is the task of the last chapter.

This book could not have been written by one person. The collective expertise of each specialist was needed. I appreciate the willingness of the contributors to write and carefully research the manuscript for theoretical as well as practical chapters. To Harjie Likins, Hedwig Pregler, and especially Clara Lou Kerr I am grateful for their suggestions to improve the manuscript. There is a special word of appreciation to Leon McKenzie and James Michael Lee for their constant support and encouragement throughout the project. To my husband, and my sons Drayton and Nelson, who put up with my hours at the desk to complete the manuscript, I am grateful.

This handbook was once a thought wished and dreamed about at the castle!

Chapter 1

The Purposes and Scope of
Adult Religious Education

LEON McKENZIE

Any examination of the purposes and scope of adult religious education must begin with the question, "What is adult religious education?" At first glance the question seems irrelevant and even impertinent. Adult religious education, after all, is being "done" by thousands of religious educators. Graduate programs in religious education purport to prepare religious educators for the work of adult religious education. The positing of the question, "What is adult religious education?" seems to imply that what is being done in the field of adult religious education is somehow lacking.

My immediate intent in addressing the question is neither to prejudice the work of religious educators of adults nor to call into doubt the saliency of graduate programs in religious education. I hasten to emphasize this because at least one reviewer of my recent book on adult religious education indicated that my critique of the practice of adult religious education was replete with "vociferous chidings."[1] Evidently my remarks anent the status quo in adult religious education were interpreted as querulous and negative.

Progress in any professional field is gained only through criticism of the status quo and the paradigm that supports the conventional wisdom in that field. A professional field can grow only when the body of theory and knowledge that constitutes that field is subjected to systematic scrutiny. Fundamental questions need to be raised to preserve a professional field from sclerosis and stagnation. My immediate primary intent in raising the question,

"What is adult religious education?" is to contribute to the advancement of the field of adult religious education. This must be clearly understood from the beginning of this chapter. I know full well that the remarks of persons perceived to be curmudgeons possess little credibility.

The question, "What is adult religious education?" may be viewed as irrelevant for another reason. We live in a technological-pragmatic culture. Everyone is fascinated by techniques, methods, procedures, and prescriptions. Discussions of a theoretical nature are discounted in the marketplace of ideas. This is true in the general field of adult education and also in the specialized field of adult religious education. Unfortunately the linkage between theory and practice is seldom a concern of practitioners of adult religious education. And yet, one cannot have good practice without good theory. One's practice of adult religious education is an instantiation of theory. Bruce Suttle has shown that theory and practice are co-relational. Educational theories are practice-oriented; effective educational practice is theory-dependent.[2] Spencer Maxcy has argued that philosophy or theory governs the relationships between instructor and learners, between learners and subject matter, and between subject matter and world at large. Theory enables educators in the making of choices that separate what is worthwhile from what is trivial in education.[3] Educational practice devoid of a theoretical foundation is akin to the implementation of a series of gimmicks. The question, "What is adult religious education?" is, then, the most *practical* of questions. This may seem paradoxical, but the most profound truths are perhaps framed in paradox.

What Do Human Beings Want?
We can best approach the question regarding the nature of adult religious education by addressing another question: What do human beings want out of life?

In the early part of this century Sigmund Freud claimed that the driving forces of personality were instinctual urges represented in what he called the id, or the "pleasure principle."[4] Followers of Freud, perhaps in an oversimplification of his ideas, suggested that the repression of instinctual urges led to psychological problems. The way was then open for popular writers to develop full-blown philosophies of hedonism. Popular hedonism maintains that what human beings want more than anything else is pleasure.

No doubt there are adults who relentlessly pursue pleasure as if pleasure were the *summum bonum*. We may be forgiven for thinking, however, that these people have not developed fully as human beings, that they have become fixated at an early stage of adult development or have regressed to an early stage of development. Anyone whose experience of life has moved beyond infantile and early adolescent levels of consciousness is aware that pleasure cannot qualify as the ultimate goal of life.

Alfred Adler, an erstwhile disciple of Freud, had another idea of what human beings really wanted. He rejected Freudian orthodoxy and argued that people really wanted power.[5] They want to overcome feelings of inferiority that originate in childhood. They want to be recognized as masters of their destinies and as achievers of notable goals. Perhaps Adler was correct to some extent. We have all known individuals whose every waking hour was devoted to the accumulation of wealth, the attainment of honors and social prestige, or the acquisition of political, social, economic, or ecclesiastical power. Again, it is fair to assume that such persons have not fully developed as human beings. They have failed to think seriously about their last end, death, which is to say that they have failed to think seriously about life.

The psychotherapist Viktor Frankl learned in a Nazi death camp that pleasure was fleeting and power ephemeral. He proposed that what human beings really want is existential meaning. Man is a logothropic animal.[6] His insight was keen. Meaning is crucial for human beings. The total orientation of the practical hedonist toward pleasure is little more than a misdirected attempt to secure meaning. The urgent striving for power is largely a clumsy endeavor to locate meaning.

What Is Meaning?

The concept of meaning has many facets and different levels of connotation, perhaps as many levels of connotation as the Greek word *logos*.[7] Meaning is a framework for understanding life, a ground upon which life can be situated, a perspective that yields an integrated vision of the world. Meaning is a source of clarity that makes the cumulative events of a person's life coalesce into a coherent totality. Meaning is a polar star that provides a sense of direction. Meaning is a model that helps us shape our behavior and respond to life events in a particular way. Meaning is a theory of existence based on a commitment to an all-surpassing ideal, to an overarching value, to a regnant cause, or to a person or persons who occupy positions of centrality in our worldview.

I view meaning specifically as an interpretive structure or framework that defines a person's being-in-the-world and his or her existential stance toward reality. A religious framework is based on a definite faith commitment and on a set of faith affirmations and values that serve as first principles for reflection and action.

Meaning can also be apprised in a philosophical or nontheological sense. That is, a person can develop an interpretive framework that is based on purely rational assumptions. Faith affirmations can be replaced by philosophical assumptions that serve as first principles for reflection and action. The difference between a purely philosophical framework and a religious framework relates to the nature of the first principles which serve as a ground for the framework. Philosophical first principles are derived from a rational analysis of reality; religious first principles are conceived as deriving from a person's response to revelatory events, a response that implies a loving relationship with God. Nonreligious persons, then, can and do possess meaning structures. In the present context, however, meaning is defined in terms of its religious connotation.

MEANING AND RELIGIOUS EDUCATION

The notion of meaning is crucial to human existence. The notion of meaning is also essential to any attempt at delineating the purposes of religious education. I view religious education as a process that enables persons: 1) to acquire meaning, 2) to explore and expand meaning, and 3) to express meaning in a productive manner. The religious educator is a facilitator who helps people gain meaning, explore and expand the meaning structures they possess, and express their meanings effectively.

The Acquisition of Meaning

We come into the world with question marks in our heads. We strive for intelligibility and purpose. We seek a perspective or framework for our being-in-the-world. The first purpose of religious education is to make a particular meaning framework available to children and neophytes in the faith community. Religious education provides a structure for living. Children and adult neophytes need to know their roots. Children need to know and experience the religious tradition into which they were born. Adult neophytes need to know more fully the religious tradition they are to embrace formally.

Having meaning, having an initial meaning framework, provides learners with order and stability in their lives. Having meaning assists a learner in developing his or her identity. One's existential stance toward reality is founded on a particular tradition and continuity with the past.

Exploring and Expanding Meaning

To have meaning signifies that a person has an initial framework for defining his or her being-in-the-world. A person can have a meaning structure, however, and still seek further meaning. The question marks in our heads are never fully erased. The religious educator, particularly the religious educator of adults, can help learners in the quest that is mandated by a seeking faith. This is done in a number of ways.

First, learners can be helped in the exploration of the richness of their religious heritage. The vast richness of any religious tradition cannot be assimilated in an initial meaning framework. Any given religious tradition is finely nuanced and deserves ongoing study to the end that one's initial meaning framework is expanded.

Second, learners can be helped to explore and expand their initial meaning structures by relating the religious tradition to their life experiences. The events of a person's life can be elucidated in terms of the tradition. This is an extremely important kind of learning. The simple transmission of tradition will be perceived as irrelevant if the tradition is not shown to be linked to life as it is lived by the learner.

Third, and most important, adolescent and adult learners should be helped to question the religious tradition critically. If the unexamined life is not worth living neither is the unexamined faith. If we look at our life experiences in terms of the religious tradition, we must also look at the religious tradition in terms of our life experiences. It is only by means of critical reflection on and evaluation of one's religious commitment that faith becomes truly personal and more than a mere submission to religious convention. The large numbers of adults who are only conventionally and nominally religious may be attributed to the fact that some religious leaders have stressed obedience to religious leadership over adult critical reflection. This problem is particularly endemic in Roman Catholicism.[8] As a result, many adults go through life equipped solely with the meaning framework they acquired in childhood, a meaning framework that is inadequate for the living of a personal adult faith.

There may be some who object to the proposition that a person should submit religious tradition and teachings to critical scrutiny. It should not be forgotten, however, that the critical appraisal of meaning structures is a process that is an integral part of many adult lives. We cannot effectively forbid adults to be critical. Willy-nilly, many adults will subject their childhood beliefs to critical analysis in spite of exhortations to the contrary. Further, it is better to help adults appraise religious tradition from within the confines of church than to fail by default and allow them to critique religious teachings outside the context of church. Critical inquiry need not be adversarial, mean-spirited, or filled with the hubris that characterizes contemporary agnostic scientism. Critical inquiry can be undertaken constructively or destructively. It is the task of the religious educator to help adults understand this difference.

What is at issue here relates to what Jack Mezirow calls perspective transformation. Mezirow defines a meaning perspective as "the structure of psycho-cultural assumptions within which new experience is assimilated and transformed by one's past experience."[9] Mezirow suggests that the continuing maturation of the adult is associated with perspective taking and perspective sharing. The adult who remains outside the ongoing process of perspective transformation does so at the risk of remaining immature as a human being.

Expressing Meaning

The third purpose of religious education revolves around helping learners become adept at expressing meaning. We live in a world that is terribly disordered, a world experienced by some as meaningless in its totality. Our world is filled with evidences of alienation, hatred, violence, and exploitation. The world in many of its aspects is meaningless. The process of religious education should prepare learners to interpret these evidences of meaningless as situations that call for action.

Religious education should help learners recognize their mission as bringers of meaning to the world. Religious education must be action oriented. It is not enough that learners are equipped to interpret the world; they must be prepared to change the world under the guidance of their religious convictions.

NOTIONAL AND RELATIONAL LEARNING

The religious educator assists learners in the acquisition of meaning, helps learners to explore and expand their meaning structures, and aids learners in recognizing that they must live their faith. These purposes are served by means of the systematic facilitation of learning. But what kinds of learning are to be facilitated?

There are two fundamental modes of learning in group or classroom situations. I call these modes notional learning and relational learning. We are all familiar with notional learning. Notional learning involves the discussion of ideas, concepts, religious teachings, biblical symbols, and doctrinal propositions. When we think of adult religious education we ordinarily think of bible study classes, discussion groups that attend to religious themes, or lectures that focus on explicit theological topics. We think of the *manifest* content of instruction and what topics are covered in a curriculum or program. The notional approach to learning is not without its power and relevance. But I wish to emphasize here relational learning: the often hidden learning that occurs from relating to others in a community of learners.

Relational Learning

Gabriel Marcel stated that for human beings *esse* is *co-esse,* that is, "to be" means "to be with."[10] It is impossible to be an individual absolutely. We define ourselves only in relation to others. "To be" means we participate in life with others. We gain our perspectives, our values, and our beliefs not in isolation but rather in terms of social intercourse.

The social psychologist Edgar Schein noted that our opinions and beliefs are influenced by others in the group or subculture to which we belong.[11] The very image we have of ourselves is conditioned by our membership in a community. Our fundamental values depend to a great extent on the support we receive from those we perceive as significant others. The way we think, our basic assumptions about life, the way we feel and behave, all of these are influenced by social processes.

George Kneller defined enculturation as "a process by which a person absorbs the modes of thought, action, and feeling that constitute his culture."[12] The operative word in the definition, I suggest, is *absorbs.* Relational learning, in contrast to notional learning, is learning that takes place as a consequence of the learner's exposure to contextual meta-language.

The interpersonal environment in which we find ourselves speaks a subtle language all of its own. The social milieu in which we move has a vocabulary and grammar all of its own. Edward Hall, in writing about proxemics, or the communicative function of spatial distance between people, called attention to "the silent language" of communication.[13] In a wider and more profound sense, any time a person is in a more or less continuing association with others, a meta-language is addressed to each member of the community. The relational ambience in which we are situated conveys subtle but dramatic messages.

The idea of relational learning is really not new except in nomenclature. Karl Marx claimed that a person's consciousness is determined by his social being and in so doing stated the root proposition for the study of the sociology of knowledge.[14] John Dewey wrote of the "unconscious influence of the environment" that is so pervasive that it affects "every fiber of character and mind." He also wrote that "social environment forms the mental and emotional disposition of behavior in individuals by engaging them in activities that arouse and strengthen certain impulses, that have certain purposes and entail certain consequences."[15] James Michael Lee has shown that the instructional process is also a definite content of instruction. "Process . . . is not simply a way to achieving content; process is itself an authentic content."[16]

What should be common knowledge among religious educators does not commonly guide the activities of most religious educators because of their tendency to become totally involved in the facilitation of notional learning. The consciousness of many educators, including religious educators of adults, is almost fixated at the level of notional learning. Contrary to the assumption that the manifest content of instruction is most important in religious education and that the best religious educators are subject matter specialists, I suggest that the social environment formed when learners come together in a group can have greater impact on the learners than the impact produced by the learning of explicit subject matters. The context of religious education is the kind of content that is most influential vis-à-vis meaning frameworks.

Marshall McLuhan was right but we probably valued his observation only as a well-turned slogan: The medium *is* the message. Regarding the religious education of adults, the community of learners *is* the kerygma. The social process *is* the proclamation. The context *is* the communication. We do not acquire meaning, explore and expand meaning structures, and learn how to express meaning primarily on the basis of the study of religious abstractions (although such studies are important and influential), but rather on the basis of lived experiences in a community of shared values. The primary dimension of religious education is delineated by the New Testament concept *koinonia:* fellowship.

The existence of church-related schools, from the elementary to university levels, attests that the context of education has been recognized by many as relevant to religious learning. Students in church-related schools acquire, explore and expand, and learn how to express religious meaning even when they are engaged in such apparently mundane endeavors as math, spelling, and English grammar. These students live each school day in a context that is fraught with meaning. Their association with teachers and other students in a community shaped by specific religious values communicates meaning. The pervasive influence of environment of which Dewey wrote impinges subtly on the awareness of the student and contributes powerfully to the development of a faith consciousness.

Kerygma, Diakonia, and Koinonia

Allow me to approach an analysis of adult religious education from a slightly different perspective, a perspective that may have more appeal to those accustomed to the language of theology. The purposes of adult religious education may be delineated in terms of three New Testament concepts that identify the mission of the church. The church exists to make meaning available, to assist people in exploring and expanding meaning structures, and to facilitate the expression of meaning through actions that remediate human problems. The church accomplishes these tasks by reason of its kerygmatic, diakonic, and koinoniac functions.

In its kerygmatic function (*kerygma* = message) the church heralds the announcement that Jesus stands-present-again in the world (*anastasis* = resurrection), and that this standing-present-again is a sign of Yahweh's affirmation of Jesus and humanity. The resurrection is also an attestation that ultimate meaning revolves around the teachings of Jesus. Christian meaning, and its acquisition, exploration, and expression, finds its norm in the standing-again of Jesus as present in the world. Corresponding to this function in an explicit sense, educational programing will address biblical themes and theological reflections that elucidate the resurrection as the key to the meaning of human history.

In its diakonic function (*diakonia* = service) the church is the instrument by which the resurrected Jesus attends to the spiritual and corporal needs of human beings. The servant church is ideally a healing presence that reaches out to anyone who is in need. Corresponding to this function educational programing will focus on the learning needs of people, however mundane these needs may appear. Those who learn, for example, how to prepare nutritious meals or how to balance their home budgets in the context of the parish or local church come into contact with the resurrected Jesus no less than those who study Matthew's gospel. The message of Jesus' standing-again as present in the world is implicit in any educational programing that aims to serve the needs of learners.

In its koinoniac function (*koinonia*=fellowship) the church is a community that points to the eschatological community that is to come in the Absolute Future and a community that serves as a model for the ideal human community. We have already seen that the church as community supports and sustains the acquisition, exploration, and expression of meaning through the relational learning that occurs in the church as context for learning. Further, the message of Jesus' standing-again is implicit in this context.

All three of these functions are absolutely necessary to the mission of the church. Lacking the kerygmatic function the church would become simply a social agency; there would be no reason for Christians *qua* Christians to form a community that serves as a model for humanity and as a prolepsis of the Absolute Future. Lacking its service function the church would be reduced to the status of a vast discussion club that bears no fruit in real life. Lacking its koinoniac function the church could not effectively proclaim the message of Yahweh's affirmation of Jesus and humanity in a language that transcends rational-discursive modes of communication.

What is important to understand in the light of this reasoning is that religious learning takes place not only as a consequence of rational-discursive treatments of theological topics but also as a result of learners being-served and being-together. This is to say that the kergyma is instantiated in the serving community in a trans-discursive or existential mode. While programs that address explicit theological subject matters are altogether appropriate, programs that bring people together in the context of church and programs that address the everyday needs of people also explicate the implications of the resurrection at a different level of experience.

No doubt theologians and others whose orientation toward meaning is rational-discursive possess a learning style that serves them well in the acquisition, exploration, and expression of meaning. But the majority of people, I suggest, attend to meaning at a level of experience that is largely emotive, interpersonal, and nondiscursive. The two orientations are not mutually exclusive, but they are dramatically different. Most adults, I submit, attend to the acquisition, exploration, and expression of meaning in terms of being-with others, social intercourse in the everyday world, and liturgical celebrations. Meaning becomes available in the experience of being-with others and in the experience of serving or being-served. Not to understand this opens the probability of fallacious thinking. In literature we come across the use of the pathetic fallacy quite often. By means of the pathetic fallacy the writer attributes human feelings and emotions to inanimate objects. To speak of the anger of the December wind helps convey a dramatic image of the wind. Similar to this is the fallacy of attributing our thoughts and feelings to others on the assumption that our thoughts and feelings are universal. Religious educators sometimes assume that their rational-discursive learning styles and their interest in theological speculation is representative of the learning styles and interests of most adults. Such an assumption should be disputed.

We arrive, then, at a conclusion that has already been advanced: Educational programing in the local church or parish need not be restricted to subject matters that are commonly perceived as "religious."

THE SCOPE OF ADULT RELIGIOUS EDUCATION

Adult religious education may be religious in several senses. Education is obviously religious when the explicit content of instruction or subject matter is religious. Education may also be religious by virtue of the intentionality of the teacher and learners. The Methodist clergyman and educator John H. Vincent enunciated in the nineteenth century the proposition that for the religious person all education is religious.[17] Finally, as I have tried to show above, education may be religious by virtue of the context of education and the interpersonal processes that occur within that context. The implications of this for program planning in the local church or parish deserve full consideration.

The religious education of adults need not be restricted to the study of theological, biblical, or liturgical topics. Any legitimate educational topic can qualify as religious education when the instructional process occurs within a religious context. Some religious educators are quick to grasp the validity of this viewpoint. Experience has taught me, however, that this position meets with immediate rejection by many religious educators of adults. Many religious educators narrowly trained as subject matter specialists in theology are seemingly unwilling or unable to espouse a perspective that calls for a departure from the status quo.

The chief objection raised to education that does not treat explicitly religious themes is that the local church or parish should not compete with other agencies that provide adult education in the community. At this writing I am involved in research regarding homophilous adults. Homophily is the psychological construct that characterizes adults who prefer to associate with others who are similar to themselves. Initial research findings indicate that many adults do not participate voluntarily in education because they do not wish to associate with others who are perceived to be "different" in terms of values and demographic variables. Many homophilous adults will not attend educational activities sponsored by college continuing education departments or other community agencies. Opportunities for education can be made available to these adults only by those social institutions with which they are familiar, institutions such as the local church or parish.

Of course, if the question is framed in terms of whether churches should compete with other community agencies in attempting to influence the values of adults, there can be only one answer to the question.

Another objection refers to the distinction between the sacred and the secular. "Adult religious education should not deal with secular subject matters," is the rejoinder. Such an objection, of course, evidences a deficit of understanding vis-à-vis relational learning and an exclusionary concern for notional learning. The objection is also based on a neo-Platonic bifurcation of reality into two spheres: the sacred and the secular. Such a distinction, carried to its logical consequences, would have us believe that religion must not be concerned about politics, social justice, economic policies that affect the poor, or world hunger. The distinction must be repudiated by anyone who believes that religion must relate to real life as it is lived in the workaday world.

Finally, it is objected that it is not possible to implement activities in different program areas because of limited fiscal and human resources. "We cannot schedule four or five different kinds
of courses during the fall because our parish does not have the
money to hire the teachers," I was once told by a director of adult
religious education. It is quite possible, however, to offer a wide
variety of different programs if those responsible for adult religious education in the parish begin thinking of adults in the
parish as potential instructors. In any congregation there are
many members who are knowledgeable in many subject matters.
These people should be recruited to share their expertise with
others in the parish. As administrator and coordinator of the
total curriculum, the person responsible for adult religious education can help volunteer leaders/teachers develop simple lesson
plans and implement these plans effectively. Once we begin viewing adults not only as consumers of education but as providers as
well the problem of available resources does not appear to be
significant.

Pragmatic Considerations

If adult religious education theory does not take into account
pragmatic considerations, it is doubtful that theory can ever be
put into practice. The theory of adult religious education outlined
here is congruent with what we know about adults in respect to
educational activities.

Adults will not seek out educational activities until they have
arrived at a "readiness for learning." Adults follow their felt needs
and interests in regard to participation in education. They have
their own agendas. They are largely self-directing and vote with
their feet when they like or dislike a particular theme proposed
for study. They will respond favorably only to programs that they
perceive as relevant to *their* concerns.[18] The determination of
program topics should be based on a systematic study of the
needs and interests of the adults to be served by the educational
program.[19]

This is not to say that programs addressing theological and
biblical topics are to be ruled out. Adults have individual educational needs and interests. But they also have responsibilities as
members of a congregation and as members of the church. Cer-

tain needs may be ascribed to adults by religious educators so that adults may fulfill their responsibilities as members of the congregation and church. But such ascribed needs, and the educational objectives deriving from these needs, cannot be met until adults become willing to participate in educational programs. And they will not participate in educational programs in any satisfactory numbers until they have been *cultivated* as regular participants in education in the context of the local church. That is, the agendas of pastors and religious educators cannot be addressed until the agendas of adults are met and until they feel comfortable about regular participation in parish educational programs.

Recently a religious educator asked me to explain why attendance at a peace and justice seminar was so meager, given the importance of the topic. My initial response was perhaps enigmatic. "You did not have good attendance because of what you did *not* do three years ago." Adults must be cultivated over a period of time as clients of the educational services provided by the local church. Barriers to participation must be broken down incrementally over time by facilitating the entry of adults into learning situations. An adult may attend a parish program on first aid in the home, a program on backyard gardening, and a program on family communications before the meta-language of the context urges that person to attend a peace and justice seminar. What is needed, therefore, is a long-range view, patience, and strategic rather than tactical thinking.

I hasten to add that even if a person does not decide to participate in a peace and justice seminar, the meta-language of the religious context will probably have important things to "say" to that person.

CONCLUSION

What is sorely needed is nothing less than a thorough reconceptualization of the purposes and scope of adult religious education. This reconceptualization should be based not only on theological perspectives but also on principles of adult education, an understanding of educational anthropology and contextual meta-language, research information regarding adult development, and on the principles of marketing. The notion of marketing may be offensive to those who do not understand that the concept is largely equivalent to responsiveness to the felt needs and interests of consumers, but the central ideas of marketing must also serve as a basis for rethinking the meaning of adult religious education.[20] It is hoped that this chapter will contribute something to the reconceptualization process.

(This chapter represents an expanded version of the 1984 Gheens Lecture on religious education presented to the faculty and student body of Southern Baptist Theological Seminary, Louisville, Kentucky.)

NOTES

1. See Trenton Ferro's review of *The Religious Education of Adults* in *Adult Education Quarterly* XXXIV, no. 3 (1984), pp. 179-182.

2. Bruce Suttle, "Adult Education: No Need for Theories?" *Adult Education* XXXII, no. 2 (1982), p. 106.

3. Spencer Maxcy, "How Philosophy Can Work for the Adult Educator," *Lifelong Learning* IV, no. 4 (1980), p. 9.

4. The idea that human beings primarily seek pleasure in the initial phases of development was not original with Freud. St. Augustine observed this same phenomenon. Freud had the misfortune of too many eager disciples whose minds were not as sharp as their master's. For a fuller treatment of Freud's ideas see *The Standard Edition of the Complete Psychological Works of Sigmund Freud,* ed. and trans. James Strachey (London: Hogarth Press, 1953), Vol. XVI, pp. 320ff.

5. Alfred Aldler, *Understanding Human Nature* (New York: Fawcett Publications, 1954), pp. 65-80.

6. Viktor Frankl, *Man's Search for Meaning* (New York: Washington Square Press, 1967).

7. In a standard lexicon over five columns are devoted to explicating the various usages of *logos.* If I were pressed to render the notion of meaning into the Greek language, I would do so in terms of *logos.* The phrase *kai o logos sarks egeneto* in the Fourth Gospel (1:14) provides much food for thought when *logos* is interpreted as "meaning" instead of "word." See H. Liddell and R. Scott, eds., *A Greek-English Lexicon,* 9th ed. (London: Oxford University Press, 1958), pp. 1057-1059.

8. In a study of random samples of Southern Baptists and Roman Catholics, it was discovered that only 19.3 percent of the Southern Baptists viewed faith as obedience to religious leaders while 53.2 percent of the Roman Catholics viewed faith in these terms. See Leon McKenzie and R. M. Harton, "Faith and Its Development: A Study of Southern Baptists and Roman Catholics," *Review and Expositor* LXXX, no. 4 (1983), p. 598.

9. Jack Mezirow, "A Critical Theory of Adult Learning and Education," *Adult Education* XXXII, no. 1 (1981), p. 6.

10. Quoted in Vincent Miceli's *Ascent to Being* (New York: Desclee, 1965), pp. 1-45.

11. Edgar Schein, "Interpersonal Communication, Group Solidarity, and Social Influence, in *Groups and Organizations,* ed. B. Hinton and H. Reitz (Belmont, Calif.: Wordsworth, 1971), pp. 266ff.

12. George Kneller, *Educational Anthropology* (New York: Wiley and Sons, 1965), p. 42. Kneller goes on to point out that enculturation is a more inclusive term than socialization. The latter term refers only to the process by which a person becomes a member of society.

13. Edward Hall, *The Silent Language* (New York: Anchor Press, 1973).

14. Quoted in Peter L. Berger and Thomas Luckmann, *The Social Construction of Reality* (New York: Anchor Books, 1967), pp. 5-6.

15. John Dewey, *Democracy and Education* (New York: The Free Press, 1944), p. 16. While I am not a Deweyite, I strongly recommend this book for its penetrating insights into the theoretical foundations of education.

16. James Michael Lee, "Process Content in Religious Instruction," in *Process and Relationship,* ed. Iris Cully and Kendig Cully, (Birmingham, Ala.: Religious Education Press, 1978), pp.22f.

17. See Clinton Hartley Grattan's *In Quest of Knowledge* (New York: Arno Press, 1971), p. 168.

18. For a fuller treatment of the charactcristics of the adult learner, see Malcolm S Knowles, *The Modern Practice of Adult Education,* rev. ed. (Chicago: Follett Publishers, 1980), pp. 40-59.

19. A procedural model for the systematic study of adult educational needs and interests can be found in my book *The Religious Education of Adults* (Birmingham, Ala.: Religious Education Press, 1982), pp. 237ff.

20. See P. Kotler's *Marketing for Nonprofit Organizations* (Englewood Cliffs, N.J.: Prentice-Hall, 1975).

Chapter 2

Basic Principles of Adult Religious Education

NANCY T. FOLTZ

INTRODUCTION

The reconceptualizing called for by Leon McKenzie in chapter 1 begins with an understanding of the goals of adult religious education.

Educators are challenged to stimulate adults to exploration, expansion, and the expression of meaning. Reluctant adults most often need motivation which will cause them to participate in new educational processes. Finding the key to challenge and motivation is both the prerogative and the obligation of those who would engage in significant educational pioneering endeavors.

From the vantage point of meaning we can examine the basic principles that constitute fundamental assumptions about adult religious education. Principles can provide the insight for a new understanding of the adult. These principles add consistency to both the general task of adult education and may suggest specific program approaches. Such principles are the corrective lens for myopic vision.

Adult religious education includes not only goals and principles, but is a gentle blend of four content areas: cognitive, affective, psychomotor, and lifestyle. One content area does not operate in isolation from the other three. Each, through separate and unique, adds a dimension to religious instruction necessary for a comprehensive understanding of the educational process.

The cognitive domain concerns matters of the head. It is a way of knowing, of viewing, that is the "intellectual representation of a reality."[1] Factual information about the life and ministry of Jesus Christ, the missionary journeys of Paul, and the history of the church is cognitive content.

Affective content concerns matters of the heart. Feelings, emotions attitudes, values, love—all are embodied in the affective domain. To know God intellectually is not the same as to experience the Presence in the fullness of its mystery, power, and love. Yet neither is such knowing divorced from cognitive content. Cognitive knowing and affective knowing are different, yet each influences the other. Stated simply we must never forget that the adult learner feels as well as thinks.

The psychomotor content is the tangible action prompted by mental activity. It is the actual physical doing. Psychomotor content occurs when Jesus tells the man to pick up his bed and walk, tells the disciples to bring up the fishing nets, to feed the multitude on the hillsides. The motor action required was an essential part of the message and its meaning.

Lifestyle content describes the integration of all that we know (cognitive), feel (affective), and do (psychomotor). These elements find expression in the life lived. Jesus, Gandhi, Martin Luther King, and Mother Teresa are all individuals whose lifestyle is an integration of thought, feeling, and doing. "Lifestyle is the most important substantive content in religious instruction. To be sure, no religious instruction is truly *religious* unless it is first and foremost a lifestyle affair."[2]

In the last twenty years adult education has shifted emphasis from teaching to learning.[3] Interest in how the adult learns is central to reconceptualizing effective adult religious education. Adults are not children or adolescents. They are different in their developmental needs, in their accumulated experiences, and in their perceptions about God.

Several factors have contributed to this new role of "adult as learner." One significant factor is the shift in the age of the American population. This century finds the adult population increasing faster than the population as a whole.[4] "In the United States during the century, the number of people over sixty-five has quadrupled and now makes up almost 10 percent of the population."[5] Religious educators cannot afford the luxury of concentrating primarily on children and youth. Adults have come of age, and just as we have in the past examined the intricacies of the child learner so we now turn our attention to the adult learner.

Malcolm Knowles has added significantly to our understanding of the adult learner.[6] Once high school graduation marked the end of learning in formal settings.[7] Today, formal and informal educational opportunities are increasing faster than we can count. Statistical evidence states that adult educational activity is on the increase. Not only is the campus "greying" but the church and the society as a whole are aging. As adults perceive themselves as learners the door of possibility opens for the church. Whether or not the adult learner will be encouraged to walk into church educational events is another question. How well we perceive who the adult learner is and how well we design learning events are all a part of the answer. Make no mistake, adults will consciously select and choose in the church just as they do in other sectors of society. Automatic, instantaneous response will not occur. Our perceptions of the adult are crucial. Accurate perceptions and careful educational planning go hand in hand.

These two factors, an aging population and a perception of the adult learner, offer a double challenge to adult religious education.

Although this chapter will center primarily on cognitive learning, it will show the interrelation with the three other domains, namely, affective, psychomotor, and lifestyle. The chapter is divided into three sections: 1) the concept of development; 2) a comparison between the child and adult learner; and 3) the basic principles of adult religious education.

The Concept of Development

Religious educators have indelibly etched in their educational minds the work of Robert J. Havighurst. Who can forget his description of the child's Terrible Two's and Trying Three's? These are years marked with significant development changes for the child. Yet adults have equally significant developmental changes which have yet to be adequately explored. Daniel Levinson reminds us that "adulthood is not a single phase of life. For one thing, it lasts too long, covering the fifty or more years that people ordinarily live after adolescence. Secondly, tremendous changes occur over the course of the adult years."[8]

Not only are there differences between the child and the adult learner, but there are differences among adult learners. It is not possible to create programing or to work with adults if they are not understood as unique. One class, one program, one style, one approach will not suffice. The Baskin-Robbins thirty-one ice cream flavors model could serve us well. We may not offer all thirty-one flavors on the same day, but we know that we have the capacity over a period of time to offer them as many choices in religious education.

Colin Titmus and associates suggest a definition for adult development as "the sequence of continuous change and growth throughout the various stages of adulthood."[9] Whether we call development "changes," "phases," "stages," "passages," or "transformations," the single idea implied is that the adult does not remain static throughout adulthood.

Understanding the adult learner begins with knowledge from other disciplines such as psychology and sociology, as well as remembering that cognitive, affective, psychomotor, and lifestyle contents are golden threads woven into the magnificant tapestry of the adult learner. Neil Smelser and Erik Erikson remind us that two phenomena of adult life, work and love, are central psychological and social forces which affect persons. "On the psychological side, the adult years mark the development and integration of cognitive and instrumental capacities that enable people to reach whatever heights of purposeful, organized mastery of the world they are capable of reaching."[10] A sociological perspective points to the "spectacular development of the modern occupational bureaucratic complex that has provided the locus of most of the work activities of society."[11] Understanding adults as well as their engagements in society is the enjoinder from not only Neil Smelser and Erik Erikson, but from Leon McKenzie who states that the contemporary adult often stands in stark contrast to "churched adults." Leon McKenzie suggests that

> quite often those who are at home in the "churchy" culture appear to be unable to discuss nonchurchy issues; they seem to be sealed off from the concerns of the workaday world; they seem to be contained within a separate reality. Adults who are not concerned exclusively, or even to a high degree, with "churchy" issues feel themselves more at

home in a weekday world than the world of Sunday devotions and sermons. They apprise themselves as secularists when they are simply not "professional" religionists.[12]

When the adult comes to church we get the whole person, together with his or her need to acquire, express, and expand meaning in life. These needs are the first needs to be met.

"Adulthood has its transition points and its crises. It is a DE-VELOPMENTAL PERIOD in almost as completely a sense as childhood and adolescence are developmental periods."[13] Certainly, some of the obvious differences appear as we examine the needs of young, middle-aged, and older adults. These age-related categories are just one way of examining the adult learner. Another way to view adults is through such life experiences as singleness, separation, divorce, and death related circumstances. Adulthood is a complex mix of human existence. Whatever the approach to adult religious education, the essential point of departure is the acknowledgement that all adults are not the same. An oral assent to this notion is not enough; the practice must follow. Diversification in programing and in responding to the adult learner is the order of the day.

Myths have surrounded the work of adult religious education. Unfortunately these myths have become barriers to creative structuring of adult work. Just as James Michael Lee suggests that we must "despookify" religious instruction, so we must "despookify" adult religious education.[14] We must rid ourselves of useless, cumbersome, obsolete baggage.

One myth to be eliminated is that people retire from life at age 65. We have equated age 65 not only with retirement but, more importantly, with the completion of serious work in a productive society. We have failed to acknowledge that while retirement age may be associated with government, politics, and economy it does not apply to mental capabilities or potential for productivity. The age 65 syndrome originated "in 1889 in Germany, when Bismarck, for the first time in the Western world, introduced legislation that acknowledged the responsibility of a federal government for financial support of its older citizens."[15] The magical age of 65 has frequently done irreparable damage to the image of the adult learner. Fortunately, second and third career possiblities for adults as well as the emergence of elderhostels suggest that we have turned the corner in recognizing the potential of older adults. Not only do adults learn after age 65, but they have specific needs which can be addressed. The over-65 adult learner rejects childish or inferior learning endeavors which insult his/her intellect and provide no challenge. Ruth Weinstock suggests that "Golden age garbage" such as rhythm bands and ballroom dancing are no longer in vogue.[16] The older adult and the adult learner in general are looking for the church to offer serious, rigorous intellectual offerings.

Bernice Neugarten refers to a new category "The Young Old." These adults are approximately 55-75 as differentiated from the "Old Old" who are 75 and beyond.[17] If there are significant differences between these two groups, then our study of adulthood has only just begun.

A Comparison between the Child Learner and the Adult Learner

Malcolm Knowles' study of andragogy, the art and science of helping adults learn, although controversial, offers useful information on critical assumptions about the adult learner. The four critical assumptions Knowles makes suggest some of the differences between the child and the adult learner. Chart 1 lists the four assumptions: self-concept, experience, readiness to learn, and orientation to learning. Each concept expands progressively and developmentally as the child matures to adulthood. This progression or developing capabilities moves from left to right on the chart.

Knowles in his original writing on andragogy in 1970 did not intend to present a dichotomy between pedagogy and andragogy; however, two major factors led readers to perceive such a dilemma.

The first factor was the subtitle of Knowles' book, *Andragogy Versus Pedagogy;* the second was that prior to this book the term pedagogy was considered an unchallenged pedagogical paradigm. Malcolm Knowles' original intention was to present an alternative set of assumptions that would not be exclusive to one age level. That is to suggest, that at times some pedagogical assumptions are appropriately employed in formal and informal learning settings for the adult and, conversely, there are times when andragogical assumptions are appropriate for the child.[18]

The interesting twist in Malcolm Knowles' contribution is that while he unintentionally presented what was viewed by some as a dichotomy, he attracted the attention of adult educators. His work became a focal point around which to reconsider the basic assumptions about the adult learner. If we can use his critical assumptions as a starting point and move on, we shall be wiser for it. Valuing adult experiences, knowing that adults need to use the information they learn quickly, and offering the adult learner opportunities for decision making are part of Knowles' critical assumptions.

Basic Principles of Adult Religious Education and their Implications

One of the distinct features of adult religious education is that the center of attention is not curriculum but the learners themselves. Knowing how the adult is developing biologically, intellectually, and socially is crucial. Just as the educator responds to the child's growth in programing, curriculum development, and approaches to instruction, so it is necessary to understand and respond to changes in the adult.

Chart 1
Knowles' Four Critical Assumptions of Andragogy

Concepts

1. Self-Concept	CHILD	from dependent few decisions from other-directed	to interdependent to many decisions to self-directed	ADULT
2. Experience	CHILD	from limited experiences	to wealth of experiences	ADULT
3. Readiness to learn	CHILD	from readiness to learn the developmental tasks	to readiness to learn the developmental tasks involving social roles	ADULT
4. Orientation toward learning	CHILD	from postponed application of knowledge from subject centeredness	to immediacy of application to problem centeredness	ADULT

Biological Differences

The adult experiences changes in both vision and hearing throughout the adult years. Visual decline can be expected to begin in the twenties with the greatest amount of decline occurring between the ages of 40 and 55. Following age 55 there is continuous decline but at a decreased rate.[19] The important issue here is that although there are natural declines in visual and hearing acuity after age 40, there is not necessarily a corresponding decline in either the ability to learn or in the correctness of the learning response. This distinction is important for the self-concept of the adult learner and to those designing events for the adult.

Hearing reaches the peak of performance before a child is 15, and then there is a gradual but consistent decline until about age 65. "In no capacity except sight are there greater changes at different stages in life than in hearing acuity."[20] One valuable piece of research on hearing acuity indicates that as women age they lose the capacity to hear low tones. In the aging process men lose the capacity to hear high tones. This research suggests implications for grouping and instruction.

The ability to cope with the natural biological decrements of sensory acuity, vision, and hearing affects the learning process. One of the barriers to adult learning is a lack of accurate information about this natural decline. Not to know is to fear, and this alone can incapacitate both the learner and the educator.

Intellectual Differences

The ability of the adult to direct his own learning efforts, to make decisions, and to use time is different than for the child. The child's thinking processes are largely centered in the concrete and literal mode; but the studies of Jean Piaget suggest the capacity for abstract thought processes. An adult will select his/her learning activities whereas the child usually learns via a planned educational program established by others. The number of decisions a child makes is minimal in comparison to those required of adults. Time is thought by many adults to be more valuable than effort or money; but time to the child is of little importance.

Perhaps the most desirable combination is the best of both worlds, childhood and adulthood. Knowing the specific differences between the intellectual capacities of the child and the adult can help us to focus clearly on the adult learner and the implications for adult religious education. Planning for adult religious education is not synonymous with planning for children. Adults will not take kindly to being treated as children and conversely children are not little adults. Adults expect to make decisions, to respond both in the abstract and the concrete, to solve problems, and to use time efficiently. Religious educators need to work with adults as decision makers, abstract and concrete thinkers, problem solvers, and wise users of time.

Social Differences

The social differences between the child and adult range from the limits of childhood experiences to the rich accumulated experience of adults. Adults define themselves through their experiences while children define experiences as something that happens to them.[21] The role of experience is central to unlocking the world of learning for adults. Malcolm Knowles suggests that when we devalue an adult's experience "the adult perceives that as not rejecting his experience, but rejecting him as a person."[22] One of the adult's unique capabilities is awareness of the positive or negative influences his/her past experience offers to present learning.[23] Such influences have profound implications for adult religious education.

The adult learner is interested in the immediate application of knowledge. Generally speaking, the school child postpones applications of learning while the adult looks for an immediate use.

Chart 2
A Comparison Between How the Child
Learns and How the Adult Learns

Child (Pedagogy)	Contributor	Adult (Andragogy)
1. Biological Differences		
A. Visual	J. R. Kidd	
B. Hearing		Decline—the question is how much and how the decline affects the learning
C. Speed of responses		

Child (Pedagogy)	Contributor	Adult (Andragogy)
2. Intellectual Differences		
A. Other-directed learning	J. R. Kidd	Self-directed learning
B. Concrete and literal thought	Jean Piaget	Abstract thought
C. Subject-centered	Malcolm Knowles	Problem-centered
D. Limited perception (of world)	Jean Piaget	Expanded perception
E. Dependence	Malcolm Knowles	Independence
F. Not goal-oriented	NAPCAE-J. R. Kidd	More goal-oriented behavior
G. Time (of minimal importance)	Malcolm Knowles —J. R. Kidd	Time (as valuable as money or effort)
H. Minimal decisions made	Malcolm Knowles	Decision maker
I. Nonverbal activities	Donald Brundage & D. Mackeracher	Verbal activities
3. Social Differences		
A. Limited experience	Donald Brundage & D. Mackeracher Malcolm Knowles	Experience as resource
B. Postponed application	Malcolm Knowles	Immediate application
C. Individual action-oriented	Donald Brundage & D. Mackeracher	Corporate action-oriented
D. Limited point of view	Jean Piaget	Expanded point of view
E. Readiness Development (social pressure)	Malcolm Knowles	Developmental tasks of social roles

Chart 3
Biological Changes in the Adult

Researcher	Finding	Finding Reference
J. R. Kidd	Heart	In adults over 60, the heart increases in size and weight,

Researcher	Finding	Finding Reference
		but the capacity to increase in rate and strength of beats during intense physical work usually diminishes.[24]
J. R. Kidd	Brain	The brain enlarges throughout the life span. If the brain is not used there seems to be a loss of neural connections as well as the functioning of brain cells.[25]
J. R. Kidd	Vision	The greatest decline occurs between the ages of 40 and 55.[26]
J. R. Kidd	Hearing	The peak of performance is 15, and then there is a consistent gradual decline until about 65.[27]
J. R. Kidd	Loss of high tones Loss of low tones	Older male adults lose the capacity to hear high tones and older females adults lose the ability to to hear low tones.[28]
H. Y. McCluskey, Donald Brundage, and D. Mackeracher	Sensory acuity and speed of response	Neither the ability to learn nor the correctness of the learning response corresponding decline with loss of sensory acuity and speed of response.[29]
Donald Brundage and D. Mackeracher	Stress	Adults tend to begin learning programs under some stress. Further arousal through the actions or demands of the teachers is counter-productive.[30]
Leonard Pearlin	Stress	As life changes occur, the adult experiences stress and needs coping-resources.[31]

Chart 4
Biological Profile of the Adult Learner

Age 20-25	1. Adults over 20-25 are at the most advantageous period of learning.[32]

Low tone less	2. Women over 65 lose the capacity to hear the low tones.
High tone less	3. Men over 65 lose the capacity to hear the high tones.
New learnings	4. The loss of hearing in the adult can influence behavior and his feelings toward learning new things.[33]
Interpersonal relations	5. The loss of hearing in the adult affects interpersonal relations.
Self-confidence insecurity	6. The loss of hearing in the adult affects self-confidence and insecurity.
Accuracy of information	7. The loss of hearing in the adult affects the accuracy of information taken in.
Hearing	8. The adult over 65 declines in the ability to hear sounds, to translate, and to respond to sounds.
Speed of response	9. Adults decline in their speed of response but not necessarily in the power to react.[34]
Sensory acuity loss	10. Adult learning after 40 is most effective when the learning environment can compensate for any loss in sensory acuity.[35]
Compensation devices	11. The adult learner may be using a number of coping devices to compensate for loss in sensory acuity.[36]
Learning ability	12. The adult's decline in visual acuity does not necessarily suggest a corresponding decline in either the ability to learn or the correctness of the learning response.
Stress	13. Adults learn best when not under stress.[37]

Chart 5
Intellectual Changes in the Adult

Researcher	Findings	Finding Reference
Malcolm Knowles	Self-directing	The child is a dependent personality. As the child develops he/she moves to become a self-directed human being.[38]

Researcher	Findings	Finding Reference
Donald Brundage and D. Mackeracher	Self-directing	Self-directed adults accommodate two learning needs: 1) autonomous mastery of their life 2) belonging to and participating in groups.[39]
Jean Piaget	Abstract thought	The child thinks in concrete thought processes until age 11 when the mind is liberated and can handle abstract concepts, hypotheses, theories.[40]
Donald Brundage and D. Mackeracher	Abstract	Adults more frequently use generalized, abstract thought. Specific, concrete thought is more frequently used by children.[41]
Malcolm Knowles	Problem-centered	Current life problems are often the motivating force for the adult's participation in educational activity.[42]
B. W. Kreitlow and Associates	Problem-centered	Adults respond to learning which is problem-centered. They are trying to make sense out of experiences which bombard them.[43]
N. E. Jackson, H. B. Robinson, and P. S. Dale	Expanded perception of the world	Adults constantly struggle to recognize and prioritize the most critical features or dimensions of a complex situation.[44]
J. R. Kidd	Perception	Four of many ways an adult learner may have a different perception than a child or youth: (1) No "correct answer." Problem solving in adulthood usually means that there is no single "correct answer."

Researcher	Findings	Finding Reference
		(2) The adult associates correctness with tradition or religion. The adult is more bound than the child to the stereotypes of "correctness." (3) When adults find solutions to problems, there is likely to be immediate effects. (4) Conflicts, often arise when the expectations of the "learner" and the "teacher" differ.[45]
Donald Brundage and D. Mackeracher	Independent	The adult's self-concept and self-esteem permits the possibilities of participation as an individual separate from other selves. The child's self-concept, permits viewing self separate from others, but dependent on, others.[46]
J. R. Kidd and Malcolm Knowles	Independence	The child first sees self as being completely dependent upon the adult world.[47]
C. O. Houle and J. R. Kidd	Goal-oriented	These adults in Houle's study had clear-cut objectives. Continuing education did not occur until their mid-20's or later.[48]
J. R. Kidd	Goal-oriented	If the adult is aware of the purpose of the task there is usually increased effectiveness. Fatigue is greater and the output is less when there is work without aim.[49]
NAPCAE's	Goal-oriented	Maturity and experience aid the adult learner in more observable goal-oriented behavior than in children.[50]
Stephen Udvari	Time	Adults have their own timetable for participation in

Researcher	Findings	Finding Reference
		programs. When desire to learn and interest in what is taught peaks, adults will participate. Adults know that participation is voluntary, so they want to come and go freely and return at any time they have the urge to learn.[51]
Malcolm Knowles	Time	The different adult time perspective produces a difference in the way adults view learning, as compared to children.[52]
J. R. Kidd	Time	Time is a key influence affecting motivation. A child has a lifetime before it, and the adult views time as limited and as valuable as money or effort.[53]
Donald Brundage and D. Mackeracher	Time	Severe time constraints interfere with productive learning. Adults learn best setting their own pace. Although adults may reduce their speed they will compensate for it with improved efficiency and competencies in learning strategies.[54]
Donald Brundage and D. Mackeracher	Time	Measuring time for children and young adults tends to be "time since birth." Adults over 40 measure time as "time until death."[55]
Irving Lorge and J. R. Kidd	Speed-time	As age progresses, there is a decline in the rate of learning. The intellectual power does not change, in and of itself, from ages 20-60.[56]
A. T. Welford and J. R. Kidd	Job performance	The older adult may have decreases in the speed of a

Researcher	Findings	Finding Reference
		task, but they often have gains in both quality and accuracy.[57]
Malcolm Knowles	Decision makers	The commitment of an adult in a decision or activity is directly related to the adult's participation in or influence on its decision making and planning. This is one of the basic findings of applied behavioral science research.[58]
Donald Brundage and D. Mackeracher	Verbal	Through nonverbal activity children express their own needs and learning processes. "Expert" observers and interpreters learn for future planning. Adults verbalize their needs, and describe their learning processes through verbal activities. For adults, there is a dimension of negotiation and collaboration in the planning of their own learning experiences.[59]
Nancy Bayley and M. H. Oden	Longitudinal study over four decades	Female mental abilities stabilize at an earlier age. Male mental abilities exhibit greater stability later. Verbal scores are more stable than performance scores for both sexes.[60]
W. A. Owens	Formal education	The more the formal education, the greater the gain in test scores.[61]
Nancy Bayley M. H. Oden and J. R. Kidd	Follow-up studies on mental ability	The more schooling taken, the greater gain in test scores.[62]
C. Fox and J. R. Kidd	Vocabulary	Professional persons 60-70 years of age increased vocab-

Researcher	Findings	Finding Reference

ulary; a decrease for those for whom language was not a major factor in daily living.[63]

Chart 6
Intellectual Profile of the Adult Learner

Immediate Application	14.	Adult learners want the content or process of the learning to have an immediate and pragmatic application within their life.[64]
Learning effort	15.	Adults engage in at least one or two major learning efforts a year.[65]
Self-directed	16.	Adults plan about 70 percent of their learning projects.[66]
Selective learner	17.	The adult is selective in the learning process and his areas of interest.[67]
Speed and efficiency	18.	Adults tend to learn best when they can set their own pace. Their reduced speed is compensated for by improved efficiency and competence in learning strategies.[68]
New learning	19.	When new learning is consistent with old learning it reinforces; when inconsistent it interferes.[69]
Goal-oriented	20.	Some adults are *goal-oriented* learners who use education for accomplishing fairly clear-cut objectives.[70]
Learning-oriented	21.	Some adults are *learning-oriented.* These adults seek knowledge for its own sake.[71]
Discomfort	22.	The adult learner will experience discomfort if the learning objective is too elementary or if it is too difficult.[72]
Learning-objective	23.	A learning objective for the adult needs to be gauged as being within the possible range of accomplishment by the learner at this present level of experience.[73]
Problem-centered	24.	Adults tend to enter educational activities with a *problem-centered,* rather than a *subject-centered* approach.[74]

Sense of finite	25. Middle-aged adults have a growing awareness of time. They sense the finiteness of one's existence.[75]
Introspection Future growth	26. Middle age is a time of introspection and self-analysis. Some investigators suggest that middle age is a critical time in terms of future growth and development.[76]
Developmental tasks	27. There are specific developmental tasks during the middle-age stage of adult development.[77]
Verbal abilities	28. The adult's verbal abilities increase after age 50.[78]
Non-verbal abilities	29. The nonverbal ability in the adult does decline after age 50.[79]
Measuring success-motivation	30. Being able to measure his/her own success is perhaps the strongest motivating force for an adult to continue on to put fresh energy into the chosen study.[80]

Chart 7
Social Changes

Researcher	Finding	Finding Reference
John Schwertman	Experience	For some, the principal factor in adult learning is not only the richer experiences of the adult but also the use made of this learning.[81]
J. R. Kidd	Experience	Adults differ from the child in their sexual and social experiences. "Adults have *more* experiences. Adults have different *kinds* of experiences. Adult experiences are *organized* differently.[82]
Donald Brundage and D. Mackeracher	Experience	The adult learner organizes and integregates part of her/his past experiences into his/her self-concept and self-esteem. It is necessary for the adult

Researcher	Finding	Finding Reference
		learner to have past experiences respected and valued by others. If the adult's past experience is devalued, he/she also may feel devalued.[83]
Malcolm Knowles	Experience	Individual differences widen with experiences. Just as individual differences are important with children so they are important with adults. A group of 60-year-olds is different than a group of 40-year-olds, who in turn cannot be the same as a group of 10-year-olds.[84]
Donald Brundage D. Mackeracher	Corporate	Adults are expected to be productive and hold a responsible status in society, whereas children are assigned a nonresponsible status in society. It is expected that children will play and learn.[85]
Malcolm Knowles	Immediate Application	The adult wants to take today's learnings and use them immediately.[86]
Jean Piaget Barbel Inhelder	Point-of-view	Children have difficulty taking another's point-of-view. Grasping desired information and modifying initial comprehension is a difficult task for children.[87]

Chart 8
Social Profile of the Adult Learner

Past experiences	31. Adult learning is facilitated when past experience can be directly applied to current experience.[88]

Past experiences	32.	A unique capability of the adult learner is the ability to be aware of the potential positive or negative influences on present learning which past experiences offer.[89]
Activity-oriented	33.	Some adults are *activity-oriented* learners who select their learning experience for a social contact need.[90]
Expectation base	34.	The adult learner's past experience provides a significant expectation base for new learnings.[91]
Immediate application	35.	Adults engage in learning largely in response to pressure they feel from current life problems; their time perspective is one of immediate application.[92]
Learning for credit	36.	Adults are not learning to earn credits. Earning formal credits is not an important motive in the educational behavior of American adults.[93]
Relational learning	37.	Adults have the ability to learn relationally, that is, to perceive how facts affect themselves or others in the learning process.[94]
Matching styles	38.	Adults learn more productively and satisfactorily when their learning and cognitive styles match those of the teacher. There is no "one best way" for adults to learn.[95]
Life-application	39.	It is now well-established that learning happens with greatest efficiency where there is some similarity between the learning situation and the life situation.[96]
Aware of social behavior	40.	Whereas the child lacks the ability to differentiate "between social behavior and concentration on individual action," the adult can make this differentiation.[97]

Comparisons, Findings, Profiles

Chart 2 compares the learning of children and adults using biological, intellectual, and social differences. Charts 3-8 indicate the research information as well as a profile of the adult learner. These child-adult differences are not meant to be an exhaustive list, but rather to suggest pieces of information that can shed light on the difficult task of adult religious education.

Charts 2-8 present cognitive data. The task for adult religious educators is to consider such data as they work in formal or informal learning settings. The affective and lifestyle domains are not to be excluded. These charts are an attempt to present clear cognitive data about the adult which can inform the educator in the "doing" of adult religious education.

Knowing the biological, intellectual, and social differences is a part of the process of defining the adult learner. Out of this information come principles and implications for adult religious education. "Nothing in life is irrelevant to a person's overall religious education."[98] Therefore a viable beginning point is to integrate the content areas of cognitive, affective, psychomotor, and lifestyle domains and the biological, intellectual, and social changes of adulthood.

There are ten basic principles about the adult learner to consider. Several statements can be made about these principles. First, it is not the intent of this chapter to provide an exhaustive list but rather a modest beginning. Second, these principles are directed to the adult religious educator for using in programing, designing curriculum, and in general instruction. Third, the list integrates the work of several reseachers.

1. *The capacity to learn does not necessarily decline with age, but natural losses in hearing and seeing can affect the learning process.*

"Are you able to hear?" and "Are you able to see?" Too many adults have missed learning opportunities because they were either too far removed from the speaker, the sound system was distorted, or some outside noise was louder than the guest speaker. Whatever the reason, if they are to learn, adults must be able to hear and see.

If the adult is at home listening to an audio or video tape the same obstacle of sight and sound can pose learning barriers. A common clue to hearing loss is when the adult suggests that others "mumble when they talk."

As adults age, their field of vision narrows and the eye takes longer to adapt to dark. For the adult over 40 the increase in visual decline is considerable. Adapting to visual changes, such as maximizing contrasts in newsprints, blackboards, and television screens can be useful.

Hearing decline is second only to visual decline. Children under 15 experience about 5 percent auditory disability. This loss is sufficient to create difficulties in understanding an interview or a telephone conversation. In adults 65 or over auditory disability increases 65 percent.

We know that as women age they begin to lose the capacity to hear the low tones and as men age they begin to lose high tones.[99] When I first read this information I reflected on the number of times religious educators have tried to group the older men's and women's bible study in one room. The resistance from the older adults was usually strong enough to permit them to remain in their separate rooms. One of the factors creating this strong preference for separation in learning may be the high tone, low tone loss. When the adult is unable to hear in conversation frustration increases.

Adult religious educators can take note that both hearing and seeing can pose significant barriers to the assimilation of new learning.

2. *The loss of hearing can contribute to other problems such as a loss of accuracy of information received, a loss of self-confidence and security, a change in interpersonal relations, and the need to use coping devices.*

When an adult responds to a question with a ridiculous answer because he/she could not hear, individuals are embarrassed. The result is often a personal inward retreat in which the learner refuses to make another oral response. When the learner's self-confidence is shaken it takes time to rebuild. Often the adult then moves into a period of isolation which affects other interpersonal relationships.

The psychological problems with hearing loss are often more serious than the actual physical impairment. When, for example, an older adult is confronted with rapid speech, he or she may experience a loss of intelligibility of up to 45 percent.[100] Hearing problems are compounded when adults who need hearing aids refuse to use them.

The adult religious educator can be sensitive to the natural aging process and to the potential learning barriers.

3. *The accuracy of response is not necessarily affected by age, but the speed of response is.*

"You have ten minutes to write your answer," "We will be covering in twenty minutes what should take a week," are both statements which do not contribute to optimal learning conditions for the adult. Studies testing adults in timed tasks report that as the adult ages there is a slowing down of the speed of response, but not necessarily the accuracy of the response.

Older adults are slower to react to sounds, to translate sounds, and to respond.[101] The speed of learning is not very important in adult learning. On the contrary, there is evidence that schools overemphasizing speed have done so to the detriment of learners regardless of age.[102]

When adults can control the pace of learning, A. B. Knox concludes, "most adults in their 40s and 50s have about the same ability to learn as they had in their 20s and 30s."[103] This suggests that the adult religious educator make certain that time allocated is accurately matched to the task. Rushing the adult learner can be nonproductive. Allowing time for adults to complete their learning increases their sense of confidence. Always rushing and moving right along may not result in quality thinking and work.

4. *Adults learn best when they are not under stress.*

When unpleasant conditions dominate for long periods of time the adult experiences stress and anxiety.

Leonard Pearlin suggests three ways societies and organizations are implicated in the emotional development of adults. First, the organization may be the source of the focus with the capability to adversely (and beneficially) affect the well-being of people. Stressful situations are not equally distributed in social positions and statuses.[104]

Second, stressful situations have different effects on individuals in different social contexts. For example, retirement for an adult who is financially and emotionally prepared for the future creates one set of circumstances. Conversely, retirement for an adult who has lived to work may result in depression.

Third, social organizations can contribute as formal or informal helping agents. Adults need coping resources during times of stress.[105] When unemployment and marriage conflicts arise adults experience stress and need additional supports to sustain emotional and psychological strength.

Adult religious educators can be sensitive to the social forces which impinge on adult lifestyles. Six downtown churches in the Pittsburgh area studied the needs of the homeless. The city had several overnight locations for men, but none for women. In 1979, Bethlehem Haven, a home for women, was opened in Smithfield United Church. Each night twenty to thirty women from the city streets come into the church for food and a safe night's sleep. The lifestyle of adult religious education can be reflected in the ministry provided. How we respond to human needs in the community defines who we are.

Religious education can be a strong positive force in encouraging adults to examine their inner resources and to provide guidance.

5. *Time is valuable to the adult.*

Adults and children view time differently. A child or a young adult measures time as "time since birth"; an adult past 40 measures time as "time until death."[106] H. Y. McClusky discusses the "arithmetic of time," suggesting that each year lived is a fraction of the time experienced. Consequently, as the adult ages, one year becomes a decreasing fraction of the total time experienced.[107] It is not surprising that as adults age the value of time increases as the death of friends, relatives, and parents brings the finality of life to the immediate foreground. Issues often left for private conversations with only the closest of friends can be effectively addressed by adult religious education: "How to face retirement," "Working through grief," "Terminal illness in our family."

Patricia Cross and A. Zusman identified eight major barriers to participation for the adult learner. In descending order of mention, the eight barriers were: "(1) lack of time; (2) costs; (3) scheduling problems; (4) assorted institutional requirements/ red tape; (5) lack of information about appropriate opportunities; (6) problems with child care or transportation; (7) lack of confidence; (8) lack of interest.[108]

Adults enter learning settings on a voluntary basis. The adult is highly selective in the allocation of time. Therefore, adult educators are wise to examine how time is used.

Beginning and ending on time, setting agendas that match time schedules, and discussing expectations are all components of using time efficiently.

Adults do not want to waste their time. Educational opportunities must be varied. They may be self-directed studies using cassettes or video tapes at home. Or they may be short-term, long-term, or independent study opportunities. Flexibility in time schedules may increase the participation of the adult learner.

6. *The adult learner is problem-centered rather than subject-centered.*

"How-to" books and guides are quick sellers. They usually define a common problem and then offer the solutions in ten easy steps. Unfortunately, major problems such as nuclear war and peace issues are not as easily solved. Nevertheless, adults are problem solvers. They are interested in identifying problems and setting out to offer reasonable resolutions.

One task of adult religious education is to identify the pressing problems of interest to adults, to determine if other community groups are already exploring those problems and create new opportunities where the adult can study and resolve problems.

Researchers have examined the participation of adults in learning projects. The largest and most representative sample describing one learning project of American adults was the Penland study.[109] The projects were divided into three subject matter groups: (1) formal topics, such as, history, English, science: 6.9 percent; (2) practical topics, such as, home repairs, job related projects, hobbies/crafts: 75.9 percent; (3) intra-self topics, such as, religion, music, politics: 17.2 percent. Three quarters of the adult learners chose practical how-to projects.

Adults come to learning opportunities with problems to be solved. The more the adult has defined the problem the less satisfactory traditional learning opportunities will be.[111] For example, if an adult has lost his/her job, a class on major religions of the world might not appeal, but an informal conversation exploring job options might.

Out of the total worshiping congregation just a few persons participate in any of the adult educational offerings. We must be careful not to assume that a reasonable goal is to get all adults

from worship into an adult educational event. There are reasons
why this is an unrealistic notion. First, many adults are comfortable in the pew and uncomfortable in a classroom. Second, ongoing adult classes are often "closed groups" and would not welcome a flood of new learners. Third, learning options which
include home study, or referring to other established community
groups may be preferred. This suggests that religious educators
can save energy by examining the needs of adults in the pew and
community and then begin to determine what educational opportunities might be most useful.

One starting point is to scan the present adult programs to
determine if any problem-solving classes or seminars are offered.
If all adult educational offerings are subject-centered and none
are problem-centered then we have direction for new adult learning options.

Effective adult religious education brings together the needs of
adults with creative ways to discuss and resolve those needs.

7. *The adult learner is self-directed.*

In recent years greater numbers of adults have chosen self-
directed learning experiences. Some adults have studied foreign
languages, taken trips abroad; they have experienced something
new and different. What prompts an adult to begin a new learning venture? What kinds of new learning could be shared in adult
religious education?

Self-planned learning is differentiated from groups or private
instruction learning. Three studies concluded that self-planned
learning was not an isolated activity. In fact, participating adults
received help from at least four acquaintances, friends or family
members.[112] In reviewing over twenty research studies Allen
Tough concluded that the "learner makes the day-to-day decisions on what and how to learn in 73 percent of all adult learning
efforts."[113]

There are four basic reasons why adults select self-planned
learning: 1) to set their own learning pace; 2) to use their own
style of learning; 3) to keep the learning style flexible and easy to
change, and 4) to put their own structure on the learning project.[114] Each of these four reasons reflects control over the learning
project.[115]

Some adults are working on learning projects. They may be learning to fly, studying world religions, or enrolled in aerobic dance. Many of these self-directed adults could be encouraged to share what they are learning and how they are incorporating the new learning into their lifestyle. For my friend who is learning to fly, scripture passages telling about "soaring with the wings of eagles" have new meaning. For my husband, who has preached by the Sea of Galilee there are new insights and images of the scripture. Integration is the key word. Our task is to encourage integration of the new learning into the total lifestyle of the adult.

8. *The adult learner is interested in immediate application of the learning.*

"How can I use the information learned?" This is the central question asked by the adult learner. Adults are not interested in storing knowledge for later use or in hearing answers to questions they do not ask.[116] The assimilation of new learning is directly related to the immediate need and usefulness of the information. The adult learner looks for knowledge with "high turnover power."

New learning that is consistent with old learning is assimilated more easily than new learning that conflicts with old learning. When an educator introduces a new body of knowledge it is advisable to ground the new in information that is already known.[117] That is to say, if you are giving directions, suggest well-known landmarks to help the learner remember the information. Sorting the new concepts from the old aids the learning process.

Whereas children often delay using their new learning, adults prefer to make immediate use of it. Adult religious educators may want to prime the interest pump for adults by suggesting short-term learning opportunities. Application to lifestyle, whether it is a study of world hunger or peace with justice, is one way to acknowledge this basic principle. Extraneous information which has little or no bearing upon the adult's lifestyle is worthless!

9. *Some adult learners are goal-oriented; some learning-oriented; and some are activity-oriented.*

Adult learners have multiple motives for learning. C. O. Houle's three-way typology is the most influential motivational study today. Houle examined twenty-two case studies of men and women. Each adult was an exceptionally active adult learner. Houle wanted to know why these learners were so active.[118]

The diversity of adult learning audiences is great. Some are comfortable in groups where goals will be set and tasks defined. Others absorb information in a sponge-like fashion, intent on the joy of learning. Some adults want to do rather than talk. Adult religious education can provide opportunities for each group. Frustration often mounts when a learning-oriented group is interrupted by a few adults who wish to turn it into a social action group.

Many adults want to participate in setting their own goals. Educators who insist on pre-set goals for learning groups miss the unique dimension of a goal-oriented adult. The amount of personal ownership of a goal is directly related to the amount of energy and effort the adult has invested in the formulation of the goal.

Some adults learn because it is enjoyable.[119] Learning itself produces an educational high. They may enroll in a community course, take a short-term session at the church, or engage in self-directed study, but their orientation to learning is for the sake of acquiring new information. Adults are curious beings who find challenges in new and different learning experiences.

Activity-oriented audiences are the "doers." They want more than study and talk, they want "action." Often this group in the church is the social action audience.

Adult religious education must speak to the needs of all three groups and recognize that each group may learn and participate more fully if not categorized as one adult audience.

10. *The adult can construct an expanded perception of the world.*

The church's mission is to be lived and discussed. Our perception of the world and the church's relation to the world is our mission. Missionaries, politicians, and educators are a part of the working team necessary to have more than a provincial view of the church's mission.

Educators can encourage adults to responsibly participate in the community, state, nation, and the world. In a day when communication brings the world into our living rooms, it is dangerous for the church to neglect the world.

One church whose members travel all over the world decided to bankroll ideas and experiences. They developed questions their church wanted to ask as well as ideas they wanted to share. As each traveler visited a new country he/she would visit a church, worship with the members and exchange ideas with the congregations. Once home, the adult met with a group of church members to discuss the experience. Cross-fertilization from religious communities across town, or across the country, or across the world can strengthen our knowledge of and our participation in the church's mission.

CONCLUSION

Adults both think and feel, they "do" and they are known by the very lifestyle they live. As a first step in the work of adult religious education we must have an accurate perception of who this adult learner is. Paul Bergevin stated the essence of adult education when he said:

> The sooner we can adjust our system of education to people instead of trying to adjust people to our educational system, the sooner we will strike a blow advancing the civilizing process. Adult education can tackle social and educational ills. . . . Given the opportunity, many adult learners will respond to the idea that life is more than a frenzied scramble to earn money, to possess more, bigger, and better things. And further, adult education can help us understand the pettiness of the notion that when you've been to school, you've been educated.[120]

Adults are not children and they are not youth. Adulthood is a longer period of time than both childhood and youth together. The changes and experiences in the lives of adults are of ultimate importance in knowing this adult learner. Adult religious education must view the whole adult. Adults are not only consumers of ministry; but they have the potential to be prime producers!

NOTES

1. James Michael Lee, *The Content of Religious Instruction* (Birmingham, Ala.: Religious Education Press, 1985), p. 270.
2. Ibid., p. 701.

3. J. R. Kidd, *How Adults Learn* (New York: Association Press, 1977), p. 13.

4. K. Warner Schaie and S. L. Willis, "Life-Span Development: Implications for Education," *Review of Research in Education* 6 (1978), pp. 120-151.

5. Kidd, *How Adults Learn,* p. 8.

6. Malcolm S. Knowles, *The Adult Learner: A Neglected Species,* 2nd ed. (Houston: Gulf Publishing Co., 1978). This book presents an understanding of the adult learner and how to view learning theories.

7. For information on formal and informal learning settings see James Michael Lee, *The Flow of Religious Instruction* (Birmingham Ala.: Religious Education Press, 1973), pp. 5-9.

8. Quoted in Neil J. Smelser and E. Erikson, eds., *Themes of Work and Love in Adulthood* (Cambridge, Mass.: Harvard University Press, 1980), p. 265.

9. Colin Titmus, P. Buttedahl, D. Ironside, and P. Lengrand, *Terminology of Adult Education* (United Nations Educational, Scientific and Cultural Organization, France, 1979), p. 31. This book is an excellent guide to the language of adult education. It would be an asset if adult religious education had such a resource.

10. Smelser and Erikson, *Themes of Work and Love,* p. 4.

11. Ibid.

12. Leon McKenzie, *The Religious Education of Adults* (Birmingham, Ala.: Religious Education Press, 1982), p. 91.

13. R. J. Havighurst, *Social Roles of the Middle-Aged Person* (Chicago: Center for the Study of Liberal Education for Adults, 1955).

14. Lee, *The Flow of Religious Education,* pp. 293-294.

15. Ruth Weinstock, *The Greying of the Campus,* A Report from EFL (New York: EFL, 1978), pp. 20-21.

16. Ibid., p. 57.

17. Quoted in Weinstock, *The Greying of the Campus,* p. 35.

18. Malcolm S. Knowles, "Andragogy Revisited: Part II," *Adult Education* 30, no. 1 (Fall, 1979), pp. 52-53.

19. Kidd, *How Adults Learn,* p. 62.

20. Ibid., p. 64.

21. Knowles, *The Adult Learner,* p. 56.

22. Ibid.

23. Donald J. Brundage and D. Mackeracher, *Adult Learning Principles and Their Application to Program Planning* (Ministry of Education: Ontario, 1980), p. 99.

24. Kidd, *How Adults Learn,* p. 59.

25. Ibid., p. 72.

26. Ibid., p. 63.

27. Ibid., p. 64.

28. Ibid., p. 65.

29. H. Y. McClusky "An Approach of a Differential Psychology of

the Adult Potential," in *Adult Learning and Instruction,* ed. S. M. Grabowski (Syracuse, N.Y.: ERIC Clearinghouse on Adult Education, 1970); Brundage and Mackeracher, *Adult Learning Principles,* p. 23.

30. Brundage and Mackeracher, *Adult Learning Principles,* p. 175.

31. Cited in Smelser and Erikson, eds., *Themes of Work and Love,* p. 175. See Leonard I. Pearlin, "Status Inequality and Stress in Marriage," *American Sociological Review* 40 (1975), pp. 344-357.

32. Kidd, *How Adults Learn,* p. 78.

33. Ibid., p. 64.

34. Knowles, *The Adult Learner,* p. 159.

35. Brundage and Mackeracher, *Adult Learning Principles,* p. 23.

36. Ibid., p. 23.

37. Ibid.

38. Kidd, *How Adults Learn,* pp. 30-52; Knowles, *The Adult Learner,* pp. 27-59; Malcolm S. Knowles, *Self-Directed Learning: A Guide for Learners and Teachers* (New York: Association Press, 1975), pp. 9-58; Malcolm S. Knowles, The *Modern Practice of Adult Education: Andragogy Versus Pedagogy* (New York: Association Press, 1970), pp. 37-55.

39. Brundage and Mackeracher, *Adult Learning Principles,* p. 115.

40. Lee Edson, *How We Learn* (New York: Time-Life Books, 1975).

41. Brundage and Mackeracher, *Adult Learning Principles,* p. 115.

42. Knowles, *The Adult Learner,* p. 58.

43. B. W. Kreitlow & Associates, *Examining Controversies in Adult Education* (San Francisco: Jossey-Bass Publishers, 1981), pp. 4-5.

44. N. E. Jackson, H. B. Robinson and P. S. Dale *Cognitive Development in Young Children.* (Monterey, Calif.: Brooks/Cole Publishing Company, 1977), p. 23.

45. Kidd, *How Adults Learn,* pp. 37-38.

46. Brundage and Mackeracher, *Adult Learning Principles,* p. 12.

47. Kidd, *How Adults Learn,* p. 36; Knowles, *The Adult Learner,* p. 55.

48. C. O. Houle, *The Inquiring Mind* (Madison, Wis.: University of Wisconsin Press, 1961), p. 16; Kidd, *How Adults Learn,* p. 445.

49. Kidd, *How Adults Learn,* p., 86.

50. NAPCAE's Information Guide (Washington, D.C., 1974), p. 59.

51. Stephen S. Udvari, "Applied Research Innovations," *Materials and Methods in Adult Education* (New York, 1972), p. 237.

52. Malcolm S. Knowles, *The Modern Practice of Adult Education: Andragogy Versus Pedagogy* (New York: Association Press, 1970), p. 48.

53. Kidd, *How Adults Learn,* pp. 104-105.

54. Brundage and Mackeracher, *Adult Learning Principles,* p. 108.

55. Ibid., p. 35.

56. Irving Lorge, *Review of Educational Research* XI (December, 1941); XIV (December, 1944); XVII (December, 1947); XX (June, 1950); Kidd, *How Adults Learn,* p. 83.

57. A. T. Welford, *Skill and Age: An Experimental Approach* (Lon-

don: Oxford University Press for the Nuffield Foundation, 1951); Kidd, *How Adults Learn,* p. 83.

58. Knowles, *The Adult Learner;* p. 115.

59. Brundage and Mackeracher, *Adult Learning Principles,* p. 12.

60. Nancy Bayley and M. H. Oden, "The Maintenance of Intellectual Ability in Gifted Adults," *Journal of Gerontology* (1955); Kidd, *How Adults Learn,* p. 87.

61. Ibid. See also William A. Owens, Jr., "Age and Mental Abilities: A Longitudinal Study," Genetic Psychology Monographs 48 (1953), pp. 3-54; William A. Owens, Jr., *Life History Correlates of Age Change in Mental Abilities* (Lafayette, Ind.: Purdue University Press, 1963).

62. Bayley and Oden "The Maintenance of Intellectual Ability in Gifted Adults," *Journal of Gerontology,* 1955; Kidd, *How Adults Learn,* p. 86.

63. C. Fox, "Vocabulary Ability in Later Maturity," *Journal of Educational Psychology* (1947); Kidd, *How Adults Learn,* p. 85.

64. Brundage and Mackeracher, *Adult Learning Principles,* p. 109.

65. Allen Tough, *The Adult's Learning Projects,* 2nd ed. (Toronto: Ontario Institute for Studies in Education, 1979), p. 1.

66. Ibid., p. 6.

67. Ibid., p. 24.

68. Brundage and Mackeracher, *Adult Learning Principles,* p. 108.

69. Kidd, *How Adults Learn,* p. 275.

70. Houle, *The Inquiring Mind,* p. 16; Knowles, *The Adult Learner,* p. 44.

71. Houle, *The Inquiring Mind,* p. 16; Knowles, *The Adult Learner,* p. 45.

72. Kidd, *How Adults Learn,* p. 277.

73. Ibid.

74. Malcolm S. Knowles, "Program Planning for Adults as Learners," *Adult Leadership* (1967), p. 278; Tough, *The Adult's Learning Projects,* p. 38.

75. Sharan Merriam, "Middle Age: A Review of the Literature and Its Implications for Educational Intervention," *Adult Education* XXIX, no. 1 (1978), p. 49.

76. Ibid.

77. Ibid., p. 50.

78. Brundage and Mackeracher, *Adult Learning Principles,* p. 110.

79. Ibid.

80. Kidd, *How Adults Learn,* p. 290.

81. John Schwertman, *I Want Many Lodestars* (Chicago: Center for the Study of Liberal Education for Adults, 1958); Kidd, *How Adults Learn,* p. 45.

82. Kidd, *How Adults Learn,* p. 46.

83. Brundage and Mackeracher, *Adult Learning Principles,* p. 98.

84. Knowles, *The Adult Learner,* p. 57.

85. Brundage and Mackeracher, *Adult Learning Principles,* p. 12.

86. Knowles, *The Adult Learner,* p. 58.

87. Jean Piaget and Barbel Inhelder, *The Psychology of the Child* (New York: Basic Books, 1969), p. 121.

88. Brundage and Mackeracher, *Adult Learning Principles,* p. 99.

89. Ibid.

90. Houle, *The Inquiring Mind,* p. 16; Knowles, *The Adult Learner,* p. 45.

91. Kidd, *How Adults Learn,* p. 46.

92. Knowles, "Program Planning for Adults as Learners," p. 278; Allan Tough, "Major Learning Efforts: Recent Research and Future Directions," *Adult Education* XXVII, no. 4 (1978), p. 38.

93. J. W. C. Johnstone and R. J. Rivera, *Volunteers for Learning: A Study of the Educational Pursuits of American Adults* (Chicago: Aldine Publishing Company, 1965), p. 68; Tough, *The Adult's Learning Projects,* p. 19.

94. Kidd, *How Adults Learn,* p. 46.

95. Brundage and Mackeracher, *Adult Learning Principles,* p. 110.

96. Kidd, *How Adults Learn,* p. 274.

97. Piaget and Inhelder, *The Psychology of the Child,* p. 119.

98. Lee, *The Content of Religious Instruction,* p. 625.

99. K. Patricia Cross, *Adults As Learners* (San Francisco: Jossey-Bass, 1981), pp. 156-157.

100. C. Calearo and A. Lazzaroni, "Speech Intelligibility in Relationship to the Speed of the Message," *Laryngoscope* (1957); Cross, *Adults As Learners,* p. 156.

101. Kidd, *How Adults Learn,* p. 65.

102. B. S. Bloom, "Mastery Learning," in *Mastery Learning: Theory and Practice,* ed. J. H. Block (New York: Holt, Rinehart & Winston, 1971); K. Patricia Cross, "Old Practices and New Purposes," *Community and Junior College Journal* 50, no. 1 (1979), pp. 4-8; Cross, *Adults As Learners,* p. 115.

103. A. B. Knox, *Adult Development and Learning: A Handbook on Individual Growth and Competence in the Adult Years for Education and the Helping Professions* (San Francisco: Jossey-Bass, 1977); Cross, *Adults as Learners,* p. 155.

104. Leonard I. Pearlin and Morton A. Lieberman, "Social Sources of Emotional Distress," in *Research in Community and Mental Health,* ed. Roberta Simmons (Greenwich, Conn.: JAI Press, 1979); Smelser and Erikson, eds., *Themes of Work and Love,* pp. 174-177.

105. Smelser and Erikson, *Themes of Work and Love,* pp. 174-177.

106. Brundage and Mackeracher, *Adult Learning Principles,* p. 35.

107. H. Y. McClusky, "The Adult as Learner," in *Management of Urban Crisis,* ed. McNeill and Seashore (New York: The Free Press, 1971); Knowles, *The Adult Learners,* pp. 155-156.

108. K. Patricia Cross and A. Zusman, "The Needs of Nontraditional

Learners and the Response of Nontraditional Programs," in *An Evaluative Look at Nontraditional Postsecondary Education,* ed. C. B. Stalford (Washington, D.C.: National Institute of Education, 1979); Cross, *Adults as Learners,* p. 146.

109. P. Penland. *Individual Self-Planned Learning in America* (Washington, D.C.: Office of Education, U.S. Department of Health, Education, and Welfare, 1977), p. 59; Cross, *Adults as Learners,* p. 188.

110. Cross, *Adults as Learners,* p. 188.

111. Ibid., p. 193.

112. Allen Tough, *Intentional Changes: A Fresh Approach to Helping People Change,* (Chicago: Follett Publishing Company, 1982), p. 69.

113. Ibid., p. 124.

114. Ibid., p. 125.

115. Ibid.

116. Cross, *Adults As Learners,* pp. 90-91.

117. David Ausubel, Joseph Novak, and Helen Hanesian, *Educational Psychology: A Cognitive View* (New York: Holt, Rinehart & Winston, 1968), pp. 67-68.

118. Quoted in Cross, *Adults As Learners,* pp. 82-83.

119. Ibid., p. 83.

120. Paul Bergevin, *A Philosophy for Adult Education* (New York: Seabury Press, 1967), pp. 97-98.

Chapter 3

Working with Young Adults

SHARAN B. MERRIAM AND TRENTON R. FERRO

Since high school, Bob has held a number of jobs, all in retail sales, including positions as manager of a record department in a large discount store and salesperson in a national chain of toy stores. His dedication, however, is to music, especially organ, and he serves as both regular organist and substitute in a number of churches.

Lori is completing her freshman year in college. She is a serious student, yet outgoing and interested in the world about her. Although she has not yet decided on a career choice, she should do well in whatever vocation she may select.

Don and Joyce were married upon completion of college. They are both in their second year of teaching at the high-school level. In addition, Don is responsible for the instrumental music program and chess club, while Joyce coaches the junior varsity volleyball team and handles the choral music.

Sue is the mother of an eleven-year-old and a three-year-old girl. Her first husband died of cancer while yet in his twenties, and she is divorced from her second. She is presently attending college, pursuing a degree in art.

Jim completed his high-school requirements in January and immediately entered the Navy. While the rest of his class was participating in graduation exercises, he was completing basic training, receiving his diploma *in absentia*. He has been on leave three times in the last year and comes back to visit his former schoolmates each time he is in town.

The six individuals highlighted in these vignettes are quite diverse, yet they have one important characteristic in common: they all fit into the category labeled "young adult," that segment of the population which is in the age range of 18 through 35 years.[1] This group, in both its commonness and diversity, provides the focus for this chapter.

There are two major emphases in this chapter. First, an effort will be made to describe the young adult, both in his/her uniqueness and in his/her commonality with the rest of the population. Then some directions will be outlined for working with young adults in the church, including some parameters and paradigms.

THE YOUNG ADULT: A DESCRIPTION

In order to better understand the young adult, one must first try to describe what it is that establishes young adults as a group apart from other segments of the population. There are, indeed, certain developmental tasks and issues that are more descriptive of this age group, while there are others that might fit other groups as well. The three psychological issues unique to young adulthood are independence, identity, and intimacy.[2] These issues relate to the various social tasks mentioned in the vignettes at the beginning of the chapter: marriage, college, serving in the armed forces, seeking a job or deciding upon a profession, and establishing a new relationship with one's family of origin and with society in general. While most of these social tasks are not limited to this age group, the *clustering* of these tasks within the period of young adulthood helps set that stage of adulthood apart from others.

Psychological Issues

As the individual passes from adolescence into young adulthood, his/her concern turns from preoccupation with self, brought on by the tremendous physical, emotional, and psychological changes of adolescence, to finding one's place in community and society, attention switches from being like everyone else (peer pressure) to a more conscious awareness of one's uniqueness. The chief issues with which the young adult struggles are independence, identity, and intimacy.

Independence

Possibly the most noticeable characteristic of this stage of development is the necessity for young adults to separate themselves from their families of origin, a sometimes trying task for both parents and young adults, and to establish themselves in society with their own identity. This effort can lead to conflict with parents, on the one hand, and to a feeling of separation and being alone, on the other. As the individual establishes his/her independence, she or he may adopt a value system that is other than that of his/her parents, thus possibly heightening the conflict that might exist.

This need for establishing psychological independence is often accompanied by an actual physical separation from the family of origin: going off to college, entering the military, or moving into a separate apartment. These moves are not necessarily final. The young person in the military and the student return "home" at periodic intervals; the young person who moves out may do so several times, with periodic returns to his/her "home" before the final physical break is made. Physical separation does not automatically lead to psychological separation, however, and independence does not depend solely or primarily on physical separation. Healthy adult development, however, does require the establishment of psychological independence.

Identity

As indicated above, the searching out and establishing of one's own unique identity is part of the transition from adolescence and a natural concomitant of independence. As is the case with independence, the search for identity is not a smooth, linear progression from identity submerged in family of origin or peer group to self-identity. This journey, too, has its hills and valleys and cyclical reoccurrences of submergence and emergence of individual identity.

Defining "identity" is not an easy task, but it is related to what we call "maturity," to ego and moral development, and to self concept. It is that which gives coherence to one's thoughts and actions; it is attached to one's system of values; and it provides a base for decision making and status in society.

These observations are borne out by those who have studied

the developmental stages of humans. In her identification of the eight milestones of ego development, Jane Loevinger indicates that her fourth stage of "conformist" is typical of most adolescents and that the fifth stage of "conscientious" ego development is congruent with young adulthood identity formation.[3] Similarly, W. G. Perry describes a relativism stage of cognitive and ethical development in which the individual develops a toleration of the diversity of opinion, values, and judgments which exist in society.[4] Lawrence Kohlberg's studies on moral development reach parallel observations.[5]

Identity, then, is a conscious state of personal awareness in which the young adult moves away from a self-centered world in which moral choices and value decisions are dominated by the group with which he/she identifies into a broader context in which many options and values for coping with the world are recognized. Young adults identify, affirm, and espouse those choices and values which are now part of their worldview.

Intimacy

Independence and self-identity should not be equated with isolation or separation. Rather, the third psychological issue faced by each young adult is the achievement of an intimate relationship with another. It is the inability to do so that leads to separation and isolation. According to Erik Erikson, identity implies a structural integrity in which one is aware of the boundaries of the ego.[6] Once the individual is secure about his/her own boundaries, then one is ready to establish an intimate relationship with another without risk of losing one's own identity.

This ability to achieve intimacy with another while still maintaining a personal identity and independence is probably the most significant indication of maturity in young adulthood. Possibly this stage of development could properly be called interdependence; the individual retains a personal identity while at the same time entering into a meaningful relationship with another that calls for giving and even sacrifice if that relationship is to be successful. In fact, healthy intimacy requires the continuance of identity by both parties. Should one lose a sense of identity by becoming submerged in a relationship with another, intimacy in its best sense cannot be achieved. A couple may be in physical proximity while experiencing considerable psychological separation.

E. Douvan provides insight into the role which intimacy plays in fostering growth in young adulthood by making a distinction between intimate relationships and role relationships. Examples of role relationships would be those between co-workers and among family members in which each person carries out expectations placed upon him/her because of the position he or she holds in the social structure. One's role is limiting. Intimate relationships, however, do not depend on prescribed norms or expectations. Value is placed on the person and the relationship itself rather than on the person's role or task or on the goal or purpose of the relationship. Role relationships, therefore, are confining and restricting while intimate relationships lead to further personality growth.[7]

Intimacy is a lifelong issue, but the establishment of an intimate relationship is normally a task of young adulthood. Several other of life's major decisions which are made during the period of young adulthood hinge on the establishment of intimacy: selection of a marriage partner, beginning a family, selecting a job or career, choosing a college, and deciding where to live. Conversely, the inability to enter into a relationship of intimacy can leave scars which hinder and even damage the successful conduct of these other developmental tasks of young adulthood.

Sociocultural Tasks

"No man is an island." The psychological development of the young adult is not carried out in isolation, in a vacuum; this development takes place in a society or culture which places its norms and expectations upon this developing and maturing young person. Young adults in contemporary North America are expected to become financially self-sufficient through work, to set up a family unit of their own, and to make some commitment to the larger community.

Occupation

A nearly universal task of young adulthood is the choosing of an occupation or career and the planning and preparation necessary for entering that chosen field of work. Young adulthood is traditionally a time of extended training or settling into a particular job or career. Included in this process may be entering an apprenticeship program, attending a trade or vocational school, or matriculating at a college or university. Some enter directly into the job market, either with a clear concept of vocational choice or by just taking the first opportunity that comes along. Others may decide to join one of the branches of the military, either because they have not been able to come to a career decision, or they see the armed forces as the means of receiving training and experience necessary for entering the work force, or they have decided to make a career of the military.

While the selection, exploration, and settling-in process has been rather standardized for men, the situation has been more fluid for women. In the past the woman's developmental tasks during young adulthood, even if she had a career, still centered around the tasks of childbearing and motherhood. Today a woman will not necessarily relegate her career to a second-place status. She may choose not to have children at all, or continue her career while raising a family, having reached an accommodation and understanding with her spouse as to the care of home and family or by making use of a child-care facility. As a result of this greater flexibility on the part of women in creatively dealing with the dual roles of career and parenthood, men have also had to make role adjustments.

Accompanying this greater flexibility in handling roles is a change in attitude toward work from that held by previous generations. Today's young adults are much more concerned about their work providing a sense of personal worth and self-fulfillment. They want their work to be meaningful in and of itself and not just be a means of providing support of one's life outside of work. Young adults want to see the result of their work, to participate in decisions, and to do work that is interesting. At the same time, young adults, especially those who intend to enter the blue-collar market, are looking at a decreasing job market, and the jobs available offer opportunities much below their expectations.

Family

The occupation or profession that a young adult chooses often helps in the process of establishing his/her independence and identity. The need to develop intimate relationships most often finds its expression through the establishment of the primary social unit of the family. Although people today marry at slightly older ages, have fewer children, divorce more often, and become involved more frequently in alternative family styles, nearly all men and women in our culture still marry at some point in their adult lives, usually in their twenties, and most have at least one child.

Young people marry for a variety of reasons. Biologically, marriage provides each partner with a regular sexual outlet, and young adulthood is the optimal time for producing children. Socially, there is a need to find someone with whom to share the work and expense of living independently of family. Many still get married because it is "the thing to do," while yet others have a need for a "safety net," need to get away from home, or desire to fill some vacancy within themselves.

Readiness for first marriage occurs in young adulthood, but certainly not all young adults marry. Remaining single is much more of an option today than in the past. Furthermore, there are many alternatives to marriage for sustained interpersonal relationships in young adulthood. One must be very careful, however, to not equate singleness with young adulthood. Many young adults are not single, and many of those who are single are not young adults. This is a factor that must be kept clearly in mind as one works with young adults.

Parenthood is another developmental task of young adults that is undergoing change. Childless marriages, single parenthood, and delayed parenthood are becoming more acceptable options. The bearing and rearing of children has been ranked by young adults as being the least important task out of eight to be accomplished during young adulthood.[8] For those who do have children, there are social class and sexual differences in the effect of children on their lives. Working-class couples have children at a younger age and find parenthood more rewarding than do middle-class couples. Finally, while the major responsibility for child-rearing still falls upon the mother, there are signs of change as more emphasis is being placed on the role of the father.

Community

The psychological issues and the social tasks of young adulthood necessitate the widening of a person's life to include the larger community—one's neighborhood, state, and nation. The establishment of independence leads to taking up residence in the community and becoming dependent on the community for services and support. One's career and profession leads to involvement in community and professional organizations. Marriage and parenthood lead to increased involvement in the community.

This widening of one's awareness of the larger world is one of the characteristics of maturing young adults. They become more conscious of community, national, and world issues and problems, especially as they are affected by them. Young adults grow as they become involved in the debate on an issue and take part in the process of reaching a solution.

This growth process is marked as well by the expansion of oneself through serving others in the community, by growing civic concern and involvement, and by becoming more politically aware and active. Yet this growth often leads to tension and conflict as young adults adopt positions and values at odds with those of their parents or those of the community.

As is the case of all age groups, these generalizations about the psychological issues and sociocultural tasks of young adulthood are just that—generalizations. While they are generally descriptive of young adulthood as a whole, they certainly do not describe every individual between the ages of 18 and 35. As is the case with any age group, there exists a great diversity among those who fall into this category. Failure to recognize this diversity within the larger framework described above could lead to disastrous results in working with young adults.

Theological and Religious Considerations

It is important, while looking at those factors that mark the uniqueness and distinctiveness of young adulthood, to also consider those areas which young adults share with all other adults and, in fact, with all humanity. Since the focus of this volume has to do with adult religious education, it seems most appropriate that this commonness be considered within a theological framework.

The Human Condition

A basic tenet of the Christian faith is that there are certain universals that affect all people. No matter how one may personally interpret Genesis 1-3, the common confession of Christianity is that the source of all life lies with God and that this life has been jeopardized by the willful disobedience of humanity. Thus human pride has disrupted the harmony that God intended and has introduced disharmony into all human relationships: with God, with self, with others, and with nature. Since young adults are a subgroup of humanity, they, too, share in this common human condition. Religious educators and others who work with young adults must recognize this as one of the givens as they determine the direction they will take in working with this particular group.

The Message of Salvation

The Christian message is twofold. On the one hand, it stresses humanity's separation from God; on the other, it offers the hope and promise that God has offered a significant, in fact the only, solution to this dilemma of human existence in the person of Jesus Christ. Since this is the core purpose of the Christian church—to proclaim this message of salvation to all people—this purpose must also underlie all aspects of the congregation's programs, including those designed for distinguishable groups such as young adults.

The combination of these two points provides the parameters of the Christian view of the believer, as Martin Luther noted in his famous description of each person as being *simul justus et peccator,* "at the same time saint and sinner." Young adults, as is the case with every human being, share those common struggles of humanity that can lead to disruption of life and play havoc with the emotions. Likewise, they need, and if a Christian may desire, the Good News of Hope and help that is provided by the sensitive and meaningful proclamation of Jesus Christ as savior and the application of this gospel message.

The difference in applying this message to young adults comes in recognizing that the struggles of life are played out more prominently in those areas outlined above: The young adult is striving to achieve independence, identity, and intimacy. To the extent that the young adult needs assistance in these pursuits, the congregation is afforded the opportunity to serve that individual. The congregation can also play a significant role in assisting young adults as they meet their sociocultural needs of occupation, family, and community.

Stages of Faith

Building on the works of Jane Loevinger, W. G. Perry, and Lawrence Kohlberg which were introduced above, as well as other studies in the developmental stages of the human life cycle, James Fowler has outlined the various stages in which a person's faith develops. As is the case with other developmental studies, stages cannot be closely connected with chronological age. People at all different ages can be at all different stages of development. This is particularly true of faith. If, however, young adults have backgrounds in the congregation, they may already have passed through those stages normally related to childhood into those more closely related to the adult experience: synthetic-conventional faith (faith which seeks security in adhering to established norms), individuative-reflective faith (faith which doubts, questions, and examines the assumptions of parents and religious tradition), or conjunctive faith (faith which brings into meaningful reconciliation the variety of fatih dynamics that have played an important role in the earlier faith development of the individual).[9]

Those working with young adults are presented with an excellent opportunity to assist in the establishment of faith or in its development. Possibly the difficulty in the past has been that congregations have not been prepared or able to deal with that stage of faith development which questions and challenges rather than simply accepts the tradition. Now that research has shown that such a stage is a necessary and important aspect of the individual's development, not only should such questioning be encouraged and accepted, but young adults could even be given a lead in helping others move into that stage of faith development.

Diversity of Gifts

These new insights into the stages of faith development help highlight what Christian theology has espoused for centuries, even though Christians and congregations have found it hard to put into practice. Every believer has been gifted with his or her own, unique set of abilities, talents, and capabilities. This is one of the core concepts of Pauline theology in which Christ is the head of one body which is made up of many members, each having an individualistic yet important task to perform for the well-being and proper functioning of the body as a whole (see

Romans 12, 1 Corinthians 12, and Ephesians 4).

Being mindful of this concept serves two functions in working with young adults. First, young adults are seen, both individually and as a group, as having significant contributions to make to the health and well-being of the total body of believers. Second, awareness of the diversity of gifts will keep the practitioner from making shallow assumptions which would categorize young adults and place them all into a common mold. Even as there are common elements which draw young adults together, there are also quite diverse traits and characteristics among young adults. There will be many circumstances and situations in which a young adult person will feel more comfortable with someone of a different age who shares a common problem or life experience than with someone his/her own age who is, however, experiencing life in quite a different manner.

Unlike the psychological issues and sociocultural tasks described previously as being basically germane to young adults as a group distinct from other age groups, the theological considerations presented here place young adults within the larger context of humanity. All persons, regardless of age, share in the human condition and are in need of the message of salvation. Each believer is at some stage of faith, but this is not dictated or controlled by age. Each believer, as well, has received unique gifts as a child of God, and these, too, are not age related.

The church, therefore, in developing a ministry with young adults, recognizes both the unique psychological and sociocultural circumstances of young adults as well as their common bond with all other persons. Hence, the congregational functions which will be described below are the same functions carried out by the congregation vis-à-vis all age groups. While the functions are the same, however, their particular applications are dependent upon the sociocultural and psychological situations of each age group. In this case, we illustrate and expand upon the application of congregational functions to that group defined as young adults.

THE YOUNG ADULT AND THE CHURCH

It is most intriguing that adults feel at such a loss in trying to relate to those younger than themselves—children, teenagers, and young adults—when they themselves have passed through these stages of growth and development. Although they have been there, they now find themselves uncomfortable in, and even incapable of, dealing with those who are now there. How strange!

Upon further investigation, this may not be so strange after all. How unfortunate it would be if each individual did not move beyond these various stages. More mature adults have accomplished the tasks and moved through the developmental stages connected with younger years. They no longer deal with the same issues of life in the same way. Yet this does not explain the uneasiness with which many look upon their younger counterparts.

Possibly the answer lies in the fact that each age level has trouble understanding other age levels because each has its own tasks and concerns, much as those described for young adults above. Furthermore, many at each age level are unable to allow others to act their age; all others are seen through the filters of the current situation. Teenagers have trouble relating to their parents and vice versa because each struggles with a different set of tasks. The same would hold true, to some extent, for young adults and those who have reached middle age. This recognition alone might help ease the concern of adult religious educators and others in congregations who are working with young adults. Both the similarities of all humans, especially of all adults, as well as the differences that exist between age levels must be recognized and even upheld. Older adults who wish to work with young adults cannot become younger and ought not to try to be younger than they are, nor should they expect younger adults to be other than young adults. Thus working with young adults requires recognizing one's position as an adult religious educator, as well as taking into account the circumstances of young adults.

The Congregation

Those within the church who wish to establish meaningful programing with and for young adults must be very clear, first of all, about their base. Where do they start, what is their purpose, and what is their goal? This requires an examination and awareness of overall purpose and rationale for existence and also a clear conception of how the congregation is organized to carry out its function.

Statement of Mission or Purpose

Undoubtedly every congregation has within the first few paragraphs of its charter of organization or constitution a statement which clearly defines the reason(s) for its coming into existence. This statement should be examined regularly, for every undertaking of the congregation should be in keeping with its stated purpose. Careful consideration of this statement may cause the leadership to reconsider its purposes and goals and to draw up a new mission statement. That new statement, then, will become the cause and guide for all subsequent programing and should lead, as well, to a reexamination of programs already in existence to see if they now are in keeping with this newly revised mission of the congregation.

Although this is a consideration that is important for all aspects of a congregation's work, it is certainly appropriate for establishing a meaningful program for working with young adults. As young adults strive to gain independence, identity, and intimacy, they also seek integrity. Young adults are not interested in sham. They can spot insincerity very quickly and are soon turned off by any approaches that claim to have the interest of the young adult at heart but in fact have other motives for wanting to solicit young adults for their programs—to increase the number of members on the roles, to broaden the financial base, to find "new blood" for boards and committees—whatever.

By reviewing, revising, and adhering to its statement of mission or purpose, the congregation has established a firm foothold in its attempts to minister to the young adult. Whatever it does will be in keeping with its stated purpose for existence. If young adults are turned off, the reason will be that they do not agree with or accept that stated purpose for the congregation's ministry. Others will be attracted because they agree with the mission and appreciate the coherence between statement and practice.

Congregational Organization

If a congregation is to properly carry out its stated purpose, it does need to have some organizational pattern. It needs to decide what major functions are necessary for carrying out its mission, and these functional decisions will have a bearing on how all programs are developed and carried out. A couple of models are mentioned here.

Avery Dulles has suggested that there are five distinct ways that individuals, and individuals joined together as congregations, view the church; there are five models which describe the varying vision that different Christians have of the church.[10] None is necessarily better than the other, nor should any be considered to be worse. Dulles is merely giving formal expression to what we all know—people go to church for different reasons and seek different types of resources and support from the church. Many congregations are plagued by a schizophrenia because they are trying to be all things to all people and are unable to figure out whom they really want to serve and what their purpose really is. How much better it would be to recognize what a congregation's basic model is and to work at becoming the best congregation it can become within the framework of that model.

The models that Dulles suggests are the following: 1) The church as institution emphasizes organization, management, and efficiency. This model has appeal for those who place high value on logic, knowledge, and the historical continuity of the church. 2) The church as mystical communion or community highlights fellowship, prayer, and interpersonal relationships. 3) The church as sacrament concentrates on liturgy, worship, symbol, and the beauty that is attached to both the place and process of worship. Central to this model is the recognition of God's offering of grace and man's response of faith. 4) The fourth model depicts the church as herald. The focus of this model is upon the communication of the Word of God, especially in the form of proclamation, but also in teaching, bible study, and the passing on of tradition. 5) The church as servant emphasizes the role of the congregation as an agent for human betterment and as a responder to human needs. Central concerns are those of justice, peace, brotherhood among people, and the development among its members of those skills needed to meet these concerns.

Although the congregational leader will quickly recognize that the church attempts to do all of these tasks, Dulles' typology would suggest that a congregation should determine what its major emphasis is and make that model the central focus of its efforts, ministry, and programing. Others will be less inclined to take this route of special emphasis, preferring to accomplish its mission by consciously carrying out a variety of tasks at the same time. What keeps this approach from splintering is the constant, conscious attempt to keep the congregation's statement of purpose clearly in sight and to see that each area of activity derives its rationale from that purpose, which also serves as the goal of any given program.

This approach draws upon New Testament terminology to define the various functions that a congregation carries out as it seeks to accomplish its purpose or mission. In his chapter Leon McKenzie delineates three of these terms: *kerygma, koinonia,* and *diakonia.*[11] A fuller description of the task outlined in the New Testament should probably also include two additional terms: *didache* and *martyria.* These terms, in order, describe the congregation's functions of proclamation, fellowship, ministry or service, teaching, and witness.[12] Possibly two other terms could be added: *leitourgia* (ministry or service) and *latreia* (service). The modern derivates of these words have become associated with the service of worship, but in their original meanings they can easily be related to the concept of *diakonia.*[13]

These congregational functions were referenced briefly during the discussion of theological and religious considerations. What is the relationship between those considerations which were described as the common possession of all and these functions of the congregation? Primary and basic is the message of salvation which must be brought to bear on the human condition. This is accomplished both through the proclamation *(kerygma)* of Jesus Christ as Lord and Savior and by meeting the various social, emotional, physical, mental, and psychological needs of individuals through dedicated service *(diakonia).* By so doing, the church follows the example of its Lord who proclaimed the presence of the kingdom of God and confirmed that presence by meeting the immediate needs of those who attended him.

Those who are moved to accept the concept of this proclamation—that Jesus Christ is Lord and Savior—become members of, and participate in, the fellowship *(koinonia)* of believers. This fellowship is expressed in corporate worship *(leitourgia)* of the God who has revealed himself in Jesus and by serving *(diakonia)* the needs of fellow believers and nonbelievers alike. By so doing, they give witness *(martyria)* to their faith and make use of the particular gifts which they now recognize as coming from their God. Each one serves and witnesses in keeping with the particular talents and abilities God has given.

In addition, each member of this fellowship *(koinonia)* of the Christian congregation needs to grow in faith and must progress from a initial, child-like faith through the several stages of faith development to a more mature faith. This becomes part of the educational or teaching *(didache)* function of the congregation. Throughout the life of both, the whole congregation and of each individual is a constant emphasis on the need for continuing growth if faith is to remain alive, well, and active.

This five-fold framework of *kergyma, koinonia, diakonia, didache,* and *martyria* will be used to suggest some of the more specific ways that adult religious educators and congregations can work with young adults. They provide the constituent parts of one face of a three-dimensional matrix for program planning and evaluation.

Programing with and for Young Adults

The discussion up to now has concentrated on providing the framework within which the congregation can carry out its work with and for young adults. This framework is all-important, for without it whatever program is developed will be without rationale or purpose. This framework will now be given a visual form, and programing directions will be outlined.

A Conceptual Matrix

Those who work with young adults must take into account psychological concerns, sociocultural circumstances, and congregational functions as they plan their work with young adults. Each of these constitutes one face of a three-dimensional matrix, diagramed in Illustration 3-1. Using such a diagram as this will help the practitioner keep in mind the three foci that will lead toward meaningful ministry and programing. Some activities will be much more specific and selective, while others will be broader and more general in intent. Whatever the plan, one or more items from each face of the matrix must intersect, thus assuring the program planner that appropriate consideration has been given to each of the foci.

By way of illustration, the adult religious educator might respond to interest shown in presenting a course or workshop on sexuality. Using the matrix, the determination can be made that this would certainly fall within the framework of congregational concern and purpose. In terms of psychological concerns, it certainly relates to identity, in many cases to intimacy, and maybe even to independence. It relates to such sociocultural circumstances as single or married and has bearing on the workplace and school setting as well as to military service. It would certainly fit into the *koinonia* (fellowship) function of the congregation, and could be seen as relating to the *diakonia* (service) and *didache* (teaching) functions, as well. Furthermore, such a course can be firmly based on sound theological and biblical foundations as it takes into account the purposes of creation and the nature of humanity.

Illustration 3-1
Program Planning and Evaluation Matrix

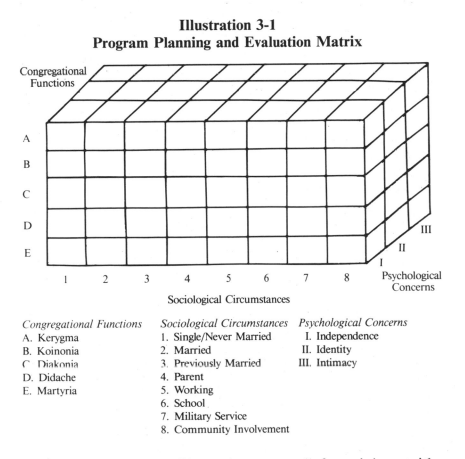

Congregational Functions	Sociological Circumstances	Psychological Concerns
A. Kerygma	1. Single/Never Married	I. Independence
B. Koinonia	2. Married	II. Identity
C. Diakonia	3. Previously Married	III. Intimacy
D. Didache	4. Parent	
E. Martyria	5. Working	
	6. School	
	7. Military Service	
	8. Community Involvement	

This matrix, then, will not be a cure-all for ministry with young adults, but it can be used to help keep programing on course, and it can be consulted further to determine how narrow or broad one's work with adults has become. Current programs can be checked off against the matrix, determining which functions, issues, and circumstances are being served. Gaps might be discovered. The decision must be made whether to leave these gaps in existence or to develop a ministry to fill them. A congregation might discover, for instance, that it has done very little to relate to the work situations of its young adults. This particular parish may decide to address this issue by establishing discussion groups centered around occupational fields such as education, health care, and industry. These groups could serve several purposes. Chief and foremost would be their function as sharing and support groups in which group members could discuss the various problems, concerns, and cares that relate to their particular profession or occupation. In addition, however, there might be opportunities for fellowship and bible study. Such a closeness might develop that the group could decide to take responsibility for developing a worship service highlighting its profession or to undertake a pertinent project in the community. The matrix, then, can be used to both check and generate ideas.

Programing Suggestions

Before outlining some specific ideas for young adult programs, two general comments are in order which arise out of the foregoing discussion. The first may have already struck the reader. The circumstances of young adulthood, especially the sociocultural tasks, are not limited to this age group. Being single, married, previously married, working, a parent, in school, involved in community, and even in the military are functions true of many age groups. Many worthy efforts of a congregation will be directed toward these various tasks without regard to age. In dealing with young adults, it is most important not to separate them out from the congregation just because they are young adults. Some will feel most comfortable with their peers, but others will be much more interested in the task at hand. A widow of 25 may well have more in common with a widow of 55 than with one her own age who has never married.

A common danger is to equate "single" with "young adult." Although there is a strong intersection of these two descriptions, they are certainly not coterminous. Single, in particular, ranges across the age spectrum and includes persons in a variety of other sociocultural situations; widowed, divorced, and single parent join the ranks of those who have never been married under the banner of "single." Great care must be taken not to confuse these. If a ministry to singles is desired, this must not be limited to young adults.[14]

The second comment has to do with the relationship of the congregation with its young adults. Although the adjective is "young," the noun is "adults." These individuals must be treated and respected as adults. To approach them with an attitude of condescension is to ring the death knell for any viable program for working with young adults. Rather, it is important to recognize the significant psychological issue of independence and make young adults part of the programing team. The preposition "with" has been frequently used. This is by design. Young adults don't need to have something done *for* them. They are capable and intelligent human beings who have a fair idea of what they want and need. They must be involved in the total process of developing a young adult ministry. In fact, failure to seek their input and take it seriously could well lead to a program which never takes off. Treat them as adults; accept them as peers; and they will come through.

After the appropriate groundwork has been laid by taking into account the various concerns that have been expressed here, the education planner can give consideration to appropriate possibilities for the congregation in its ministry with young adults. Actual directions and programs will arise most naturally out of each congregational setting and situation as young adults are consulted and brought into the planning phase and due consideration has been given to the descriptive and prescriptive analyses arising out of the use of the program planning and evaluation matrix. Some general suggestions and guidelines are provided here to aid in the planning process.

Counseling

The survey of psychological issues and sociocultural tasks relating to young adulthood suggests to a congregation the possibility of establishing or expanding its counseling function if this is seen as one of the important aspects of that congregation's mission. Some of the counseling would be dealing with crises relating to young adults' struggles to find independence, identity, and intimacy. Much of it could be programatic and directive, helping young adults in the decision processes in which they are presently involved. Possible areas include career and vocational guidance, premarital planning, marriage enrichment, and dealing with such struggles, when they arise, as facing the draft.

If such a course of action is decided upon, several directions present themselves. One consideration is the type of counseling to be offered. Will it be by a person properly trained? Will it be a current staff person? Will a new staff position be created? What about the possibility of using group and peer counseling techniques where these are appropriate? It is certainly possible to provide a meaningful counseling service without increasing professional staff. There are a number of excellent programs in which pastors or key congregational leaders receive intensive training. They in turn conduct an extensive training series for fellow members in such activities as listening skills, assertiveness, caring and support skills, and dealing with special situations. Often a person so trained will have experienced what another is now going through and is capable, with this training, of providing meaningful and extended help. For example, a widow can provide special help to a young woman who has recently lost her spouse.[15]

If a congregation decides to use current staff or to add new staff for the purpose of expanding a counseling ministry, new directions of help are provided. A trained professional can administer and interpret any number of tests and instruments that provide help and insight both to the counselor and the young adult. There are any number of instruments that are most useful in career and vocational planning. Others provide a basis for engaged couples to properly plan for married life together, while still others give each individual a clearer picture of his/her personality traits and preferences. Most of these inventories can be used both under clinical conditions and in workshop and retreat settings, provided that the tests have been taken in advance so that they could be scored and graphed appropriately. Such instruments can lead to meaningful insight and discussion.[16]

Issue and Content Focused Classes, Workshops, and Retreats

Young adults will most likely not be attracted to weekly, or even monthly, group meetings which have no termination and no apparent focus. Young adults in the local setting should be consulted on this, but they will probably be more interested in programs that have both a time terminus and content that relates to their current needs and interests. Illustrations have been given previously of share and support groups centered around occupation and workshops or retreats based upon the explanation, discussion, sharing, and planning connected with some personality, vocational, or premarital inventory.

Depending upon local concerns, topics of possible interest might include budgeting, money management, and financial planning; sexuality, relating to one's family of origin; marriage enrichment; parenting and parenting preparation; and personal development. Special study groups and task forces might develop around such issues as atomic energy, nuclear warfare, national and world hunger, and other topics of local and national interest. Committed, Christian young adults will also be open to learning and applying theological and biblical understanding and insight to these matters of concern. Some will also desire opportunities for spiritual development and growth in personal faith and biblical knowledge.

Fellowship

A congregation is in a position to make a major contribution to the psychological development of young adults by providing young adults the opportunity to gather for purposes of fun and fellowship. Often little is needed beyond support and encouragement—and access to the secretarial, duplicating, and mailing services of the congregation. In their search for independence, identity, and intimacy, young adults need environments that are both supportive and nonrestrictive, environments in which they feel comfortable and yet in which they can spread their wings and try to fly. American society offers few places for young people to gather outside of drinking and eating establishments. If they have arenas in which they can meet together in order to get acquainted and to plan activities of mutual interest and benefit, they will be able to develop optional activities to those which are designed for commercial, not developmental, purposes.

Service and Ministry

If young adults are to be accepted and treated as the adults they are, and if they are to be looked upon as full members of the congregation, they should have the same opportunities as other members of the congregation to participate in the full ministry of the congregation. On the other hand, there should not be greater expectation of participation than there is with any other segment of the congregation. The Pareto (80/20) Principle applies here as elsewhere: 20 percent of the people do 80 percent of the work; 20 percent of the members provide 80 percent of the budget support. Within these expected parameters, however, one can reasonably expect to find young adults who have a willingness, desire, and capability to enter into positions of congregational leadership and service.

Certainly high on the list of prospective areas of service is that of education: Sunday School, Vacation Bible School, catechetical instruction, and the full scope of growth offerings for adults, including those for young adults. Young adults oftentimes make excellent youth workers and counselors. Their talents can also be tapped profitably for worship, music, outreach, building and grounds repair and upkeep, and the whole host of other duties related to a congregation's functions. Effective use of the Planning and Evaluation Matrix can uncover such possible areas of ministry as effectively as it can open doors to other areas of programing. If the young adults find ways to serve which make use of their interests and strengths, their sense of worth and identity is enhanced.

Ministry among young adults can be a meaningful, while at the same time challenging, experience. Proper consideration of psychological issues, sociocultural factors, and congregational functions provide appropriate directions for keeping such a ministry on course. Full involvement of those being served will keep the congregation from treating young adults as a group outside the mainstream of congregational life. Rather, they will prove to be significant participants in the overall mission of the congregation, no longer ministered to but ministering.

NOTES

1. While there is not uniform agreement on the age span of young adulthood, most writers agree that it begins in the late teens (graduation from high school is a natural starting point) and concludes in the early

thirties. The adult religious educator will ultimately have to decide on the actual parameters as his/her own situation dictates.

2. The psychological issues and sociocultural tasks described in this chapter are drawn largely from Sharan B. Merriam, "Developmental Issues and Tasks of Young Adulthood," in *Meeting Educational Needs of Young Adults,* ed. Gordon Darkenwald and Alan Knox (San Francisco: Jossey-Bass, 1984).

3. Jane Loevinger, *Ego Development* (San Francisco: Jossey-Bass, 1976). Those who engage in the study of stage development, such as Loevinger, Perry, and Kohlberg, do not identify various stage levels with chronological age. Each individual has his/her own timeclock for achieving each stage, and some never achieve the highest stages of ego, cognitive, ethical, and moral development. Nevertheless, there are general age categories which sometimes fit stage descriptions, as is the case here. Many young adults do achieve the stage of "conscientious" ego development.

4. W. G. Perry, Jr., "Cognitive and Ethical Growth: The Making of Meaning," in *The Modern American College,* ed. A. W. Chickering (San Francisco: Jossey-Bass, 1981).

5. Lawrence Kohlberg, "Moral Stages and Moralization: The Cognitive-developmental Approach," in *Moral Development and Behavior: Theory, Research and Social Issues,* ed. T. Lickona (New York: Holt, Rinehart & Winston, 1976).

6. Erik Erikson, *Childhood and Society* (New York: Norton, 1950).

7. E. Douvan, "Capacity for Intimacy," in *The Modern American College,* ed. A. W. Chickering (San Francisco: Jossey-Bass, 1981).

8. S. Merriam and L. Mullins, "Havighurst's Adult Developmental Tasks: A Study of Their Importance Relative to Income, Age, and Sex," *Adult Education* 31 (1981), pp. 123-141.

9. James Fowler, Sam Keen, and Jerome Berryman, eds., *Life Maps: Conversations on the Journey of Faith* (Waco, Tex.: Word, 1978). See also James Fowler, *Stages of Faith: The Psychology of Human Development and the Quest for Meaning* (New York: Harper & Row, 1981), and Kenneth Stokes, ed. *Faith Development in the Adult Life Cycle* (New York: W. H. Sadlier, 1982).

10. Avery Dulles, *Models of the Church* (Garden City, N.Y.: Image Books, 1978). Several articles in Loretta Girzaitis, *The Church as Reflecting Community: Models of Adult Religious Learning* (West Mystic, Conn.: Twenty-Third Publications, 1977) use Dulles' models as a base for suggesting approaches to adult religious education and parish planning.

11. See above, chapter 1 by Leon McKenzie, "The Purposes and Scope of Adult Religious Education."

12. For similar models, see Henri J. M. Nouwen, *Creative Ministry* (Garden City, N.Y.: Image Books, 1978), where he outlines the ministerial task under the headings of teaching, preaching, individual pastoral

care, organizing, and celebrating, and James B. Dunning, *Ministries: Sharing God's Gifts* (Winona, Minn.: Saint Mary's Press, 1980), who describes ministries of the Word, of building community, of celebrating, and of serving-healing.

13. See Alan Richardson, ed., *A Theological Word Book of the Bible* (New York: Macmillan, 1950) for a fuller descriptions of these concepts.

14. See below, chapter 7 by Richard Hunt, "Working with Single Parents," and chapter 8 by Neil Paylor, "Working with Adults in Separation and Divorce."

15. An example of this type of congregational ministry is *The Stephen Series.*

16. Examples are the Myers-Briggs Type Indicator and the Taylor-Johnson Temperament Analysis.

Chapter 4

Working with Middle-Aged Adults

R. E. Y. WICKETT

Middle-aged adults frequently experience new challenges and unprecedented growth in the spiritual aspect of their being. Many adults who are confronted with the realization that they are in the second half of life have reached what Robert Havighurst called a "teachable moment."[1] Taking the adult learner's perspective on this situation, Malcolm Knowles refers to this mid-life experience as a moment of "readiness to learn."[2] In order to work effectively with middle-aged adults at the "teachable moment," religious educators need to understand their distinctive developmental and learning characteristics. The first part of this chapter will review the characteristics of the middle-aged learner with particular reference to psychosocial development, religious or faith development, adult learning, and the interconnection between these three aspects of life. In the second part of the chapter, the roles and functions of the religious educators who are involved with middle-aged learners will be examined.

THE MIDDLE-AGED LEARNERS IN OUR SOCIETY

It is difficult to provide precise bench marks for the beginning and ending of middle age. Perhaps Bernice Neugarten encapsulated the position best when she suggested that "Middle-aged people look to their positions within different life contexts—body, career, family—rather than to chronological age for their primary clues in clocking themselves."[3] For the purpose of this chapter, I suggest that we assume the late thirties for the beginning and mid-fifties as the ending of middle age.

83

The number of middle-aged adults in our society is growing rapidly. Recent statistics indicate that the middle-aged sector of American communities will be the largest overall by the year 2,000.[4] Certainly all forms of adult education will face new demands generated by the shifting age structure of the population.

Since there is clear evidence from studies of adult participation in educational and other activities involving learning, we know that middle-aged adults have a continuing capacity and desire to learn.[5] The research on learning also indicates that adults can learn quite effectively during middle age.[6]

THE PSYCHOSOCIAL DEVELOPMENT OF THE MIDDLE-AGED LEARNER

Religious educators should understand the nature of the adult learner in order to be successful in the facilitation of the learning process. The following paragraphs examine the definition of middle age and the nature of psychosocial development during middle age through the views of certain key researchers.

There have been changes in the definitions of middle age from Robert Havighurst[7] to Daniel Levinson and his associates[8] which parallel the perception of lengthening life spans from the 1940s to the 1970s. Robert Havighurst defined middle age as the period from 30 to 55 years of age, which Daniel Levinson delays to the period from 40 to 60 years of age (See Figure 1). Gail Sheehy suggests that there is experience or realization which culminates in the "beginning" of the middle-aged period during the late thirties.[9]

It should be noted that recent authors differentiate between periods of time within the life stage of middle age. While Havighurst defines middle age as a lengthy, continuous period of time,[10] Levinson[11] and other recent authors subdivide this period into two or more periods. Erik Erikson suggests that stages include times of turmoil or crisis which are followed by times of rest and stability.[12] It does not seem possible for the normal person to experience turmoil for a period such as middle age which lasts approximately two decades.

Levinson and his colleagues perceive the period of middle age as incorporating two "transitions" and two periods of relative calm (See Figure 1). The first transition is the critical adaptation to life in the new, middle years while the second transition appears to be less traumatic.

The experience of middle age can be divided into two basic periods: the initial time of turmoil and the subsequent return to stability. The first half of middle age is the period which receives the most attention because it is the period of activity and change. This is the period of reflection and action in response to the desire or need for change in one's life.

Equally important for educators is the period of stabilization which follows the changes. This is the second half of middle age which occurs in the mid/late forties or early fifties. Most people adjust to the changes and settle into their new life situation after the changes and adjustments have been experienced.

Both the periods of change and stability are of importance to educators, but it is difficult to find precise bench marks in time which are universally accepted. The fact that there are individual differences among adults makes a precise definition quite elusive.

THE NEED TO CHANGE

Adults experience a number of physiological, social, and psychological changes after they reach the "midpoint" in life. The combination of these changes creates stress and the need to learn new strategies for coping with life. Adults learn to cope in a variety of ways and they can be assisted to cope by educators who appreciate the nature of the change and the "readiness" to learn which is associated with developmental change in mid-life.

Physiological changes range from the simple to the complex. Most adults experience some decrease in hearing and sight. Men experience a decrease in strength and the ability to learn and perform related large psychomotor skills. Women lose the ability to have children at some stage during middle age. All of these changes can create stress for the learner as the effect creates an awareness of change and of the aging process which will lead to death.

The social changes which occur during middle age arise from increasing pressures in the home, at work, and from within the broader circle of friends and acquaintances in the community.

FIGURE 1
Developmental Periods in Early
And Middle Adulthood

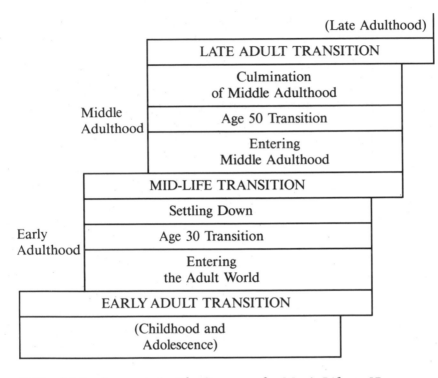

© Daniel Levinson et al., *The Seasons of a Man's Life,* p. 57.

Teenage children and spouses have expectations of continuing support as they pursue their interests. The community also places additional demands upon its "established" citizens of the middle years. Typically, the pinnacle of a career is achieved at this time of life.

In the midst of these changes, many adults at the midpoint of life must come to terms with mortality.[13] It is not possible to delay indefinitely the tasks which are to be accomplished. Mid-life is an appropriate time to examine both the meaning of life and the values and priorities which we have held to this time. The psychological stress of confronting mortality which results in the rethinking of meaning, values, activities, and relationships can be lessened through learning.

Erik Erikson's theory of psychosocial stages provides us with insight into middle age.[14] For Erikson, middle age corresponds to the age of "generativity versus stagnation." He recognizes the vital importance of this stage in the developmental process of the person.[15] This stage is more than sexual in nature, although the process of reproduction and continuation of the species is a part of generativity. Creativity has many manifestations in the human social context, and the person who experiences the positive side of this stage will feel much more positive about his or her life.

The psychosocial stage of middle age is characterized by change and the potential for growth. The search for new understanding and the meaning of life is a central activity for adults in the middle years.

RELIGIOUS DEVELOPMENT AND PSYCHOSOCIAL DEVELOPMENT

The religious educator needs to be aware of the nature of both psychosocial *and* religious development. There is a vital connection between these two forms of development which can assist us to have a better understanding of the learner.

Leon McKenzie suggests that we can not assume that religious development and "total human development" occur simultaneously. However, he continues to argue that there are links between these aspects of development.[16] It is clear that one may not expect exact parallels, but there may be moments when certain aspects of psychosocial and religious development have links.

James W. Fowler makes an important connection between psychosocial development and the development of faith which is central to religious development. Fowler juxtaposes Levinson's three adult eras and Erikson's last three stages against his last three stages of faith (See Table 1).[17] Daniel Levinson's era of middle adulthood and Erik Erikson's age of "generativity versus stagnation" are seen as an "optimal parallel" to the period of "conjunctive" faith.

In the Levinson mode, the middle-aged adult experiences the need to search for the meaning and purpose of life. This search will involve the examination of the life situation including relationships, values, priorities, and activities for work and leisure. The accepted previous situation with its relative comfort and convenience is reexamined. It is even rejected in certain instances.

As the search for meaning proceeds, we move beyond the boundaries and understanding of our previous life situation. We both reject and retain parts of our previous life situation. That which is retained becomes part of a new life situation with a different understanding of life and its meaning.

One can draw a similar parallel to the change which occurs as an individual departs from Fowler's Stage Four and embarks on Stage Five. Just as the latter stage "involves going beyond the explicit ideological system and clear boundaries of identity,"[18] The mid-life reexamination goes beyond the boundaries to incorporate new information and options.

Table 1
Psychosocial and Faith Stages: Optimal Parallels

Levinson's Eras and Erikson's Psychosocial Stages	Fowler's Faith Stages
Era of Infancy, Childhood, and Adolescence	
Trust vs. Mistrust	Undifferentiated Faith (Infancy)
Autonomy vs. Shame & Doubt	1. Intuitive-Projective Faith
Initiative vs. Guilt	(Early Childhood)
Industry vs. Inferiority	2. Mythic-Literal Faith (School Years)
Identity vs. Role Confusion	3. Syntetic-Conventional Faith (Adolescence)
First Adult Era	
Intimacy vs. Isolation	4. Individuative-Reflective Faith
	(Young Adulthood)
Middle Adult Era	
Generativity vs. Stagnation	5. Conjunctive Faith (Mid-life and Beyond)
Late Adult Era	
Integrity vs. Despair	6. Universalizing Faith

© Fowler, Stages of Faith, p. 113.

According to Fowler's concept of Stage IV, which coincides with younger adults, the person wishes to control the situation of a faith kept within a specific set of meanings (the so-called "circle of light"). All other information is reduced to meaning within this "circle of light." Conjunctive faith, or Stage V, incorporates new aspects through an expansion of the "circle of light." There is an organic dimension to Stage V within which meaning cannot be reduced without some loss of understanding. In Stage V, one can approach things which previously threatened the limited definition of faith. New experiences are accepted even when they defy explanation.

The relationship between psychosocial development in middle age and faith development at the conjunctive stage exists mainly on the expansion of the frame of reference for people. The "meaning of life" is a phrase which is common to both the psychosocial and religious contexts.

ADULT LEARNING

Before we can begin to work effectively with learners, we need to have a clear picture of the process of adult learning. The seminal work of Allen Tough, described in *The Adult's Learning Project*,[19] has had a major impact on the way in which all educators of adults view learning. Other researchers who have received both direction and inspiration from Tough's work used his approach to examine the learning of a wide range of groups and topics. Specific comments about the author's study of middle-aged adults and spiritual growth will be addressed later in the chapter.

Tough, and other researchers, found that the vast majority of adults, including middle-aged adults, participated in some significant, deliberate learning each year. These learning projects, as Tough called them, involve a wide range of subject matter ranging from the job to personal skills. The learning project approach should be of interest to religious and other educators because it is concerned with deliberate learning which involves a significant time commitment for the learner.

A key finding of Tough and other related researchers was the amount of self-directed learning undertaken by adults. More than two-thirds of the major planning of the learning activities was performed by the learner. It is indicated from this research that the professionally planned learning activity is only a part of the total picture—and not totally important as educators previously had believed.[20]

Although Tough's research is important for an understanding of all adult learning, it is of particular importance to the adult learners in middle age. The type of highly personal learning required to respond to developmental needs and tasks will require a mixture of learning in individualized and group activities.

ADULT LEARNING PROJECTS AND
RELIGIOUS DEVELOPMENT

The only study which examined adult learning projects on religious development was conducted by R. E. Y. Wickett several years ago.[21] John Elias confirms that it is the first and, to date, only study which involved self-directed learning and religion.[22] The study also included learners who participated in organized courses. It should be noted that all participants in the study were in the middle-aged range (35 to 55 years of age) described at the beginning of this chapter. Data not reported in the article of 1980 is also included in this chapter.

One of the findings of the study which supported the linkage between psychosocial development and religious development was the inability of some respondents to distinguish between learning involving their spiritual growth and other aspects of their learning.[23] Respondents frequently described a wide range of topics for their learning, related to many parts of their lives. Respondents were asked to make the distinction between those learning efforts involving a spiritual dimension and others which did not. When the interviewer probed for the reason behind this inability to make such a distinction, approximately 20 percent of all respondents stated that they could not separate the spiritual part of their being from the other parts.

Perhaps an even more important finding of this study supported the linkage between psychosocial development and religious development with particular reference to middle age. A number of respondents indicated that a traumatic event or life crisis had caused their involvement in their learning activities. These events or crises included marital stress and/or breakdown, the death of a person who was close to the respondent, alcoholism, and aging.

Three respondents indicated that their marital situations had influenced their participation in the learning project. The complete breakdown of a marriage, for example, had resulted directly in psychotherapy sessions with a spiritual dimension.

The death of a person who was close to them was reported by two respondents as a major factor which influenced their involvement in a learning project. One respondent indicated that the death of her mother had had a strong impact on her life and her thoughts, resulting in serious questioning about her own future.

Alcoholism and membership in Alcoholics Anonymous had influenced the lives and learning of two respondents. Life crisis situations created by alcohol had resulted in their attempts to understand better the spiritual dimension of their lives. Both of these respondents saw their experience with Alcoholics Anonymous as having a strong spiritual dimension. They sought assistance through Alcoholics Anonymous from a spiritual power to help them overcome their problems and to shape their future lives.

A number of respondents discussed the recognition of the aging process as an important event which influenced their involvement in a learning project. One respondent indicated that the event was her fortieth birthday. Two other respondents pointed out that they suddenly realized that they were getting older. Their awareness of the aging process necessitated a reassessment of their life situation and its spiritual dimension.

As noted earlier, the mid-life transition can be a traumatic period for a significant number of adults.[24] Examples, which have been cited in previous paragraphs, indicate the same type of crisis situation which precipitates the mid-life transition in the psychosocial aspect of human development. The answers for these respondents were to be found in the subsequent learning projects which were triggered by the events.

It should be noted at this time that most respondents in the study could not identify a "traumatic" event as a spur to learning. Some respondents suggested events which were as simple as the receipt of information concerning the availability of a course. Nevertheless it is clear that some people do experience "traumatic" life experiences which precipitate learning leading to growth and development.

When the content of the reported learning projects was analyzed, it was observed that 28 percent of the respondents described learning for spiritual growth rooted in themselves, or in others in conjunction with themselves. The grouping of content projects was as large as the very comprehensive category of God/Religion which also represented 28 percent of the respondents.

A summary of certain projects described by respondents is available in "Adult Learning and Spiritual Growth."[25] The topics of the learning projects which were discussed in the interviews ranged from a seven-year study of Hinduism to a study of the religious and spiritual implications of racism to psychotherapy and the occult. Some of the projects were very clearly related to the spiritual growth of the respondents. In other instances, the interviewer had to probe into the nature of the spiritual growth of the learning.

In several situations, the "most important project" related to spiritual growth for some respondents tended to be his or her most exciting learning activity during the past year. Others were a bit disappointed when they could not report a project which had occurred two or three years earlier. The projects reported by these persons were often an outgrowth of the spiritual development which had occurred as a result of an earlier learning project.

As noted previously in this chapter, Tough observed the extensiveness of self-direction in learning projects. Wickett's study of middle-aged adults who were involved in learning projects for spiritual growth recorded a high incidence of learner-planned activities (see Table 2). Forty-four percent of reported projects were primarily learner planned. Although this figure is not as high as Tough's reported figures for the main planner of a project, it was much greater than any other main planner in the author's study.[26]

Table 2
The Primary Planner

Primary Planner	Total (N=50)
1.a Group/Peer	8
1.b Group/Leader	11
2.a Expert	1
2.b Non-Expert	0
3. Object	1
4. Learner (Self)	22
5. Mixed	3
6. No Response	4

It is clear from these data that group situations were prominent in the decisions about how and what to learn from this group of learners. Either peer groups or group leaders were prominent in the planning of almost two out of five learners. This is a clear indication of the valuable support which learners can gain from their church and other groups.

Thirty-three percent of the respondents who answered the question in this study indicated that they had spent a considerable amount of time in the planning of their learning. Yet 40 percent spent less than one hour.[27] There is an obvious bimodal distribution which requires further investigation for clarification.

The implications are clear from this study and from other related work by Tough and his associates. *Educators of middle-aged adults need to understand that self-directed learning is a fact. Middle-aged adults want to be involved in decisions about their learning. They will take what they wish from activities which are planned by others and, when necessary, they will plan the learning which they require.*

The primary sources of content or subject matter in this author's study were groups (including formal classes) and written material (including books). Other research[28] and our own experience bear witness to the importance of these sources (see Table 3). The high incidence of group activity may be derived from the fact that the respondents came from several sources involving groups.

Another important finding of the study may be seen in the main way in which learning happened for the respondents. Twenty-eight percent of the respondents indicated that they could not identify a single method. These respondents said that two or more were equally important methods. Reflection and discussion were the next most important methods (see Table 4).

Learning Project research has indicated that far more learning is self-planned and motivated by factors other than credit.[29] R. E. Y. Wickett's study found that credit courses were used by a small number of respondents but the primary purpose of taking the course was for the content made available in that context.[30] Learners who are engaged in a process of growth are more likely to regard such matters as credit as unimportant.

Perhaps the most important finding involved the answers to a question concerned with the "ideal" learning situation for the learner. Each learner was asked to comment on possible assistance which could have improved the learning situation in the particular project

Table 3
Main Source of Subject Matter

Main Source	Total (N=50)
Group (instructor of learners)	15
Friend, relative, or neighbor	2
Expert	3
Books, pamphlets, newspapers	14
Television and/or radio	0
Programed materials	0
Displays, exhibits, museums, or galleries	0
External sources of revelation (e.g. God)	1
Internal sources (memories of life experience)	5
Mixed	4
Other (music)	1
No response	5

Table 4
Main Method of Learning

Main Method	Total (N×50)
Reading	4
Discussing	8
Doing	3
Observing (including listening)	4
Television and/or radio listening	0
Meditating (formal)	0
Praying	1
Contemplating or reflecting	12
Mixed	14
No Response	4

previously described in the interview (see Table 5). The most important improvements mentioned were the opportunity for input from a content or resource person and more time for group involvement, including discussion.[31]

The respondents who wanted more input on a one-to-one basis with an expert would have liked to have had a knowledgeable person with whom they could discuss the spiritual part of their lives. Some of these respondents noted that they were not seeking specific advice. A more suitable form of input would have come in the suggestion of possible sources of information or directions for future searching related to spiritual growth.

Thirteen respondents indicated that group discussion would have had value for their learning projects. The opportunity for discussion appeared to be less than adequate even for those respondents who had been part of a group learning activity. It was of some interest to this author to note that only one respondent wished to have a spiritual experience to improve her learning. There was an absence of comments on spiritual experience throughout the interview.

Table 5
Improvements for an Ideal Learning Project

Improvements	
Input (some, more, or better) from;	
a) Content resource person or advisor, one to one basis	20
b) Group, including discussion and/or materials	13
c) Nonhuman resources or materials	7
More agreeable life situation (e.g., more time or freedom)	6
Travel	2
Other [a]	4
No improvement identified	7

[a]This category included; a spiritual experience, the writing of poetry, new life experiences, and a better sense of direction.

THE ROLES AND FUNCTIONS OF ADULT RELIGIOUS EDUCATORS

The intention in this section is to provide a description of both the roles and functions which the adult religious educator should undertake in relation to the learner for the provision of a wide range of educational services. The functions or activities of the educator are also described. The roles and functions should be consistent with the research and ideas expressed previously.

It is important to clarify the nature of the role which is expected of the religious educator *in the context of the learner's situation.* Is the religious educator the primary resource for learning? Does the learner wish to have a dependent or an independent relationship with the religious educator? These key questions must be addressed before an effective relationship can develop with the learner.

The religious educator may determine after an examination of the learner's situation that there is no other primary resource person available to the learner. It is not unusual to find that the religious educator is the primary learning resource person for some adult learners. However, situations may arise where middle-aged learners are experiencing a situation which contains a spiritual dimension but includes another focus. For example, a person involved in marriage counseling at a secular agency may wish to address spiritual issues which have arisen from the marriage situation. The spiritual or religious need parallels the psychosocial developmental need. Careful role clarification on the part of the religious educator is required if these distinctions are to be understood.

Whether the religious educator is seen by the learner as the primary resource person or not, the degree of dependence between the learner and resource person should be established. Is the learner's intention to have the religious educator direct the learning activity? The research of Allen Tough[32] and R. E. Y. Wickett suggests that many situations arise where the learner wishes to direct his or her own learning. Many learners may wish to make their own decisions while still having access to a knowledgeable resource person who can assist in the learning process.[33] It cannot be assumed that all middle-age learners are dependent learners. It would be safe to assume that a significant number want a degree of independence in their learning activities.

Both individual and group learning situations require that these key questions be considered. Groups are composed of individuals who, in most church settings, attend as volunteer learners. Each individual learner brings his or her life experience and learning needs to the group. The fact that a religious educator is faced with a group situation will *not* diminish the necessity to be concerned with the learning style of each individual.

The ability to define one's role as a religious educator will be enhanced by active listening. Counselors seldom take action in a meeting prior to the client's presentation of the problem. A similar opportunity needs to be made available for individuals who come to a group or an individual session.

There is one other factor which must be considered in defining the role of the religious educator. Many religious educators are required to work in the context of an institutional situation. If someone is expected to function in a classroom, that person must develop the relationship with the middle-aged learner in that context. The availability which occurs through "office hours" or a similar arrangement can be of benefit. That religious educator should attempt to reach the most flexible arrangement possible in order to meet the learner's needs. When the relationship is established, the person is ready to work with the learner.

In certain instances a religious educator of middle-aged adults will be required to function in a traditional manner. It appears that this traditional situation should not occur too frequently. Should a religious educator be required to function in a traditional manner, there are ample materials to read to provide assistance. This chapter will review adult religious education approaches which are more appropriate for middle-aged adult learners.

Malcolm Knowles has established key functions to assist the adult educator who is working with "self-directed learners." These functions include setting a climate for learning, defining a new role for the "teacher," and assisting the learner to develop the ability to be self-directed.[34]

The establishment of a good relationship for learning is the purpose of climate-setting whether the religious educator is working with an individual or a group. The demonstration of openness to the learner's ideas and needs creates the opportunity for the learner to share relevant life experiences and for the religious educator to develop a better understanding of the learner.

A redefinition of the role of teacher must occur because many learners see the "teacher" as the sole person who will purvey the content from accumulated wisdom. Should the teacher wish to become a facilitator, he or she must assist the learner to adjust to the new relationship. One key change in this process is that the religious educator ceases to be the major or sole purveyor of the content. The role of facilitator requires an ability to identify other resources—including people who will assist in the learning process. This is not to suggest that any facilitator should never be a resource person. There will be moments when a facilitator can and should share in the transmission of content. The research indicates that emphasis should be placed primarily on the facilitative function rather than on content delivery.

The facilitative function will be rejected by learners who assume that the teacher is to fulfill his or her traditional role and perform traditional teaching functions. Learners must be assisted to assume the appropriate style of learning for their situation. For many learners, this will mean assuming the self-directed approach, which is quite normal and natural when they are not influenced by the presence of traditional educators, "experts," and formal classes.

To achieve the most effective form of self-directed learning, the learner needs to have a sense of direction, knowledge of appropriate resources, and ideas about how to use the resources. The facilitator assists the learner with a chance to express his or her own ideas and by sharing appropriate responses.

PROGRAM RESPONSES TO MIDDLE-AGED LEARNERS

Various attempts have been made to describe the kind of programs which are appropriate for middle-aged learners. One of the most comprehensive lists of developmental tasks and educational responses was provided in an article by Virginia McCoy[35] during the period shortly after the publication of Gail Sheehy's book, *Passages*. If there is an acceptance of some connection between psychosocial development and spiritual development as suggested earlier in this chapter, it is possible to respond to developmental tasks from both the psychosocial and spiritual areas with programs which are interrelated. What we are recommending here is that courses concerned primarily with developmental tasks in one area can include elements of the other area.

Courses planned for group learning can range over many topics related to developmental tasks. The following topics include McCoy's suggestions.[36]

1. Personal growth (to examine the meaning of life)
2. Marital relationships (including divorce)
3. Career planning for mid-career persons
4. Family relations (teenage children and aging parents)
5. Human relations (friends, colleagues, etc.)
6. Values clarification
7. Financial planning
8. Basic survival skills
9. Creative problem solving
10. Stress management

Each topic can be addressed directly from a learning event designed to assist in the performance of a developmental task. Spiritual development may be directly or indirectly associated with the learning event. The facilitator can assist the group to pursue spiritual aspects in the group or on an individual basis as is appropriate in each situation.

The middle-aged learner will identify the relationship between certain psychosocial developmental tasks and spiritual development quite early. It may be more difficult for the facilitator to see the ways in which the learner is making these connections through the learning process.[37]

In a recent study of vocational change during mid-life, Donald Smith indicates that a decision to change a career can have a much broader meaning. Smith states that almost two-thirds of his sample indicate a relationship between vocational change and the issue of "the meaning and purpose of life."[38] He also states that the religious connotation was clearly present for a number of his respondents.[39]

Human relationships are a key focus in many learning activities for middle-aged learners. The number of groups and workshops which focus on every aspect of relationships from marriage to friends to colleagues is evident to anyone who reads adult education advertisements. These learning activities are organized under the auspices of both secular and religious agencies.

Henri Nouwen has examined the ability of people to reach spiritual understanding through human relationships.[40] This aspect of human relationships and the contribution to spiritual learning was confirmed in Wickett's study where 12 percent of the respondents identified this as a focus for the learning.

There can be little doubt that the search for meaning in life through personal growth is, in part, a process of coming to terms with the spiritual dimension of life. People who engage in this direction of personal growth in their learning must examine the spiritual dimension. Should they fail to do so, the search will have missed an important aspect of life.

We can consider learning activities related to values clarification as a subset of the broader issue of renewed concern for the meaning of life. Perhaps this is where some people begin their search, through an examination of specific values and attitudes, before moving on to explore the broader issues of the meaning of life. Certainly those persons who develop a new sense of self through a new direction for their lives will need to restructure their values and attitudes in accordance with this new direction.

It is appropriate for adult religious educators to assist people to examine the roles, values, and attitudes which they bring to their lives. Should the opportunity or the need arise within the workshop on group situations, it is necessary to do more than merely facilitate exercises in values and clarification.

INDIVIDUALIZED FACILITATION FOR MIDDLE-AGED LEARNERS

Cyril Houle describes the various categories of learning situations in his book, *The Design of Education*.[41] "Tutorial teaching" is Houle's major category which refers to one-to-one teaching. In this category, there are four subdivisions. They describe various one-to-one patterns from the most structured to the least structured arrangement.[42] The most useful pattern for the religious educator of middle-aged learners is "nondirective" instruction. This is the least structured form of one-to-one interaction.

The description of this pattern of interaction between learner and facilitator (teacher, instructor, etc.) is that "the learner asks for help but the person who guides him (counselor, therapist, teacher, or any other) knows that the seeker must find his answers within himself."[43] Houle suggests that Carl Rogers approach to counseling provides an excellent example for the facilitator who uses this pattern.[44]

Carl Rogers identified certain characteristics of a counselor which should apply to the "nondirective" teacher or tutor.[45] These characteristics would include the ability to accept and respect the client, to speak and act clearly and sensitively, and to free oneself from the limitations of the past and the institutional framework. Obviously, we cannot free ourselves totally from a religious framework, with its roots in history, nor should we attempt to do so. We need to free the learner to find his or her own way to the essential aspects within the appropriate framework.

If adult religious educators are engaged in helping the learner to grow spiritually, *and* if there are parallels between spiritual and psychosocial development, it would seem appropriate to use a similar approach to assist in both forms of development. Because many church workers involved in religious education have some training and experience in counseling, the approach may be developed more rapidly and effectively for that group of facilitators. It is also clear from the previously mentioned research findings that this is the kind of relationship which many middle-aged learners seek.[46]

Working with the Individual Learner

Although the adult religious educator may assume a "nondirective" role as facilitator, it is important to note that learners may have differing opinions about how they would like to engage in the learning process. Some learners will prefer a plan which provides them with a sense of direction while other learners prefer to be flexible. When the religious educator encounters the latter type of learner, it is easier to be nondirective. When the encounter is with the former type of learner who wants a clear sense of direction, it will require an effort to assist the learner to achieve his or her own sense of direction.

When the encounter is with a middle-aged learner who requires a firm plan, you may wish to consider the development of a learning contract. The learning contract approach has been described by Malcolm Knowles in his book on self-directed learning.[47] Learning contracts have been utilized with a wide range of adult learners in many settings. It provides a workable framework for a self-directed learner and a nondirective facilitator.

GROUP FACILITATION FOR MIDDLE-AGED LEARNERS

There is a wide range of methods and techniques available to the religious educator working as a group facilitator with middle-aged learners. A useful source is "40 Ways to Teach in Groups," by Martha Leypoldt.[48]

A technique called "nominal group" process may be particularly helpful because it allows the learner to review his or her feelings, ideas, attitudes, and experiences. One can readily see how the application of this technique for middle-aged learners begins to work on developmental tasks such as the search for meaning or values clarification. The facilitator must work effectively with the results of this introspective process.

Other useful techniques are those which are designed to promote sharing directly with the other members of the group and the facilitator. Techniques such as brainstorming and buzz groups can provide many opportunities for sharing.

There are certain situations where some form of simulation, such as role playing or a simulation game, can assist the middle-aged learner to gain insight to life through expanded experiences. Situations may be devised, but a wide range of simulation games and exercises are available from many sources.

Many exercises have been developed over the years to assist the learner in the process of values clarification. There may be occasions when specific instruments or tests are available and useful. Middle-aged learners may not react favorably to some forms of "testing" unless they see the test clearly as a tool which meets their particular needs.

CONCLUDING STATEMENT

This chapter has reviewed the life situation of the middle-aged learner including psychosocial development, religious development, learning theory in general, and learning theory with reference to spiritual or religious learning. The middle-aged adult does engage in psychosocial development through the search for meaning of life which closely parallels religious development. The learning which is appropriate for this situation involves a degree of self-direction and opportunities for discussion.

Specific recommendations have been made for religious educators of middle-aged persons with reference to the roles and functions appropriate to various learning situations. The most appropriate role for the religious educator is the nondirective facilitator who responds to learner needs. The facilitator's functions which encourage exploration of the meaning of life through self or group planning and sharing will fit this role quite well. It is anticipated that these ideas, suggestions, and guidelines will be helpful to adult religious educators who engage in the exciting process of working with middle-aged learners.

NOTES

1. Robert J. Havighurst, *Developmental Tasks and Education,* 2nd ed. (New York: David McKay, 1970), p. 5.

2. Malcolm S. Knowles, *The Modern Practice of Adult Education: From Pedagogy to Androgogy* (Chicago: Follett Publishing, 1980), p. 51.

3. Bernice L. Neugarten, *Middle Age and Aging* (Chicago: University of Chicago Press, 1968), p. 94.

4. K. Patricia Cross, *Adults as Learners: Increased Participation and Facilitating Learning* (San Francisco: Jossey-Bass, 1981), p. 3.

5. Ibid., pp. 50-52.

6. Jack Botwinick, *Aging and Behaviour,* 2nd ed. (New York: Springer Publishing, 1978), p. 307.

7. Havighurst, *Developmental Tasks and Education,* p. 83.

8. Daniel J. Levinson et al., *The Seasons of a Man's Life* (New York: Ballantine Books, 1978), p. 57.

9. Gail Sheehy, *Passages: Predictable Crises of Adult Life* (New York: E. P. Dutton, 1976), p. 242.

10. Havighurst, *Developmental Tasks and Education,* chapter 7.

11. Levinson et al., *The Seasons of a Man's Life,* p. 20.

12. Erik Erikson, *Childhood and Society,* 2nd ed. (New York: Norton, 1963), pp. 189-190.

13. Roger L. Gould, *Transformations: Growth and Change in Adult Life* (New York: Simon and Schuster, 1978), p. 217.

14. Erikson, *Childhood and Society,* chapter 7.

15. Ibid., p. 266.

16. Leon McKenzie, *The Religious Education of Adults* (Birmingham, Ala.: Religious Education Press, 1982), p. 20.

17. James W. Fowler, *Stages of Faith: The Psychology of Human Development and the Quest for Training* (San Francisco: Harper & Row, 1981), p. 113.

18. Ibid., p. 186.

19. Allen Tough, *The Adult's Learning Projects: A Fresh Approach to Theory and Practice in Adult Learning,* 2nd ed. (Toronto: The Ontario Institute for Studies in Education, 1979).

20. Ibid., pp. 96-97.

21. R. E. Y. Wickett, "Adult Learning and Spiritual Growth," *Religious Education* 75, no. 5 (July-August, 1980), pp. 452-461.

22. John L. Elias, *The Foundations and Practice of Adult Religious Education* (Malabar, Fla.: Robert E. Krieger Publishing, 1982), p. 94.

23. Wickett, "Adult Learning and Spiritual Growth," p. 459.

24. Levinson, *The Season's of a Man's Life*, p. 199.

25. Wickett, "Adult Learning and Spiritual Growth," pp. 455-457.

26. The discrepancy can be accounted for through the selection process used to obtain respondents. The author obtained respondents from several groups including university extension courses and church groups.

27. Wickett, "Adult Learning and Spiritual Growth," pp. 458-459.

28. Roger Hiemstra, *The Older Adult and Learning* (Lincoln, Neb.: Department of Adult and Continuing Education, University of Nebraska, 1975); and Patricia Coolican, *The Learning Styles of Mothers of Young Children* (doctoral dissertation; Syracuse University, 1973), p. 569.

29. Tough, *The Adult's Learning Projects,* p. 19.

30. Wickett, "Adult Learning and Spiritual Growth," p. 458.

31. Ibid., p. 460.

32. Tough, *The Adult's Learning Projects,* p. 86.

33. Wickett, "Adult Training and Spiritual Growth," p. 460.

34. Malcolm Knowles, *Self-Directed Learning: A Guide for Learners and Teachers* (Chicago: Follett Publishing, 1975), Part II.

35. Virginia McCoy, "Adult Life Cycle Change," *Lifelong Learning: The Adult Years* 1, no. 2 (October, 1977), pp. 14-18 and 31.

36. Ibid., p. 17.

37. Wickett, "Adult Learning and Spiritual Growth," p. 457.

38. Donald E. Smith, "Intentional Mid-Life Career Changes," Ed.D. dissertation, University of Toronto, 1984, p. 86.

39. Ibid., p. 87.

40. Henri J. M. Nouwen, *Reaching Out: The Three Movements of the Spiritual Life* (Garden City, N.Y.: Doubleday, 1975), p. 46.

41. Cyril O. Houle, *The Design of Education* (San Francisco: Jossey-Bass, 1972), chapter 4.

42. Ibid., pp. 96-101.

43. Ibid., p. 100.

44. Ibid.

45. Carl R. Rogers, *On Becoming A Person* (Boston: Houghton Mifflin Co., 1961), pp. 50-55.

46. Wickett, "Adult Learning and Spiritual Growth."

47. Knowles, *Self-Directed Learning.*

48. Martha M. Leypoldt, *40 Ways to Teach in Groups* (Valley Forge, Pa.: Judson Press, 1967).

Chapter 5

Working with Older Adults

LINDA JANE VOGEL

Older adults have described their participation in school- and church-sponsored classes in significantly different ways. Education is seen as:

"Just filling time" and "making me a more compassionate person."
"One activity among many" and "making me more aware of the needs of the world."
"A place to associate with more people and make new friends" and "an experience that gives me a broader perspective on life so I'm not as narrow-minded."
A way of "avoiding stagnation" and an experience that "helps me grow in my faith."[1]

This wide range of responses illustrates the fact that older persons bring a variety of needs and expectations to learning experiences. Planning a comprehensive adult religious education program with older adults requires an examination of the special needs and the unique resources they bring to such a program.

In this chapter, we will seek to examine the physical, psychological, and social needs of older adults, as well as the experience and wisdom which older adults can bring to a teaching/learning encounter. We will examine a model for engaging in religious education with older adults. Then we will focus on strategies for developing adult religious education programs.

105

SPECIAL NEEDS OF OLDER ADULTS

Aging is a complex and gradual process that brings specific changes, physically and mentally. Since these changes tend to be incremental, most persons are able to adapt; their social functioning is not seriously limited well into the seventies and beyond.[2] With advancing age, however, persons do become more vulnerable, and adaptations may need to be made in program planning to meet the special needs of persons in the last third of the life span.

Older adults today, as a cohort, have had less formal education than younger cohorts. Education in the past tended to emphasize mastery of knowledge rather than learning to learn.

As the rate of change in our world continues to accelerate, older persons can benefit greatly from nonthreatening learning opportunities which emphasize the *process* of finding answers and making adjustments in a high-technological society.

When older adults participate in formal adult education opportunities today, they give reasons related more to expanding personal knowledge, while younger learners are more apt to say they are seeking job-related information or skills.[3] The need for education that is holistic becomes critical. The affective as well as the cognitive must be considered as one examines beliefs, values, and attitudes in a relational context. Persons can then grow toward wholeness and self-actualization.

Much is being written about the stages of human development. As our population continues to age, more attention is being given to developmental theories which relate to later life. As we have seen (in chapter one), Erik Erikson maintains that older adults are in a position to develop "a sense of ego integrity" which involves making meaning of and accepting one's life; if they fail to do this, they are overtaken by "a sense of despair" and the fear of death.[4]

Robert Peck has expanded on Erikson's final stage (integrity versus disgust or despair). Peck maintains that retirement leads persons to face the issue of "ego-diffferentiation versus work-role preoccupation." Those whose identities are irrevocably tied to their work will have difficulty adjusting to, and finding meaning in, life beyond retirement. As persons begin to experience failing health, they need to deal with the issue of "body-transcendence versus body-preoccupation." Persons who are able to focus beyond their own physical fraility have the potential for continued growth and meaning in their lives. Finally, Peck asserts that in old age persons confront the issue of "ego-transcendence versus ego-preoccupation." Those who are able to find meaning and to see beyond their own inevitable death, have found a sense of well-being and integrity that negates despair.[5]

It will be helpful to keep in mind Abraham Maslow's hierarchy[6] as we examine the needs of older adults. It can be illustrated in the following way.

Figure 5.1
MASLOW'S HIERARCHY OF NEEDS

Maslow's hierarchy illustrates the necessity of meeting persons *where they are.* For example, education focusing on esteem needs will not intersect in any meaningful way with persons who are struggling with how they will cope and can maintain their own home now that their spouse is institutionalized.

Building on the insights of Erikson, Peck, and Maslow, Howard McClusky organizes the needs of older persons in this way. First, *coping needs* must be satisfied. Physical and economic needs must be addressed before attention can be focused on a person's higher needs. Education may provide coping skills to enable persons to focus on their *expressive needs.* At this point, persons are able to share themselves with others and it is possible to engage in community building. Beyond this, persons can address their *contributive needs*. There is a human need to give and to be needed which can now be addressed. Beyond this, persons may express *influence needs* which allow persons to engage in changing the environment and focusing on societal issues. Finally, persons are able to face the *need for transcendence* as they seek to make meaning of death and, thereby to make meaning of life.[7]

Some special needs which those learners in their 70s and beyond face include 1) seeking dignity and self-control, 2) discovering satisfying activities that one can do, 3) finding ways one can continue to make contributions to society, 4) seeking ways to interact with younger people, and 5) remaining physically and mentally alert.[8]

It becomes clear, then, that persons in later life have age-related physical, psychological, and social needs. Persons age at different rates and in different ways. Adult religious educators and those who work with older adults must know the persons with whom they work and must relate in ways that acknowledge the special needs and concerns of the older adult.

UNIQUE RESOURCES OF OLDER ADULTS

Older adults are, by definition, survivors. Too often, attention is focused on the problems and needs of the elderly; not enough attention is given to the unique resources which older adults have and are. They may bring rich life experiences and wisdom to the teaching/learning opportunities in which they participate.

The older adult embodies particular beliefs and a lifestyle that they have developed and for which they accept responsibility. When these persons come to the faith community they bring who they are—their past experiences and their capabilities and needs—to a situation which can be designed to enable knowledge, understanding, and personal transformation.

The elderhostel is one of the most exciting arenas where one can experience the unique resources older adults bring to teaching/learning encounters. The elderhostel is one of the fastest growing educational movements of our time. In 1975, five colleges in New Hampshire held week-long programs for 200 persons aged 60 and over who wanted to ask questions, to explore new ideas, to learn new skills, and to increase their sense of accomplishment. These persons brought a lifetime of experience, and when all their experience and excitement about learning intersected with the expertise of the professors, the results were electrifying. By 1985, over 700 colleges and universities in the United States, Canada, Scandinavia, and Europe were offering elderhostel classes and more than 160,000 older adults had become hostelers.

Elderhostel participants pay an inclusive low-cost fee, live in college dormitories, eat in campus dining halls, and generally take three classes which meet daily for one week. Lack of formal education has proved not to be a barrier to successful participation.

Learners I have worked with at Westmar College's Elderhostel have studied computer, Old Testament, microbiology, creative writing, cultural geography, painting with watercolors, and sociology. To see persons—some in their eighties—tackle the computer and then watch them as a letter they wrote to their grandchildren comes off the printer illustrates real excitement over learning. Listening to learners in a creative writing class read pieces they wrote about childhood experiences makes history live.

A perspective on life and society that is enhanced by years of widely varied experiences, and an awareness and strength that come from coping and adapting to life situations, enrich opportunities for learning through dialogical interchange. A drive to overcome losses and to make life meaningful again is one of the unique characteristics older learners often bring to educational settings. Older adults have generally moved beyond the need to move ahead in a career and that brings a freedom to learn for learning's sake that fosters creativity and personal growth.

By acknowledging the potential for personal and social growth in later life, the door is opened for new excitement as persons experience the possibility of growing toward human maturity. Evelyn Whitehead focuses on six religious images which she believes may be especially rich for persons in later life who are addressing the issue of integrity versus despair. These images, include 1) personal salvation, 2) hope, 3) a religious sense of time and personal history, 4) God's unconditional love for the individual, 5) the spiritual discipline of "emptiness" and "letting go," and 6) the image of the Christian as pilgrim-on-the-way.[9] The life experiences older adults have had make them better able than most to appropriate these images in deep and powerful ways. Education within the context of a faith community can provide opportunities for older adults to examine and explore these images in light of their personal life experiences and their hopes.

Integrity implies a new kind of freedom. Persons who achieve a sense of integrity are able to accept themselves as they are; they are also able to accept others who may be different. Integrity frees persons from being slaves to conformity. That freedom enables older adults to deal with questions of meaning and purpose and hope in honest and probing ways.

So it is that older adults may come to teaching/learning experiences with a perspective enriched by experience and with a single-mindedness wrought out of a maturing awareness of who they are and what life is and means. That is a resource that challenges adult religious educators who seek to work with older adults in the setting of a faith community.

A MODEL FOR RELIGIOUS EDUCATION WITH OLDER ADULTS

Religious education always occurs within a social and personal context. The following diagram illustrates one way we may visualize the social and personal context for engaging older adults in religious education.

Religious education takes place in the lives of older adults when their needs intersect with the Story and Vision of the faith community so that growth in knowledge, understanding, and transformation can occur.

We engage in religious education with older adults when persons in the last third of the life span participate in a teaching/learning setting within a particular faith community. Older selves bring who they are (their personal stories and visions) and their personal needs into a faith community which embodies a larger Story and Vision.[11] This Story and Vision manifests itself in

Figure 5.2[10]
A MODEL FOR RELIGIOUS EDUCATION
WITH OLDER ADULTS

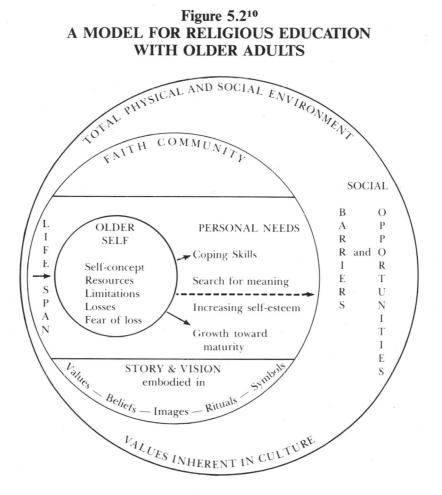

values, beliefs, images, rituals, and symbols. The particular faith community must itself be seen within the larger societal context which includes the often conflicting values inherent in the culture, as well as a wide range of social barriers and opportunities. This model, then, can provide us with a beginning point for examining ways of engaging older adults in religious education.

Assumptions underlie every model and approach to religious education. It is assumed here that persons must address their physical, psychological, and social needs within the context of their communities and the world. Older adults continue the process of seeking to make sense of their own lives and of life in general. Everyone brings who they are and all are capable of growing toward wholeness as they seek to resolve the issue of integrity versus despair in their lives.

The theological assumptions and the lifestyle stance of particular faith communities provide a context out of which persons engage in religious education. Much of the content to be studied, as well as the teaching/learning strategies which are used, are determined by the Story and Vision of each faith community.

DEVELOPING PROGRAMS WITH OLDER ADULTS

Older adults bring rich resources to the faith community. Programing for them is a task that can best be done mutually by planners, teachers, and learners. Because older adults have lived many years and make a myriad of choices, we can expect an extremely wide range of interests and needs. This necessitates a multifaceted adult religious education program.

Program planning[12] requires that the specific needs of the older adults in a particular faith community be determined and prioritized. Prioritizing is critical since a program which seeks to meet all the needs of all the people will be fragmented and is doomed to fail.

One of the first things that should be done in the planning process is to determine if there are existing programs within the faith community or in the larger community which are or could quite easily address the prioritized needs.[13] If it is determined that the faith community ought to develop a specific program, then a committee of interested persons should engage in the planning process.

Once priorities are established, specific plans can be made to meet the needs that have been identified as most important. Then those involved in planning can find the necessary resources to achieve the goals that have been set. Many older adults are themselves important resources and must not be overlooked. Draw on the expertise of older adults in the group and in the larger community. Other resources which must be located include curriculum materials, financial resources, and adequate facilities.

Ongoing evaluation is essential to the planning process. An

identification of new needs may grow out of the evaluating process. As needs change, goals may appropriately change since evaluation is more than an end product.

Addressing Needs of Older Adults

The Shepherd's Center[14] in Kansas City, Missouri, provides a helpful model for developing and implementing a comprehensive, ecumenical program with older adults. This program was conceived in order to provide an opportunity for persons in later maturity to use their experience and resources in performing significant social roles as volunteers in the program. At the same time, the program was designed to advocate the rights of persons beyond retirement to a fair share of the society's resources. It became an effective vehicle for increasing life satisfaction in later life by engaging older persons in developing their inner resources, continuing to involve them in artistic and learning experiences, promoting caring relationships, and tapping their experience and knowledge to serve community needs.

The Shepherd's Center approach correlates with insights from Abraham Maslow, Erik Erikson, Robert Peck, and Howard McClusky. Its program is organized around four areas of need: life maintenance, life enrichment, life reconstruction, and life transcendence.

Life Maintenance

If the assessment shows that older persons need assistance and coping skills in the area of life maintenance, this should be given a high priority. Life maintenance activities may deal with basic human needs like hunger and shelter. Programs such as meals-on-wheels, handyman, and hospice address needs persons have at this level.

Hospice[15] provides a good example of an approach that cuts across all four levels of need. However, since terminally ill persons in severe pain do not have energy to focus on questions dealing with God's mercy or judgment, hospice first attacks the problems of pain control and fear of abandonment.

Comprehensive adult religious education programs, like hospice, must first address issues which will enable persons to cope successfully with maintaining whatever level of independence they are capable of and meeting the day-to-day demands of life. If we are to engage in an holistic approach to ministry, maintenance level needs must be met. At this basic level, then, programs for grocery shopping and doing errands for homebound persons may need to be developed. A telephone reassurance program might be one specific need.

To decide that "these kinds of things" are not the business of faith communities is, in my judgment, a serious error. While we should avoid duplicating services provided by others, a faith community—which emphasizes wholeness—ought to put people in touch with existing services and should provide such services where they are not available.

Our understanding of adult human development leads us to conclude that unless these life maintenance needs are met it is quite useless to expend energy and money doing what might be more generally understood to be adult religious education.

Life Enrichment

The Shepherd's Center program focuses a great deal of time and energy in this area through the development of an educational program called "Adventures in Learning." More than 1400 persons participate in their winter term. This program tends to be stimulating and nonthreatening and draws larger numbers of older adults. A wide range of courses are offered one day a week for ten weeks. Volunteer teachers—most of whom are older adults—share their excitement and expertise with others. A sampling of courses from one term includes creative writing, wood carving, international affairs, macrame, French, beginner's bridge, bible therapy, defensive driving, and building self-esteem.

For a minimal enrollment fee ($5.00), persons can participate in as many courses as they choose. These opportunities provide older adults with ways of meeting their expressive and/or contributive needs. Again, this is a necessary component in a holistic approach to comprehensive ministry with older adults.

Life Reconstruction

Persons in the last third of the life span are vulnerable to experiencing loss—employment, income, health, spouse, friends, and independence. Significant losses necessitate a restructuring of life. Older persons often turn to a faith community when they face crises and experience loss.

Some programs which may be developed for persons who feel

the need to put their lives back together include addressing issues like alcoholism, widowhood, institutionalization, divorce, and marriage enrichment. It is crucial to begin where persons are. When persons first experience a major crisis, they need someone to listen and care; they need a place where they can express their anger and frustration without fear of rejection. The faith community can provide such a caring environment.

Peer support groups may be an appropriate approach for many persons who need to engage in life reconstruction. It is a fallacy to assume that persons dealing with issues like these need a class on the nature of God! Theological answers to personal crises rarely connect because persons must use all their available energy and resources to cope with life. Reflection can precede or follow a period of crisis, but persons are rarely able to engage in such activity while they are dealing with a crisis in their lives.

It is possible, however, to provide teaching/learning options for persons prior to their experiencing significant losses. For example, classes on preretirement planning and enabling families to cope with dying and death can be extremely beneficial for persons who later find themselves in such a position. This is an appropriate time to explore theological questions dealing with life crisis issues.

Another important aspect of a comprehensive adult religious education program is to offer study groups and training sessions for persons who want to be better equipped to relate with and help other persons in crisis. Examples of this kind of program include peer counseling training seminars for widows, hospice volunteer training programs, and lay visitation training sessions.

Taking adult religious education opportunities to persons where they are can be a vital form of ministry. For example, care and share groups which are held in a nursing home and which involve both institutionalized and noninstitutionalized elderly may be beneficial to persons in both groups.

Faith communities seek to enable persons to grow toward a wholeness that is a gift from God and is not dependent on physical strength, beauty, or human achievement. They are, therefore, in a unique position to help persons accept limitations while expanding their visions. It is possible, in the Judeo-Christian tradition, to both accept loss and find fulfillment. So it is that faith communities, drawing on expertise from a variety of disciplines and fields of study, can enable persons to be become whole.

Life Transcendence

Persons seeking to experience a sense of integrity rather than despair, may be looking for answers to questions about the meaning and purpose of life. How can older adults, looking back over their life and their world and facing the knowledge of their mortality, affirm life with joy and hope? Groups may engage in bible study or in studying classical or contemporary books. Significant issues such as the problem of evil, the nature and mission of the church, nuclear war and the future of humankind, or the meaning of death and life might be examined and discussed.

Adult religious education is the primary arena where issues like these can be examined and debated. Developing an open atmosphere where it is acceptable to raise questions is important. It may be necessary to combat earlier socialization which conditioned some older adults to believe that certain questions are taboo and that there are some things Christians should not think or say. Such attitudes can inhibit growth and be guilt-producing. If we are to enable persons on their spiritual pilgrimage, openness to new ideas and the life experiences of others are important prerequisites for growth.

Other older adults may be more interested in attending lectures by inspirational speakers rather than seriously engaging in study or discussion. Still others may just want to celebrate life through worship and music.

Making peace with one's life and death can come in many ways. Faith communities can provide resources and experiences as persons seek to experience the mystery and beauty in creation.

TEACHING OLDER ADULTS

The first guideline for anyone who teaches older adults is to know the persons they teach. The physical limitations, mental capabilities, educational levels, and expectations and needs of individuals and groups vary. Knowing one's audience is a cardinal rule for any effective communication; it is absolutely essential for persons who teach older adults.

Mature learners want to share responsibility for determining what methodologies are used. Some groups may want lectures; others may want a format that involves the entire group in discussion. In general, older learners do *not* want

- to be manipulated.
- to be talked down to.
- to lose control over their own lives or their group.
- to be seen as receiving ministry but having nothing to give.

Older adults want a setting that recognizes their special needs. This may include

- accessibility (e.g., no steps, close to parking and/or unloading zone, availability of transportation).
- a well-lighted, warm room that is not drafty.
- restrooms nearby.
- chairs that are firm and some with arms to assist one in getting up.
- daytime rather than evening meetings.

Older adults want to hear what is going on, but they do not want to be shouted at. This means it is important to

- create a comfortable environment with no distracting background noises.
- speak distinctly, not too rapidly, and lower the pitch of one's voice.
- rephrase statements when someone asks to have something repeated so that hard-to-hear sounds might be avoided.
- sit so everyone can see the mouths of persons who are speaking.

Never lose sight of the fact that learning is relational. The key to meaningful learning is engaging the learners in the teaching/learning process. This is crucial with older learners who bring rich life experiences to the group. The following guidelines can facilitate learning by older adults.[16]

- Choose activities and methods which make use of and build on the life experience of the learners.
- Make use of visual images and mental pictures in order to facilitate older persons in making associations with prior learning.
- Encourage self-pacing since feeling pressured seriously impairs successful learning of older adults.

- Identify a clear focus since distractions are a more serious problem for older learners.
- Make use of verbal abilities and skills since these are least susceptible to decline as persons age.
- Plan problem-centered learning activities since older learners prefer being able to see how new learning can be used in life situations.
- Engage in ongoing evaluation which involves all of the participants and which leads to adjustments in future teaching plans.

These guidelines can all contribute to a dialogical approach to teaching/learning which is responsive to the special needs and abilities of older adult learners. Dialogical education is education that requires being open to the needs of persons and to new ideas; it necessitates honesty and caring. Dialogue can transform persons and experiences while opening learners up to a future that involves growth and new possibilities.

TEACHING/LEARNING STRATEGIES

Selecting appropriate teaching strategies[17] to achieve our educational goals is important. Since religious education for older adults is, at its best, holistic, it needs to take cognitive, affective, and normative responses into account.

Strategies that enable learners to draw on the life experiences of persons in the group are desirable. New material can be appropriated best if it is linked in some way to knowledge persons already possess.

Strategies that make use of more than one of our senses are most effective. For example, a demonstration or a film is better than giving verbal instructions. Placing cue cards with key words or phrases on the wall as memory aids will improve retention of lectures.

Hymns and rituals that persons know can be effectively incorporated into teaching/learning experiences. Music often is a powerful means of communicating. John H. Westerhoff describes liturgy and ritual acts as ways to "equip and motivate persons and the (faith) community to act in the world for social change."[18]

Storytelling is an effective teaching strategy for persons of all ages. Jesus was a master storyteller. This is a strategy that is effective with older adults, including the frail elderly.

Creative writing (journaling, stories, poetry) can be an effective strategy to engage older learners in a teaching/learning setting. It enhances reflection on and sharing of individuals' life experiences as they intersect with the Story of their faith community.

Bible Study and *"prayer and share"* groups are often appealing to older learners. Using familiar formats to engage in seeking to understand what it means to be in right relationship with God and what it means to be a faithful servant of God in the world can be highly effective.

Intergenerational activities[19] can provide opportunities for older learners to share their wisdom and experience with persons of all ages in the faith community; at the same time, older learners can grow by relating with and understanding the perspectives of younger Christians.

Simulation games[20] provide an opportunity for persons to experience particular environments and conditions which are modeled after real-life situations. It is possible to experiment with possible solutions and to discover probable consequences within a safe environment.

Role-play gives older adults a freedom to experiment with possible solutions to problems that they might hesitate to explore in a discussion. Assuming an assigned role provides freedom to try on new (and perhaps unorthodox) ideas. This strategy makes use of pantomime and conversation as persons spontaneously act out assigned situations or relationships in order to develop empathy and insight as they seek to solve problems.

Lecture becomes a viable strategy when a person with good communication skills and knowledge that the group wants or needs is able to share his or her expertise. Whenever lecture is used, the speaker needs to remember the importance of providing stimuli for more than one sense. Speaking slowly and distinctly as well as checking to be sure the group can hear and is understanding is essential.

Discussion is appropriate when group members have knowledge and/or life experiences that can be shared to move the group toward its educational goals. It is important that discussions *not* be the sharing of uniformed opinions.

Media presentations (films, film strips, tapes, records, video tapes) can be effective if they address the issue being considered by the group. They must always be previewed to be sure that they are clearly audible and/or easy to see. Persons with unusual accents or who speak very rapidly may make an otherwise fine resource ineffective with older adults.

These strategies are a sampling of possible methodologies that can enhance the learning of older adults. Variety is important. Which strategies are chosen should be determined by the expectations, the physical and mental limitations, and the goals of the particular group of older adult learners.

DEVELOPING A COMPREHENSIVE
TEACHING/LEARNING PLAN

Once a faith community has decided to address the needs of older adults, it is time to put together a comprehensive teaching/learning plan. This task can best be done by a representative group within the faith community. In addition to persons charged with responsibility for educational ministry, it is crucial that older adults be involved from the beginning. The process to be followed might be based on the following outline:

1) Recognize possible need(s)
2) Contact representative persons from potential audiences to
   a. Seek to confirm need(s)
   b. Clarify what the need(s) is (are)
   c. Explore a wide variety of options
   d. Examine critically the underlying values and assumptions which undergird the development of teaching/learning plans for addressing need(s)
3) Develop a tentative program
   a. Objectives
   b. Methods or strategies
   c. Settings
   d. Timing
4) Promote program including specific teaching/learning opportunities
5) Present tentative teaching/learning plan to persons who respond

6) Implement plan with alterations as appropriate
7) Evaluate teaching/learning experience and its underlying assumptions
8) Evaluate teaching/learning experiences in light of total program objectives[21]

Short-circuiting the process at any point is apt to make a faith community's ministry with older adults less than it could be.

CONCLUSION

Adult religious education for the future must be holistic. It must address the needs and wants of older persons in our society. It is my belief that religious education

- must be deeply rooted in the tradition, values, experiences, beliefs, and vision of a faith community.
- must be informed by the disciplines of the social sciences and other fields of study.
- must join with older persons on their journey into maturity and faith-living.
- must be holistic by enabling persons to integrate the faith community's Story with their understanding of their own past, present, and future.
- must move beyond transmission of the Story to enable persons to own their faith and to make responsible decisions in light of who they are and what they believe.

Finally, religious education must seek to

Affirm the worth of every person,
Accept persons as they are,
Love the unlovable,
Offer forgiveness which makes persons new.
Proclaim release, justice, and peace
so that persons will respond by
doing justice,
loving mercy, and
walking humbly with God.[22]

NOTES

1. Linda Jane Vogel, *How Older Adults Perceive and Legitimize their Adult Education Participation in Churches and Schools,* (doctoral dissertation, The University of Iowa, 1981), pp. 46-49.

2. Robert C. Atchley, *Aging: Continuity and Change* (Belmont, Calif.: Wadsworth Publishing Company, 1983), pp. 43-65.

3. Linda Jane Vogel, *The Religious Education of Older Adults* (Birmingham, Ala.: Religious Education Press, 1984), pp. 40-42.

4. Erik H. Erikson, *Childhood and Society,* 2nd ed. (New York: Norton, 1963), pp. 247-274.

5. Robert C. Peck, "Psychological Developments in the Second Half of Life," in *Middle Age and Aging,* ed. Bernice Neugarten (Chicago: The University of Chicago Press, 1968), pp. 88-92.

6. Abraham H. Maslow, *Motivation and Personality* (New York: Harper & Brothers, 1954), pp. 80-92.

7. Howard Y. McClusky, "Education for Aging: The Scope of the Field and Perspectives for the Future," in *Learning for Aging,* ed. Stanley Grabowski and W. Dean Mason (Washington, D.C.: Adult Education Association of the U.S.A., 1976), pp. 324-355.

8. Robert J. Havighurst, "Education Through the Adult Life Span," *Educational Gerontology* 1 (1976), p. 49.

9. Evelyn Eaton Whitehead, "Religious Images of Aging: An Examination of Themes in Contemporary Christian Thought," in *Aging and the Human Spirit,* ed. Carol LeFevre and Perry LeFevre (Chicago: Exploration Press, 1981), pp. 56-67.

10. Vogel, *The Religious Education of Older Adults,* p. 100.

11. This model makes use of Thomas Groome's shared praxis approach to Christian religious education. For a careful explication of this approach see Thomas H. Groome, *Christian Religious Education: Sharing our Story and Vision* (San Francisco: Harper & Row, 1980).

12. For a helpful discussion of planning see Donald F. Clingan, *Aging Persons in the Community of Faith,* rev. ed. (Indianapolis, Ind.: Indiana Commission on the Aging and Aged for The Institute on Religion and Aging, 1980), pp. 11-17.

13. See Vogel, *The Religious Education of Older Adults,* pp. 143-189, for a more detailed discussion of developing and implementing programs of religious education for older adults.

14. Information about The Shepherd's Center located at Central United Methodist Church in Kansas City, Missouri, was gained from a personal visit to the center. Dr. Elbert C. Cole, founder and first executive director, was most helpful to me. Since that time, one of my students did an internship there. The Shepherd's Center is a process rather than a program or a place. It serves the elderly in a prescribed geographical area and fourteen of the twenty-five churches and synagogues in that area are actively involved in the process. A helpful resource for

persons desiring more information is Elbert C. Cole, "Lay Ministries with Older Adults," in *Ministry with the Aging: Designs, Challenges, Foundations,* ed. William M. Clements (San Francisco: Harper & Row, 1981), pp. 250-265.

15. Hospice is a rapidly growing movement which is committed to improving the quality of life for terminally ill persons and their families. A good resource for learning more about hospice is by Sandol Stoddard, *The Hospice Movement: A Better Way of Caring for the Dying* (Briarcliff Manor, N.Y.: Stein and Day, 1978).

16. For more detailed discussions of principles see Victor M. Agruso, Jr., *Learning in the Later Years: Principles of Educational Gerontology* (New York: Academic Press, 1978). Also see Douglas C. Kimmel, *Adulthood and Aging* (New York: John Wiley & Sons, 1974), pp. 376-386; David A. Peterson, *Facilitating Education for Older Learners* (San Francisco: Jossey-Bass, 1983), pp. 146-166.

17. A general handbook for teachers of adults is *Adult Education Procedures: A Handbook of Tested Patterns for Effective* Participation, by Paul Bergevin, Dwight Morris, and Robert M. Smith (New York: Seabury Press, 1963). Wayne Rood's *The Art of Teaching Christianity* (Nashville: Abingdon Press, 1968) provides a theological rationale as well as helpful teaching strategies for Christian religious education. A helpful book focusing on ministry with older persons is Clingan, *Aging Persons in the Community of Faith.* Another excellent resource is Leon McKenzie, *The Religious Education of Adults* (Birmingham, Ala.: Religious Education Press, 1982), pp. 190-226.

18. John H. Westerhoff III, "The Liturgical Imperative of Religious Education," in *The Religious Education We Need: Toward the Renewal of Christian Education,* ed. James Michael Lee (Birmingham, Ala.: Religious Education Press, 1977), p. 82.

19. A helpful resource which includes annotated bibliographic suggestions for planning intergenerational activities in the faith community is Donald Griggs and Patricia Griggs, *Generations Learning Together* (Livermore, Calif.: Griggs Educational Service, 1976).

20. See Dennis Benson, *Gaming* (Nashville: Abingdon Press, 1971) for information on how to create and use simulation games.

21. Vogel, *The Religious Education of Older Adults,* pp. 154-155.

22. Based on Micah 6:8 and quoted from Vogel, ibid., p. 194.

Chapter 6

Working with Educators of Adults

R. MICHAEL HARTON

The planning has been thorough. With a good turnout for the training session of volunteer children's teachers, the director of children's work is well into her outline. She has noticed that the audience is beginning to squirm and fidget just like the children they *teach in this very same room.* She seems to be having trouble keeping their attention.

The youth minister is frustrated because the volunteer youth leaders are still not using the activities and methods recommended for teaching youth. He has *explained* how to use them at least five times and asked the leaders to try the approaches, but to no avail. He presumes that they just must be a stubborn lot!

The DRE is disappointed. Not only did fewer adults than he expected show up for his course on "Developing a Christian Lifestyle," but half that crowd did not return for the second session! When he struck on the idea for the course it sounded like something his whole congregation would go for. In the publicity and announcements he *told* the adults how much *they needed* the course. His conclusion: The adults are just not very committed!

The diocesan director of adult religious education, a former parish DRE, has attracted a good crowd for his weekly discussion of "Parents and Parish Working Together." He has trouble getting them to stick to the subject, however, and never seems to cover everything he has set out for each one-hour session.

Have you noticed that the above professionals all seem to have something in common (besides their frustration)? In all the good planning they have done, they seem completely unaware of the

125

needs and characteristics of their adult students.

The intention of this chapter's wording is to focus attention beyond persons who by professional training and identification are adult educators. This includes local parish DRE's and age-group specialists, pastors and diocesan and/or regional educators. It may even include educators in colleges and seminaries.

FALSE ASSUMPTIONS

Several false assumptions seem prevalent among many educators who work with adults in religious education settings.

False Assumption 1

Mastery of a particular content means one can automatically communicate that content to others. Therefore an age-group worker who has majored in understanding and teaching that group can teach others effectively about the group because the specialist has mastered the knowledge available and is therefore the expert. Or a scholar on Old Testament studies will make an effective teacher because he or she has spent years in study of the subject. This assumption is particularly prevalent in higher education. This writer, along with twenty fellow undergraduates, once spent a frustrating semester in an investments class where the professor was equally frustrated. The prof had been a highly successful investments counselor in a well-known firm. The business school therefore automatically assumed he could teach investments. After that trial and error attempt at teaching the prof gave up and started a consulting service. Very few institutions of higher education offer any training or orientation in teaching to new faculty.

False Assumption 2

Preparation as an educator with any one age group qualifies one to teach other age groups effectively. As a DRE, this writer was speechless at the response of a teacher of young adults he was attempting to enlist for some upcoming training. The focus was to be on teaching adults. The person let it be known in no uncertain terms that she did not need the training. After all, she already had a masters degree in elementary education! No doubt she had a good grasp of *pedagogy.*

False Assumption 3

Because adults are more mature, teaching them does not require attention to *process* as does teaching children and adolescents. Adults are only interested in the content. Also, as a part of that maturity, adults are responsible for their own motivation, for paying attention to the content and determining its relevance. If they seem not to be motivated, do not attend to the content, or drop out they are just acting irresponsibly.

False Assumption 4

With adequate publicity adults will respond to almost any course regardless of their age or situation in life. Find the right "hook," turn on the "hype," and you can attract them. Such tactics succeed occasionally in getting large numbers of adults to attend—the first session. There they discover they have been over-sold or misled. Rarely do they return, either to subsequent sessions or courses!

A COUPLE OF SAFE ASSUMPTIONS

There are at least two assumptions that can safely be made. First, all religious educators, regardless of their specialization in younger age groups or given content areas will spend at least part of their time teaching and leading adults. Preschool children's and youth's ministers usually are responsible for equipping adult volunteers who work with the young. Also, while many students in higher education are "older adolescents," an increasing number are more mature persons, adults 25 years of age and older.

Second, it is safe to assume that those who work with or teach adults in any setting need to understand the characteristics and needs of those adults. In fact, a basic principle in education in general is that teachers must understand those they teach, regardless of their age.

WHAT EDUCATORS NEED TO KNOW ABOUT ADULTS

Some of the things all educators need to understand about the adults with whom they work are indicated by the difficulties experienced by the directors and teachers mentioned at the beginning of the chapter. The children's director seemed oblivious to the importance of creating a good climate for adult learning, including *physical comfort*. It might have been helpful to hold the training for teachers of children in the children's classroom, but the adults should not have been expected to sit in the child-size chairs. No wonder they squirmed! Had the youth minister been aware that adults, too, learn through *discovery* he might have held a demonstration of the new teaching approaches, or made arrangements for the youth teachers to observe a class where the approaches were being used effectively. The DRE might have experienced more success with the planned event if it had been planned *in collaboration with* adults and according to their *perceived* needs. And since social relationships are of prime importance to young adults, the diocesan director might have been less frustrated if he had built into the sessions a "fellowship period" and adjusted the schedule accordingly.

Following is a discussion of several matters to which religious educators need to attend in order to be aware of the unique aspects of teaching and leading adults. It is not within the scope of this chapter to treat each of these in depth. Rather, the intent is to identify some crucial issues which the reader may pursue by consulting the sources cited in the notes section.

Conducive Climate

Many religious educators are unaware of how important it is to create a conducive climate for adult learning. A poor physical environment, for example, can result in many *de-motivators* which hamper learning (e.g., inappropriate furnishings). But perhaps of even more importance is a healthy psychological environment. Malcolm Knowles has declared boldly, "I see the setting of a climate that is conducive to learning as perhaps the single most critical thing I do as a facilitator of learning."[1] Religious educators need to know not only the components of a conducive learning climate, but they need to know *how* it is developed. Knowles details several direct interventions that affect the learning climate.[2]

Developmental Characteristics

In light of the volumes now available on the dynamic nature of adult development, it is astonishing that an attitude still seems to persist that few changes, other than obvious physical ones, occur during adulthood. Thus in many educational activities adults are lumped together with little regard to differences due to age, stage, or circumstance. This is ironic since most religious educators have spent hours in college or seminary studying childhood and adolescent development. These educators need to take a closer look at Erikson's sixth, seventh, and eighth psychosocial stages articulating the "crises of adulthood."[3] Havighurst's celebrated "developmental tasks" of the adult years should be studied.[4] They need a survey of the current literature including Neugarten, Gould, and Levinson, for example. Life-span development theories need to be examined.[5] Effective planning for educational events for adults depends on knowing their needs. These can be derived and anticipated in great measure by understanding them developmentally.

Characteristics of Adults as Learners

The literature on adult development is rich with implications for how we treat adults as learners. These must be consciously analyzed and discussed as to appropriate response. But we must go beyond that body of knowledge to more careful exploration of adult learning. Much is known about how adults approach learning activities and generally what they expect of the activities and their leaders. Experience and research has produced helpful information on leader behavior, structure of activities, and methods and techniques to which adults usually respond best.[6] One important consideration, for example, is the learner's life experience. A challenge the educator faces is how to recognize that experience and utilize it appropriately as a resource. Of course, educational psychologists have long emphasized the need to key new learning to the learner's experience.[7] Religious educators who plan, structure, and conduct events in the light of this information on adult learning will likely elicit more positive response from adults.

Needs Assessment

Unfortunately, needs assessment is not a well-developed component in adult education. Some confusion exists over its meaning and appropriate ways to do a needs assessment. This is partially due both to the scarcity of literature on the subject and the fact that the concept is used differently in different fields. For example, many instructional developers currently look to Roger Kaufman as the guru on needs assessment. Kaufman's definition is simple and applicable to assessing learning needs: "the harvesting of gaps between What is and What Should be and the placing of those gaps in priority order."[8] However, he generally applies the term to organizational systems development. Attention to individual needs of persons is usually called "learner analysis." Even within the field of instructional development, however, there is as yet little consistent use of the term.

Malcolm Knowles and Leon McKenzie both address needs assessment as applied to the individual in the learning setting. Knowles distinguishes between learning interests and learning needs. "If a need is expressed behaviorally as a 'want' or a 'desire,' then an interest can be said to be expressed as a 'liking' or a 'preference.' "[9] Knowles provides a helpful chapter (chapter 6) in *The Modern Practice of Adult Education* which contains many examples of approaches to assessing the learning needs of individuals. Several paper and pencil tools are provided. McKenzie points to the necessity of distinguishing between *ascribed* needs and *ascertained* needs. "An ascribed need or interest is a need or interest attributed to a person by someone else. . . . An ascertained need or interest is a need or interest identified by the person who perceives a lack in himself or consciously attributes a particular preference to himself."[10] This is an important distinction for all religious educators. His discussion in *The Religious Education of Adults* of the "ascriptive" approach taken by most religious educators is indicting to us all.[11] "Sizing up" an individual or group, we often decide what they need and plan accordingly without attempting to discover the congruence with the learners' perception of need. The results are often *disastrous,* not to mention *frustrating.*

Program Planning

Just as needs are often assessed unilaterally by religious educators, they often assume sole responsibility for planning educational events for adults. Knowles, McKenzie, and several others have addressed this subject with a quite thorough treatment of alternative approaches and procedures.[12] Different authors include different numbers of components in their planning models, but they nearly all insist on involvement of the learner in the planning process. With a variety of models available in the expanding literature on planning in adult education there is little justification for religious educators to perpetuate inappropriate and ineffective approaches. There is more at stake than simply gratifying the educator's needs for a well-attended event. At stake in the planning process are not only accurately addressed learner needs, but the learner's sense of autonomy, sense of control over his learning, and stimulating and effective choices of methods and techniques.

Factors Affecting Participation

"Lack of commitment" is an often-used excuse to explain why adults fail to attend or return to our learning activities. Actually, this generalization is quite false, since nearly all adults are committed to *something*. Why people participate in adult education has been studied for a quarter of a century now. Researchers for the most part agree that commitment to a goal is the major factor leading to participation.[13] It does not necessarily have to be a learning goal per se. On the contrary, it is more likely related to something beyond that learning setting.[14] The achievement of the goal is seen as being at least partially facilitated by learning.

T. Shipp and Leon McKenzie studied reasons for nonparticipation in adult religious education.[15] Their research has been replicated by numerous of their graduate students from several religious persuasions. Generally, the same patterns have been found by these researchers. Just as adults often give a variety of reasons for participating, those who stay away usually give several reasons for doing so. For example, in the Shipp and McKenzie research some respondents did not like those in charge of the activities. Some perceived the learning activities as irrelevant while others simply felt that the sponsoring church was "out of touch." Inadequate or poor planning of events, feelings of exclusion, and disappointment with unmet expectations were often cited by those who did not return to learning activities.

Patricia Cross, Gordon Darkenwald, and Sharan Merriam have explored factors affecting participation in adult education in general. Cross posited a stimulating model which gives insight into the interaction of many variables including self-evaluation, attitudes about education, life transitions, importance of goals and expectations, information about learning activities, and opportunities and barriers.[16] Darkenwald and Merriam have proposed a "Psychosocial Interaction Model of Participation." The model shows the effect of socio-economic status, "learning press" (a function of the level of social participation, occupational complexity and lifestyle), perceived value and utility of adult education, readiness, and participation stimuli.[17] To summarize their thesis, if all the above are *high,* then *barriers* to participation are assumed to be low and the probability of participation is high. Conversely, if these factors are *low,* barriers are considered more formidable and thus the probability of participation is low. Darkenwald and Merriam also discuss the influence of initial individual and family characteristics as well as preparatory education and socialization.[18] Religious educators owe it to themselves and their constituents to be familiar with this literature.

Exposure to the Literature

Several prominent authors and research projects have been mentioned in this section. They are but a sampling of the rich body of literature in this growing field. Religious educators need more than exposure to the literature; they need to do focused reading in the foregoing subject areas. But they need help in their selection of appropriate and substantive books and journal articles. The quality is inconsistent, and there is considerable duplication and overlap. Carefully developed bibliographies would be a major asset to religious educators seeking to become effective teachers and leaders of adults. A beginning point might be the bibliographical references cited in each of this book's chapters.

SUMMARY

The assumption of this section has been that all religious educators spend at least part of their time seeking to educate adults. Even though it may seem like a small component (as compared, say, to the time spent with youth by a youth minister), the time spent equipping adult volunteers may in fact be a key to the success of the overall effort with an age group. A survey conducted several years ago in a major denomination revealed that a lack of trained leaders was the most crucial need facing the denomination's churches. This was listed number one among about twenty-five needs. The situation has probably changed very little.

The focus of this section has been on identifying and providing a rationale for some things to which religious educators need to attend in order to be effective with adults. Once again, the reader is referred to this chapter's notes for bibliography useful for a detailed reading of specific areas summarized in this section.

ADULT RELIGIOUS EDUCATION AND PROFESSIONAL IDENTITY

As may be seen in the foregoing discussion, many religious educators are involved in adult education without consciously recognizing it. Their work with adults is incidental to their primary identification with other roles or professions. There is, however, a growing segment in religious education who either by default or design are primarily concerned with planning and conducting educational activities for adults. Often responsibility for adults is shifted to the DRE as other age-group specialists are secured (children or youth directors for example). Since most of his or her work is primarily with adults, as on councils or committees, etc., it seems natural for the DRE to begin to focus more on this age group with others giving primary attention to younger ages.

Increasingly DREs and newcomers to the field of religious education are choosing to specialize in work with adults. Many are preparing themselves for this specialized ministry through graduate study in adult education. Some seminaries are offering a variety of courses in adult religious education with a major available in the field. Other persons are seeking to become specialists through self-designed reading programs and continuing education courses.

This growing specialization is showing up in an increasing number of parishes, churches, dioceses, and regional and national denominational bodies. Specialists are being hired to work with all adults or specific groups of adults, such as singles, seniors, colleges, or young and middle-age adults. It is not difficult to construct a rationale to encourage this new "profession." In a sense, there remains a huge deficit where adults are concerned because of the historic emphasis on work with the young. Most adults themselves must be convinced of the need to give attention to continued growth, spiritually and otherwise.

Two concrete factors lend weight to the rationale for the development of a new profession focusing on adults. First, population trends cannot be ignored. The 1980 census figures indicate tremendous growth in the adult segment of the U.S. population as we move toward the next century marker. The census bureau expects a 28 percent increase in the 35-59 age range and a 20 percent increase in the older segment by 1990. By the year 2000 there are expected to be more than 30 million older adults in this country.

Coupled with the population shift is a new perspective on the dynamic nature of adult development as seen in the vast body of literature and research on the subject. Both the sheer numbers and the exciting prospects for continued growth present a powerful challenge to religious educators.

With the popular and needed emphasis on lifelong learning, we must be certain adults realize the need for continued growth in the religious realm. The expanding literature on faith development indicates that faith continues to change quantitatively and qualitatively throughout life. Some (James Fowler for example[19]) have theorized steps through which one's faith passed toward maturity. While it is difficult and even dangerous to try to categorize persons according to "stages," adults deserve guidance in their efforts to achieve a more mature faith. Familiarity with Fowler's work and that of other researchers like Thomas Groome,[20] plus sensitivity to the personal faith pilgrimage of adults, can provide cues to appropriate enabling interventions.

NEEDS CALL FORTH PROFESSIONS

Professions develop in response to specific needs. Such was the case in the early development of the DRE. Those familiar with our history will recall that we owe our beginnings, for the most part, to the growth of the Sunday School in this country. In the early years pastors looked with disdain on the Sunday School, some considering it a threat to the church. Eventually, however, churches recognized the potential of the Sunday School to bring growth and adopted it as its own. Then both church and Sunday School began to grow beyond pastors' abilities to manage the growth. "Paid Sunday School Superintendents" were hired to organize, staff, and manage the school. These were not educators, however, but successful business persons who had exhibited the needed management skills in the secular field.

Quality became a major concern among those who supported the Sunday School and the need for educational expertise was recognized. William Boocock, recognized by some as the first DRE, explained, "It was felt that if the Sunday School wished to retain the confidence of parents whose children were receiving scientific instruction in the day schools, its educational work also must be conducted upon scientific principles and in accordance with efficient methods."[21]

Beyond the Sunday School there was general need for improvement of the total educational endeavors of the church. New technologies and approaches being introduced in the public schools needed to be infused into the church's educational efforts and volunteers had to be trained to use them. Expert leadership was needed.

Another significant contribution to the development of the professional religious education director was the inception of the first professional organization, called the Religious Education Association. "There were no DREs in 1903, but 1259 people concerned enough about the quality of religious education to band together to form the REA."[22] Henry F. Cope articulated the purpose of the association as being "to inspire the educational forces of our country with the religious ideal; to inspire the religious forces of our country with the educational ideal; and to keep before the public mind the ideal of religious education, and the sense of its need and value."[23] Among the charter members of the association was a notable group of educators from the University of Chicago: President William Rainey Harper; John Dewey, professor of philosophy, psychology, and education; and the dean of the Divinity School, Shailer Matthews.

In 1913 the Association of Church Directors of Religious Education was founded. That year the Association attempted to provide in its journal, *Religious Education,* guidelines for the director of religious education both as to qualifications and functions:[24]

Qualifications
1. Four years of college and three years of seminary, with courses in theological subjects and religious education, or

2. An additional two years in an approved School of Religious pedagogy.
3. Be full-time.

Functions
1. Serve as the administrative officer in charge of all religious education work of the church.
2. Rather than be an assistant pastor, the director is to be an expert educational advisor and executive head of the religious education activities.

Duties
1. Organization—organize the Sunday School and young people's societies on a graded basis.
2. Correlation—correlate the different units into a united education plan.
3. Publication—devise methods of publicity to arouse interest and issue materials.
4. Education—provide teacher training, curriculum selection, and teach classes.

Growth, Decline, Growth

Henry Cope is credited with doing the first survey of religious education directors. He found 127 directors serving in more than eight denominations. Cope predicted that the future of the profession would be good if these persons (1) continued to have a distinct function and were committed to the entire direction of religious education and (2) could be protected from the tendency to make them "errand boys, secondary factors subservient to the ambitions of the pastor, or subject to the whims of ignorant amateurs in the Sunday School."[25] The future was indeed bright as seen in the fact that by 1927 there were some 1,000 churches in the U.S. with full-time directors.

A new profession had been born in a brief decade. But its growth and development was awkward at best. There was little standardization as to function or uniformity as to background and training of those serving in positions of director. Conscientious professionals continued to provide caution and challenge: "In discussing the subject of the Director of Religious Education it is particularly necessary that we keep in mind the fact that this is a new office, a comparatively pioneer proposition with duties, qualifications, relationships all in the process of being defined."[26] Definition and standardization continued along with steady growth into the thirties. In 1930 the first book devoted exclusively to the DRE was published by Harry C. Munro. Munro addressed the principle functions of the director: organizing, developing the educational program as "executive officer," and supervising.[27] He also emphasized the cooperative relationships of the DRE and the pastor. "As pastor and director thus share the leadership of a unified program, responsibilities and functions will be shared rather than sharply divided."[28]

Continued "growing pains" and the onset of the depression brought the first serious threat to the profession. In 1938 Otto Mayer reported: "The economic depression seriously affected the status of the directors and of the churches in which they serve. One of the major changes since 1926 has been the shift toward the employment of women at lower salaries and the employment of persons to perform a variety of specific functions, often not those of educational supervision and administration."[29] As a caveat, the women who were increasingly being employed were nearly always called "educational secretaries" rather than directors! By 1936 few churches employed full-time DREs.[30]

It is interesting to note that the decline of the profession in the thirties somewhat paralleled a shift in management and administrative approaches in the business world. "Human relations" was replacing scientific management as the prevalent view and it may be that some churches used hard financial times as an excuse to get rid of some "theory X" DREs. At any rate, as interest in the profession was renewed toward the end of the thirties, there was an accompanying emphasis on people and relationships among DREs.

Evidence that the profession was becoming somewhat more secure by the forties is seen in the efforts of some churches and denominations to classify their educators as "lay ministers." In addition there was a move in some circles to certify or ordain directors. Both these moves were efforts to convince the government that these people should not be drafted into the armed forces because they were providing essential services to their churches.

An alternate title became increasingly popular in the 1950s. "Minister of Education" began to head more job descriptions for religious education professionals. Wesner Fallaw, in "The Roles of Ministers and Directors in Christian Education," described the pastor and religious educator as sharing the ministry of the church.[31] He used a public school analogy to describe the relationship, the pastor viewed as superintendent of schools, the director or minister of education as school principal.[32] Ordination became more common for males serving as local church educators, and many began to share in pastoral duties. In an article in *The International Journal of Religious Education,* June, 1955, Mary Huey asserted that the local church educator was "truly a minister."[33]

The 1960s saw a continued emphasis on the status, training, and standards of the profession.[34] In one major denomination, employing over 1500 directors and ministers of education, a survey conducted in 1975 indicated that only about 50 percent had specific training in religious education.[35] Other denominations, notably Roman Catholic, are seeking to establish standards for certifying DREs which include a masters degree in education.

Religious educators are now enjoying a degree of popularity similar to the twenties and fifties, but for somewhat different reasons. While churches continue to look to their directors and ministers of education to lead in numerical growth, they are also recognized as never before as educational specialists. Kenneth Gangel has compared the relationship of today's DRE to the total church program to that of the academic dean in a college to the curriculum and educational structure of the institution.[36] To Gangel, he or she is a specialist in "church academics." But proliferation of responsibilities has continued to plague the profession. While still largely considered generalists in education, more administrative responsibilities are being shifted to the DRE. Indeed, many share the title "Minister of Administration and Education." Associate pastor is becoming more popular in some areas. While seemingly lending increased status it also indicates increased pastoral duties, sometimes including "substitute preacher." All such trends may only serve to divert the attention and time of the religious educator from the essential tasks of curriculum development, leadership training, and close oversight of the church's total program of religious nature.

A PROFESSION WHOSE TIME HAS COME

John Dewey ushered in a "new day" in education. With that new day came a new psychology of education that insisted that children were not "little adults" and should not be taught like adults. Teaching methodologies and curriculum began to focus on the unique characteristics of children. While the application of this new theory and methodology was needed to better educate children, there seemed to be an unfortunate swing of the pendulum to the extreme. The assumption seemed to be that one approach to learning was appropriate for everyone, including adults. This assumption has remained prevalent for half a century.

If for no other reason, the sheer increase in the number of adults has caused new attention to be focused on adult religious education. The projected decrease in the under-20 generation coupled with marked increases in all three major categories of adults—young, middle-aged, and older—are causing churches to take notice of the need to enhance ministries to adults. Special groups of adults, especially singles and seniors, are receiving increased attention in society and the church.

Some churches are becoming increasingly aware of the competition for adults' attention to educational offerings. Community education offers literally hundreds of quality choices for adults, and colleges and universities are catering to adults in new ways. Recent studies in participation/nonparticipation patterns indicate that many adults no longer consider church-sponsored educational activities a viable alternative for investment of their time.[37]

SPECIFIC NEEDS

Five areas of need are discussed here which indicate the necessity of professionally trained leadership in adult religious education. In some sense these are not new, just more intense.

1 Discipleship

The old myth that we do our learning when we are young often carries over into the religious realm. Thus, many adults believe that once they have professed faith as a child and/or completed catechism there is little left in terms of religious experience. This is tragic, particularly if one holds to a dynamic view of creation. A crying need exists, in the view of this writer, for adults to understand that the dynamic nature of God's creation means that continued growth in all areas of life including the spiritual is not only possible but imperative. The "good news" many adults need to hear is that God has yet more in store for them to experience, that God has gifts yet to bestow, that there is much potential to be realized. Getting adults in touch with this reality may in itself enhance motivation to participate in religious education directed toward discovery of their gifts and potential. Emphasizing this opportunity, Lawrence Richards says, "It becomes very important, then, not to think of a renewed emphasis on 'adult education' as just the planning of a new set or series of formal classes for adults. Instead, what must be involved is to build into all experiences of the adult in the community of faith those elements of educational process which facilitate and are necessary for transformation to take place."[38]

Adult religious educators will be in touch with both the literature on adult faith development and ways of nurturing faith in community and structured experience.

2. *Leader Training and Supervision*

The church is probably the largest recruiter and user of volunteers and the greater percentage of these are adults. Yet in a day when volunteerism in society is considered a $64 billion business the church continues with "business as usual." A result is that many adults are choosing to volunteer in the community instead of church because commitments are often shorter term, supervision is better, and *they receive training* for their tasks. So often persons enlisted for leadership at church are left to learn on their own by trial and error about their job. If the church is to continue to utilize volunteers for staffing its schools and administrative bodies it must improve its service to those volunteers. This includes an approach which helps adults become more self-actualized through their volunteer activities. Professional adult religious educators will have a grasp of how to assess both the leadership needs of the church *and* the skill and personal development needs of individuals. Further, he or she will know how to plan using andragogical approaches which enhance adults' experience, involvement and ability to be self-directing. He or she will provide a positive model of adult leadership for learners to emulate.

3. *Family Ministry*

It is ironic to this writer that in the very place where families should be able to ask for and find help for problems we put on our "smiley" masks and attempt appearances that indicate all is well. We make the false assumption that church leaders who seem successful must "have it all together" with healthy marriage relationships, no parent-child problems, etc. Astute adult religious educators will possess the skills to assess needs in a nonthreatening manner while building a positive, trusting climate where problems can be addressed effectively. With a thorough grasp of adult development the adult specialist will be able to provide educational activities that address the relational and parenting needs of young adults. Adults can be helped in their struggle to enhance "generativity" and avoid stagnation while coping with teenaged children, aging parents, etc. Older adults will find in the adult educator an advocate for their continued usefulness in the leadership corps of the church, stimulation to continue learning and help in coping with the varied adjustments to old age: the death of spouse and friends, relating to adult children, finding meaning in retirement, etc. Beyond coping and problem solving the adult minister will develop programs which *enhance* life and the ability to anticipate transitions as opportunities for growth.

4. Single Adult Ministries

Estimates vary, but with approximately 60 million single adults in this country churches are beginning to take notice of this growing segment in their congregations. Denominations are producing literature which is raising the level of consciousness and one result is that a growing number of churches are adding specialists to their staffs to develop ministries to singles. More often this responsibility is assumed by the DRE or is included in the job description of the adult minister.

Single adults present some unique ministry opportunities. Self-esteem is a painful issue for many singles for a variety of reasons. Some feel unacceptable because they have not attracted a mate. Others have been treated as immature parents. Even though singleness is gradually becoming acceptable the expectation is still marriage, and thus some singles feel incomplete. Divorce is particularly damaging to self-esteem. Widows and widowers, an often overlooked segment of singles, need ministries which not only help them deal with grief but with adjustments to singleness that involve self-esteem, personal sense of security, and practical matters like handling personal finances, etc.

Adult religious educators will understand single adults developmentally and will be sensitive to helping build self-esteem and ability to cope while enhancing single's ability to become increasingly self-actualized. The adult specialists' grasp of appropriate programing skills will enable him or her to develop educational opportunities such as divorce adjustment seminars, self-help workshops, and counseling ministries for widows and widowers.

Single adults may provide an opportunity to use Leon McKenzie's idea that courses and activities may be classified as religious education either by virtue of the intent or content of the activity.[39] Thus a course on personal budgeting for singles may be religious education by virtue of the intent to help them live more productive, fulfilling lives.

5. *Senior Adults*

Older adults are no longer the neglected minority they once were. They are no longer neglected, nor are they a minority. The 1980 census predicted that by the end of the next decade 33 million Americans would be 65 and older. Not only are there *more* older adults but they are *better educated* for the most part. One implication is that the "rocking chair clubs" and groups provided to merely entertain will be less and less satisfying to older adults. This writer occasionally visits an interdenominational weekday seniors' center operated by a cooperative effort of several churches. One hundred or so elderly are involved in over twenty-five classes ranging from oil painting to conversational Spanish. Older adults have a need to learn like all other adults, and they have some particular learning needs which are not too difficult to assess. Further, adult religious education professionals will know that not only do these persons resist being treated as children, but they want to be useful. Many churches already provide a variety of ministries conducted almost exclusively by senior members of the congregation. A focused ministry to and with these persons can be most rewarding, stimulating their continued involvement *and* their continued learning.

WHAT WOULD AN ADULT RELIGIOUS EDUCATOR DO?

In the wider areas of ministry the educator is seen as a specialist, while within the field of religious education he or she is considered a generalist. Trying to "cover all the bases" can be frustrating at times as anyone who has served in that capacity can testify. Specializing with adults brings particular focus to ministry and offers opportunity to address needs more thoroughly.

A job description for the Director of Adult Religious Education (DARE) or adult minister would no doubt appear similar to that of the generalist. Alva Parks lists among the duties of the "Minister of Adult Education" budgeting, planning, leader enlistment and training, organizational coordination, i.e., duties that are common to the DRE.[40] The differences lie in the focus of these activities. The DARE budgets for adult ministries, plans a wide range of activities (including educational) specifically for adults, and enlists and trains volunteer leaders of adults. The DARE develops and coordinates the organizations (or parts of organizations) which service adults. One presumed result of this specialized focus is improved quality of ministry and increased opportunities for adult involvement. In addition, ministries with special groups of adults such as those previously mentioned can be developed. Many churches with ministries to singles and seniors find that creation of a singles council and senior adult council improves coordination, quality of ministry, and involvement of these adults. The DARE would be the primary resource for these groups and an ex-officio member of the councils.

The needs of other groups of adults may be more readily recognized by an adult specialist, such as internationals, the deaf, the handicapped, and homebound adults. Where special skills are required the DARE will be in touch with resources and persons to address special needs.

A task which should be included in the DARE's job description relates to the broader community. The adult specialist should not only develop working lists of community resources for adults but help adults relate to those resources. Thus this specialist will be in touch with counseling, welfare, medical and educational agencies, and a variety of other agencies servicing adults and their families.

Though it may be assumed, it should also be specifically stated that the professional adult religious educator will be responsible for developing a philosophy upon which to base all adult education activities and efforts. Such a philosophy should at some point be communicated concretely (as in written statement) and be reiterated from time to time, particularly with adults responsible for planning. It should include a consideration of the uniqueness of adulthood, the learning potential and learning orientation of adults, the place of the leader, and the end toward which the adult religious education ministry strives. For such a task this writer suggests the work of Edward Lindeman[41] and Paul Bergevin[42] as appropriate starting places.

SOME ISSUES FOR THE DARE TO ADDRESS

Several issues should be addressed by the adult specialist, some related specifically to adult ministries, others to a broader context.

1. Churches need to develop a holistic approach to the religious education of adults, treating more than just the traditionally religious concerns. P. Murrell points out that institutions who are successful in their training and educational efforts with constituents "take into account the learners' concerns and motivations related to life cycle, personal and professional objectives, and ways of processing information."[43] The DARE, because of his or her familiarity with life-span development, adults' growing intentionality[44] and their varied attitudes toward education,[45] will seek to make the church's offerings for adults relevant in terms of their broader life issues. Studies in patterns of nonparticipation in adult religious education indicate that many adults have an aversion to church-based education.[46] Simply put, they do not see what the church has to offer as relevant to their needs.

2. The adult religious education specialist can have a significant impact on the entire planning processes in the local church. Many church staffs do their planning in isolation, imposing their programs on their constituents with an *un*healthy dose of guilt to persuade participation. The DARE will help colleagues and planners to recognize the need for cooperative planning *with* adults, and the need for some thorough needs analysis. More effort must go into implementing what Leon McKenzie calls an analytic/subscriptive approach to program development.[47]

3. Adult religious educators have a responsibility for fostering

the idea of lifelong learning among their constituents and the community. Success in the development of such an attitude will in part lie in educating fellow staff and church officials. One way churches influence the attitudes of adults is through the priority (high or low) they place on education. Malcolm Knowles speaks to this in addressing the fact that institutions themselves teach, apart from the courses they may offer.[48] Everything from budget to schedules and visibility for educational staff are involved. Churches must give *visible* priority to religious education as a model for members and the community.

4. The importance of social relationships and interactions in attracting and holding adults will not be overlooked by the DARE. Conscious attention to dynamics which build this "fellowship," as it is known to many, rarely reach beyond the occasional "after service" get-together. The social component is an important ingredient in the educational setting and warrants attention in the structuring of learning settings. It is often through this channel that the essential climate of trust, mutual respect, and individual freedom of expression is developed. At the same time, the socializing aspect must keep in balance so that adults get the *substance* they expect in return for their investment of time.

5. Perhaps one of the greatest needs in church-based education with adults is the infusion of new educational technologies and approaches to teaching. Even though research indicates adults' general disdain for being lectured,[49] this continues to be the primary approach in much adult education. The problem is not lack of literature on alternative approaches, for this abounds. In part the problem is that volunteer teachers particularly, tend to teach the way they were taught. But also our training of volunteers often focuses on the techniques and methods without adequate attention to three crucial points: the *rationale* for their use, a *criteria* for selection of various approaches, and *demonstration* and *practice* in their use. More active learning approaches are needed.

Adult religious educators will recognize that learning can take place outside the classroom. Thus, those who prefer to learn on their own should be affirmed in their choice through provision of home-study materials and individual learning projects. The instructional development literature includes descriptions and guidance for developing a variety of learning technologies.[50]

SUMMARY

An attempt has been made in this section to provide a rationale to encourage the growth of a fledgling profession, adult religious education. It is seen as a natural extension of the generalist role of the DRE. As has been shown, the professional role of the religious educator has been a gradual evolutionary process, always moving toward the area of greatest need. Thus the population trends, the accompanying demographics, and the need for including the religious domain in "lifelong learning" point to continued evolution in the form of directors of adult religious education. Hopefully the profession's growth will benefit from the struggles and advances experienced in the DRE's early development. Giving focus to adults through provision of a specialist can mean more significant ministry to all adults and increased quality of educational efforts with them.

Several needs areas to be specifically addressed by the DARE were discussed, such as family ministry, single adult, and senior adult ministries. Also, several issues were raised which the adult specialist can address. These needs and issues emphasize the importance of the DARE being more than a promoter of denominational programs for adults or an "activities director" for adults, corresponding to what is often identified as youth ministry. The DARE must be an educator in the truest sense, establishing philosophy, cooperatively setting program objectives, assessing needs, and *facilitating* adult learning through the widest possible array of learning avenues.

NOTES

1. Malcolm Knowles, *The Modern Practice of Adult Education,* 2nd ed. (Chicago: Follett, 1980), p. 224.

2. Ibid., pp. 224-226.

3. Erik Erikson discusses his "psychosocial model" in several of his works. See three of his books, all published by Norton, New York: *Childhood and Society* (1963), *Identity, Youth and Crisis* (1968), and

Adulthood (1978). In the latter work, edited by Erikson, the model is used in an interesting discussion of "Dr. Borge's Lifecycle," the subject of Ingmar Bergman's film, "Wild Strawberries."

4. Robert J. Havighurst, *Developmental Tasks and Education* (New York: David McKay Co., 1961).

5. "The life-span developmental approach is concerned with the description, explanation, and optimization of intra-individual changes in behavior, and interindividual differences in such changes in behavior, from conception to death," according to Hultsch and Deutsch. These authors overview the research of a number of authors on the subject. See David F. Hultsch and Francine Deutsch, *Adult Development and Aging* (New York: McGraw-Hill, 1981), pp. 15ff.

6. K. Patricia Cross provides a helpful source list of major national, state, and regional studies of adult learners and potential learners between 1969-79 (pp. 136-141). An overview of much of the research is included. See K. Patricia Cross, "Adult Learners: Characteristics, Needs, and Interests," in *Lifelong Learning in America,* ed. R. E. Peterson (San Francisco: Jossey-Bass Publishers, 1980). See also Malcolm Knowles, *The Adult Learner: A Neglected Species,* 2nd ed. (Houston: Gulf Publishing Co., 1978) and J. R. Kidd, *How Adults Learn* (New York: Association Press, 1973).

7. John Dewey, *Experience and Education* (New York: Macmillan, 1938), pp. 5-6.

8. Roger Kaufman and Bruce Stone, *Planning for Organizational Success* (New York: John Wiley and Sons, 1983), p. 8.

9. Knowles, *The Modern Practice of Adult Education,* p. 89.

10. Leon McKenzie, *Adult Religious Education: The Twentieth Century Challenge* (West Mystic, Conn.: Twenty-Third Publications, 1975), p. 59.

11. Leon McKenzie, *The Religious Education of Adults* (Birmingham, Ala.: Religious Education Press, 1982), pp. 141-143.

12. See Knowles explanation of the "Andragogical Process of Program Development" (p. 59) and his fuller explanation of each step in chapters 5-10, *The Modern Practice of Adult Education.* See also McKenzie's delineation and evaluation of five approaches to programing in chapter 6, *The Religious Education of Adults.* See also John Elias' chapter 9, "Designing Adult Religious Education," in *The Foundation and Practice of Adult Religious Education* (Malabar, Fla.: Robert F. Krieger Publishing Co., 1982).

13. Cyril Houle in 1961 did the initial research into what motivates adults to participate in educational activities. He classified his interviewees as (1) goal oriented, (2) activity oriented, and (3) learning oriented. See *The Inquiring Mind* (Madison: University of Wisconsin Press, 1961).

14. After Houle, several researchers (Sheffield, 1964; Tough, 1968; Boshier, 1971) emphasized the importance of goals related to learners'

life situations which motivated participation. P. Burgess identified the importance of "the desire to reach a religious goal" among some of his subjects. See P. Burgess, "Reasons for Adult Participation in Group Educational Activities, *Adult Educational Journal* 22 (1971), pp. 3-29.

15. T. Shipp and Leon McKenzie, "Marketing Parish Adult Education," *Today's Parish* 13, no. 1 (January, 1981), pp. 29-31.

16. K. Patricia Cross, *Adults As Learners* (San Francisco: Jossey-Bass, 1981).

17. Gordon Darkenwald and Sharan Merriam, *Adult Education: Foundations of Practice* (New York: Harper & Row, 1982).

18. Ibid.

19. James Fowler, *Stages of Faith* (San Francisco: Harper & Row, 1981).

20. Thomas Groome, *Christian Religious Education* (San Francisco: Harper & Row, 1980). See also Bruce Powers, *Growing Faith* (Nashville: Broadman Press, 1982).

21. Wiliam Boocock, "Director of Religious Education," *The Encyclopedia of Sunday School and Religious Education* (New York: Thomas Nelson and Sons, 1915), Vol. I, p. 348.

22. Dorothy Jean Furnish, *DRE/DCE-The History of A Profession* (Nashville: Christian Educators Fellowship, United Methodist Church, 1976), p. 19.

23. Henry F. Cope, "Religious Education Association," The *Encyclopedia of Sunday School and Religious Education* (New York: Thomas Nelson, 1915) Vol. III, p. 902.

24. *Religious Education* (1903), p. 304.

25. Cope, "Religious Education Association," p. 446.

26. Harry Hopkins Hubbell, "The Director of Religious Education and His Church Relationships," *The International Journal of Religious Education* I (June, 1925), p. 19.

27. Harry C. Munro, *The Director of Christian Education* (Philadelphia: The Westminster Press, 1930), p. 118.

28. Ibid., p. 161.

29. Otto Mayer, "A Study of Directors of Religious Education and Their Profession," *The International Journal of Religious Education* XV (October, 1978), p. 12.

30. Oliver DeWolf Cummings, *Administering Christian Education in the Local Church* (Philadelphia: Judson Press, 1936), p. 29.

31. Wesner Fallaw, "The Roles of Minister and Directors in Christian Education," *Religious Education* XLV (January, 1950), p. 41.

32. Ibid.

33. Mary Huey, "The Director of Christian Education," *The International Journal of Religious Education* XXXI (June, 1955), p. 18.

34. Randolf Thornton, "If You Want A Director," *The International Journal of Religious Education* XXXVI (June, 1960), p. 18.

35. Lewis Wingo, *Educational Director Profile* (Nashville: Research Services Dept., Baptist Sunday School Board, 1975).

36. Kenneth Gangel, *Leadership for Church Education* (Chicago: Moody Press, 1970), p. 89.

37. Shipp and McKenzie, "Marketing Parish Adult Education."

38. Lawrence Richards, *A Theology of Christian Education* (Grand Rapids, Mich.: Zondervan, 1975), p. 233.

39. McKenzie, *The Religious Education of Adults,* p. 133.

40. Alva G. Parks, "The Minister of Adult Education," in *The Ministry of Religious Education,* ed. John Sisemore (Nashville: Broadman Press, 1978), pp. 179-180.

41. Edward C. Lindeman, *The Meaning of Adult Education* (Montreal: Harvest House, 1961) (first published in 1926).

42. Paul Bergevin, *A Philosophy of Adult Education* (New York: Seabury Press, 1967).

43. P. Murrell, "Technologies and Human Development," *The Network News* (Center for the Study of Higher Education, Memphis State University, Vol. 3, No. 1, October, 1983).

44. Allen Tough, *Intentional Changes* (Chicago: Follett Publishing Co., 1982).

45. Cross, *Adults As Learners.*

46. Shipp and McKenzie, "Marketing Parish Adult Education."

47. McKenzie, *The Religious Education of Adults,* pp. 150-151.

48. Knowles, *The Modern Practice of Adult Education.*

49. For an overview of research see Peterson and Associates, *Lifelong Learning in America.*

50. See R. Heinich and Associates, *Instructional Media and the New Technologies of Instruction* (New York: John Wiley and Son, 1982).

Chapter 7

Working with Single Parents

RICHARD A. HUNT

More single parents are in our communities than we may think. While the number of single parents in a community increases and fluctuates, these adults fit into several categories in addition to that of "single parent." As we understand ourselves and single parents more completely, and as we link these understandings to foundations of religious education ministry and religious education, we can create religious education ministries to meet needs of single parents, work on their behalf, and join with single parents in ministries they offer.

There are three major components in ministry and religious education with single parents:

1. *Feelings:* The professionals' (and other leaders') personal experiences and perspectives concerning single parents.
2. *Interpretations:* Some conceptual frameworks for understanding single parents and their concerns.
3. *Goals* and *Actions:* Resourcing and implementing programs for religious education ministry with, from, to, and on behalf of single parents.

The focus of this chapter is upon implementing single parent religious education ministries (goals and actions) on the basis of your own personal views about single parents (feelings) and interpretations of single parent situations.[1]

1. Feelings: The professionals' (and other leaders') personal experiences and perspectives concerning single parents.

The religious educator can be sensitive to her or his own personal feelings and reactions to single adults. The topic of single parents may carry more meanings than we think. Let's begin with some frank talk about possible personal biases, stereotypes, and sins that some professionals may unknowingly harbor in regard to single parents.

How do you *really* feel about "single parents"? Pleased? Positive? Excited? Puzzled? Frustrated? Sad? Relieved? Suspicious? Worried? Envious? If you now are a single parent, would you prefer to be otherwise, either married or not a parent? If you are not in this category, would you choose it as a highly desirable status for you?

Perhaps for most professionals in the church, single parents (as a concept or program unit, not as individuals) present something of a dilemma, if not a threat, in two ways.

First, most leaders probably assume that it is best for children to have a "good" mother and a "good" father who are happily married to each other. To have only one parent is usually assumed to be a disadvantage to all concerned. The biblical concern for the widows and the fatherless not only emphasizes a response to the economic and emotional deprivations of broken families but may also imply a bias against single parents.

Second, with few exceptions, churches have traditionally assumed that sexual intercourse is available exclusively in marriage and that marriage is primarily for the nurture of the spouses and the procreation of children who will grow up to increase the number of faithful persons in the church. If the childless couple is still somewhat suspect, the unmarried adult, especially with previous (and possible current) sexual experience, is much more a potential threat to the traditional assumptions about sexual and parental values.

The hidden double threat may be that (1) single parents cannot do as good a job with their children as do "double parents" (perhaps this is a useful term for families with both parents present), and (2) that single parents are either celibate (which may seem unlikely) or sexually active (which implies several negative judgments).

For some professionals who may secretly perceive themselves to be in unhappy marriages, a third possible threat may emerge: a satisfactorily divorced person is evidence that with more courage, or in a different career, or if something else were different, the professional could make good an escape from his or her own not-so-satisfying marriage.

The presence of single parents may also strain the typical arrangement of church groups that are constituted on the basis of age, sex, and marital status. Churches with adult classes and groups organized primarily for couples may have difficulty assimilating single parents, but may not know enough interested single parents to organize a class for them. If one assumes that single parents should, or could, be comfortable in same-sex groups, even in most women's or men's groups program topics often are still focused on two-parent family concerns. Although couples groups and one-sex groups may genuinely attempt to include single parents, many single parents do not feel comfortable with program topics and social conversation that often relate to "wife-husband" issues and structures.

By contrast, some parallel reverse biases may take hold. Some leaders may even wonder why anyone would stay married when the single life seems more inviting, less complicated, and otherwise may appear so advantageous. Why struggle with the disagreements between parents when being a single parent seems to eliminate at least one major source of family discord? After all, marriage is declining and the nuclear family concept is outmoded, so single parenthood should be one of the great new waves of the future.

I want to be very clear that I do not hold to these and similar biases against or favoring single parents, although at times some of these temptations in disguise may knock at my emotional doors.

Since some major blocks to effective religious education ministry often lie in the unhealed areas of our own lives, it is best to begin here and then move into a more coherent analysis of religious education ministries with single parents. It does not matter

how much that certain percentage of some group favors or op-
poses one or another of these perspectives or assumptions. What
does matter tremendously is one's own private, very personal
feelings, interpretations, and attitudes about single parents, since
these directly affect the priorities and energies that the professional gives to working with single parents.

2. Interpretations: Some conceptual frameworks for understanding single parents and their concerns.

The adult religious educator can deepen and expand his or her
conceptual understandings of single parents. Some interpretations
of demographic characteristics relating to single parents will assist
us to create a conceptual framework for religious education ministry among single parents.

The Number and Percentage of Single Parent Households Is Increasing

The religious educator can be aware of the increasing percentage of single parent families. The number of households in the
U.S. increased from 52 million in 1960 to nearly 80 million in
1980. In 1960 74 percent of these were two-parent households.
This percentage declined to approximately 61 percent in 1980.
During this same period the number of one-person households
increased from 13 percent to 22 percent, while the number of
households with nonrelatives present (including unmarried living
togethers) increased from just under 2 percent to just over 3
percent. The number of families with a male head only (with no
wife present) decreased slightly but remained as approximately 2
percent of all households, while the percentage of families headed
by a female only (with no husband present) increased from 8
percent to 11 percent.[2]
Approximately 18 percent of all households with children are
single parent households. Some estimate that one out of every
two children will live with only one parent during at least part of
childhood. In 1960 approximately 14 percent of children under
18 experienced a parental divorce, but some projections are that
by 1990 some 33 percent of all children under 18 will experience
the divorce of their parents.

After Divorce, Single Mothers Usually Have the Children

Religious educators need to remember that single mothers are more likely to have primary responsibilities for child care. Although an increasing number of fathers have primary custody of children after divorce, still 85 percent of single parents with children in the home are mothers. It is thus no surprise that the increasing number of one-person households and unmarried persons living together include a large percentage of divorced fathers who do not have primary custody of their children.

Some Single Parents Are Widows and Widowers

Between 5 and 10 percent of single parents under age 45 have lost their mates by death. Society tends to provide more positive social support for the parent whose partner has died than for single parenthood resulting from separation, divorce, or desertion. In addition, the family dynamics around death of a parent preclude issues of custody, disagreements, living arrangements, and the possibility of reconciliation between expartners.

Religious educators can increase their awareness of the systemic reasons that underlie divorce situations. The reasons behind divorce rates certainly impact single parents. Patterns of conflict resolution, types of communication skills, family backgrounds, conflicting goals, isolation, personal invalidation, feelings of anger and betrayal, and many other deep and important dynamics are part of the divorce process. By contrast, the dynamics of a single parent whose spouse has died, perhaps after an extended illness, are often considerably different.

A Few Single Parents with Children Have Other Partner Issues

From 1970 to 1980 the number of unmarried persons of opposite sex living together tripled (although still less than 2 percent of all households), and 27 percent of these households had children (usually the children of one of the adults) living in them.

A small percentage of single parents may never have married. They may adopt children or choose to keep children born out of wedlock. Occasionally a few women deliberately choose to conceive, break off with the father of the child, complete the pregnancy, and keep the child, or may achieve this through artificial insemination. Another unknown, but relatively small, percentage

of single parents are probably dealing with their own homosexual
identities.[3]

Single Parent Households Face Greater Economic Difficulties

Church educators can be sensitive to the probability that most
single parent households have lower incomes with which to face
the same financial standards as do two-parent households. Children living with one parent are much more likely to be in homes
in which the family income is lower. By 1980, among white
children, approximately 5 percent of households with income
over $20,000 were one-parent homes, while some 60 percent of
households with income under $6,000 were one-parent homes.
Among black children, the corresponding percentages were 10
percent and 80 percent.

Divorce Rates Are Increasing Slightly

By contrast with U.S. recent history prior to the 1970s, a
marriage today is more likely to be ended by divorce than death.
In 1978 the divorce rate per 1,000 population was 5.1, and the
marriage rate was 10.4. Among the approximately 48 million
marriages in the U.S., however, are many that last until one
spouse's death and many second marriages that also last until the
death of one spouse. Many factors contribute to divorce rates, so
statements that compare number of divorces to number of marriages in a given year are half-truths and overlook the dynamics
of divorce.

Religious educators can help question the accuracy of "scare
statistics" about divorce. Depending on a variety of socio-
economic, educational, religious, and other factors, between 55
percent and 75 percent of all first-time marriages last until the
death of one spouse. This percentage is affected by the ages,
incomes, education, personal competence, commitment to marriage, and other characteristics of the spouses.

Single Parenthood Is Often Temporary; Most Single Parents Marry Again

A person may be a single parent this year and within a few
years be married and learning to live with a new spouse in a
blended family. For every divorced single parent with children

there is an ex-spouse, also technically a single parent, who does not live with the children most of the time. In addition, more varied and flexible options for custody of children, such as managing, possessing, or joint custody (or conservatorships), also affect single parents.

In 1980, of the total U.S. population including children and youth (over 215 million), 47 percent were married. Of the population age 18 and older, 65 percent were married (a substantial minority of these are remarried), 20 percent were single, 8 percent were widowed, and 6 percent were divorced. The unmarried portion of the U.S. population is composed primarily of single never-married young adults under 25, elderly widowed, and a smaller number of divorced adults in midlife. In the age range 25-29, one out of three men and one out of five women is single. Eventually nearly 95 percent of all adults marry at least once, and some 80 percent of all divorced persons marry again. Since it is likely that the majority of the U.S. adult population will continue to be married, single parents will likely continue to be a minority in the general society.

Single Parents Have Other Statuses As Well

Adult religious educators need to be careful to view single parents as individuals, not as a category. Single parents are part of at least two categories—single adults and parents of children. It is obvious, however, that they are also wage earners, professionals, community volunteers, and members of extended families, as are married parents. In trying to describe single parents, it is important to remember that they, like married parents, are more than just parents, and more than just single (or married) adults. The relationships of marriage and/or parenthood do not fully describe single parents.

Although marital and parental status are the chief criteria for categorizing "single parents," individuals in this category are, first of all, *persons,* and the two categories of "single" and "parent" offer little help in working with these persons. It makes a big difference whether one is single by choice, accident, or rejection. Like two-parent families, the age and sex of the single parent and the ages and sex of her or his children also influence her or his responses to being a single parent.

Toward a Theological Interpretation of Marriage and Family

This chapter is not intended to develop a general theoretical framework for understanding single parenthood in our society. Such theory must be drawn from many disciplines, such as psychology, sociology, anthopology, education, and philosophy, as well as from theology. Nevertheless, it may be helpful to consider some theological elements that inform single adult ministries.

Religious education ministers can assist individuals and the church to develop a more adequate theological understanding of marriage, family, and divorce. "Single parent" refers to a real-life circumstance but does not capture the many possible meanings, faith perspectives, and coping mechanisms that persons in this circumstance have. Thus, general theories, foundations, research, and concepts of religious education with adults are also quite useful in guiding our work with single parents.[4]

Issues of meaning as described by Leon McKenzie[5] are central in working with single parents. A major goal with single parents, as with others, is to enable them to identify the meanings that they have attached to their own experiences with life, sex, marriage, and with children and to affirm and/or move toward new and/or better meanings in the context of their faith.

Age and stage approaches as represented by Erik Erikson, Lawrence Kohlberg, or James Fowler, are quite limited in their usefulness in working with single parents.[6] While these approaches offer helpful insights, they tend to ignore the wide varieties of experiences that persons of the same age may have and overlook the dynamic, family-systems understanding of single parents.[7]

A conceptual approach that assumes that individuals, out of the matrix of their experiences, create their own meanings, worldviews, and faith standpoints will probably be the most helpful approach to working with single parents. Charles Gerkin[8], although writing primarily for pastoral counselors, puts in a theological framework using many points that have been made by family-systems approaches. From this perspective, each individual is a unique, living drama (or "document") who brings her or his own specific experiences, hurts, hopes, and goals to each meeting with others—whether they are friends, associates in church, counselors, or professional educators. Neither words nor logical schema can fully express the ongoing personal drama of each individual, set uniquely in ever-changing systems of family, work, neighborhood, and world affairs. Thus, as often stated by Gordon Allport, each person eventually defies being grouped into any category.

The role of persons as interpreters of their own experience is also a major emphasis of H. Edward Everding[9] in his treatment of hermeneutical approaches to religious education. From slightly different perspectives, both Gerkin and Everding point to the necessity of allowing and assisting every individual to examine and interpret her or his own life. Faith perspectives and decisions are, of course, deeply involved in this process. This approach serves both as a caution to leaders who assume that they already know what single parents need and as an encouraging frontier for always being open to conversations with single parents.

Interpreting Marriage and Parenthood

Meanings of marriage and meanings of parenting are involved in an attempt to come to a conceptual understanding of single parenting.[10]

J. B. Nelson, from a Protestant view, and Walter Kasper, from a Roman Catholic view, point to important theological dimensions of marriage. Kasper approaches marriage theologically as an opportunity and a crisis. Personal love in the marriage community, humanizing sexuality, and continuing faithfulness in love are key elements in marriage. The sacramental dimension of marriage points to the commitment of each partner to God and the foretaste of the deepest, most extensive communion with each other before God. Marriage is not necessarily "better" or "worse" than singleness. Rather, the meaning of both singleness and marriage is given by one's faith commitment to God.

Parenthood has important theological dimensions in addition to its essential birthing and socialization functions. Many biblical metaphors for our relation to God, such as "father," "child," and "parent," are drawn directly from family experiences. Whether an adult is a married parent or a single parent, it is relatively easy to draw on mother-child and father-child experiences to increase our faith and love for God and for each other. To speak of God as our parent not only describes our need for God and our absolute dependency on God's grace. In deep ways the parenting experience teaches us much about God, thus instructing us in our own developing theologies. Whether we are in child or parent roles with others, these experiences point us toward a variety of facets of God's unconditional love and care for all persons.

By contrast, we do not often talk of being a "spouse" with God. Perhaps the metaphor of spouse is too intimate, or too sexual, or too co-equal, to permit us to use it in theologizing. Perhaps because the spouse relationship can be temporary we are reluctant to build much theological insight from it. Nevertheless, important theological insights can be discovered in the spouse relationships of marriage. While there is not room to explore these in detail, some of these include the discoveries of practicing long-term, unconditional love for one person in a co-equal situation, the values of risk and acceptance for personal growth and renewal, the uniqueness of a two-person dyad composed of one woman and one man with an extensive history together, and the discovery of commitment, forgiveness, baptism, and eucharist in the daily events of life together in marriage.

One way to build a foundation for adult religious education ministry with single parents is to explore what positive theological understanding and insight we gain from this human situation. Traditionally we have assumed that single parenthood that results from any circumstance other than death of a spouse somehow implies that one or both partners have made serious mistakes, failed in some way, or could have made the marriage work if they had tried. This, of course, could also be said for intact marriages. There just is no public divorce to emphasize these negatives.

Religious educators can discover positive good in the single parenthood experiences of persons. Are there any positive theological insights to be gained from the social "institution" of single parenthood as something of one option to married parenthood? Yes. Single parenthood reminds us all that marriage itself cannot be an idol, nor can one's spouse be the only supreme relationship that persons can have. Single parenthood reminds us that loss of one's spouse as a "most-significant" other calls society and the church to come to better terms with what constitutes the essential elements of parenting and family relationships.

While analogies of God as bridegroom and the church as bride hold some helpful teachings about God for us, we may also understand God as a "single parent" with both father and mother roles wrapped into one. To explore whether a single parent can be self-sufficient and functionally fully adequate as adult and parent also challenges us to ask similar questions about God. If single parents need certain religious education ministries and provide certain religious education ministries, then perhaps the "single-parent God" also calls us to give more attention to others as "one-parent children" and to be more sensitive to the many ways in which we can incarnate love and grace.

As we consider the various ways single parents may perceive themselves, we can also ask how these perspectives give meanings to our understanding of God and to our interpretations of the meanings of single parenthood.

Meanings: How Single Parents Understand Themselves

The chart of "Types of Single Parents" can assist leaders and groups to inventory the single parents in a congregation or community.[11] While these dimensions do not exhaust the possibilities, the multiple factors may exhaust professionals who attempt to gather a group of single parents into a class or other activity. Nevertheless, there are some common themes that most single adults confront. These themes may offer possiblities for several types of adult religious education ministries.

Several conceptual principles emerge from this survey of characteristics of single parents.

1) Single parents are a diverse group. Each person has a unique set of factors that produced his or her status as "single parent." Each person also responds to these circumstances in unique ways. Here the leader's task is to perceive accurately the meanings that these adults attribute to the many facets of their single parenthood status.

2) Single parents want to be accepted as equals in the congregation and not primarily identified as "single parents." This implies that many religious education ministries to single parents will be part of the general work of the congregation, such as parent groups, study groups, recreation and volunteer projects, and administrative committees. The leader must respond to these persons primarily as adults rather than as "single parents."

3) As single parents, these adults have at least two types of specialized needs.[12]

(a) One set encompasses the crisis dimensions of the first

two years (approximately) after becoming a single parent during which time the adult is readjusting to being single and learning necessary skills for managing work and children alone.

(b) A second set of specialized needs includes the continuing issues with which single parents must cope, such as developmental needs of children, balancing work, family, and social demands and relationships, coping with increased time demands and reduced income, and planning one's future as an individual.

3. Goals and Actions: Resourcing and implementing programs for adult religious education ministry with, from, to, and on behalf of single parents.

It is preferable to consider church leaders to be in adult religious education ministry rather than just working with single parents. This may place less distance between churches and single parents and remind all that we are co-equal persons before God and in our communities. There are at least four clusters of religious education ministries.

1) To minister "with" suggests a cooperative, equal, two-way relationship with single adults in which all are joining together for ministry.

2) At times the professional will be in religious education ministry "to" individuals or groups of single parents. In this context at times religious education ministry is, for the time being, primarily a caregiver to single parents who at the time want and need to receive care.

3) At other times the single parents will be in ministry to the professional, to the church, as well as to their own children, friends, and associates, a ministry "from" single parents to others.

4) Finally, there are times when church leaders can be in ministry "on behalf of" single parents as an advocate or facilitator in church and community organizations.

The following pages will outline some examples and possible directions in each of these four types of adult religious education ministry.

1. Ministries with Single Parents
Ministries "with" single parents actually can include nearly all of the activities that occur in a typical church. While it is prob-

ably rare for any group to attempt to exclude a person because he or she is a "single parent," most groups will need to increase their consciousness concerning single parents. This may involve taking more initiative to contact them and get acquainted, offering rides for them, and appropriate child care during meetings. Opportunities may arise through children's groups at church and at schools. The similarities between single parents and married persons are much more than the differences, so here both types of persons can choose to work together on most topics. For instance, some singles and some married might prefer lectures instead of discussions, informal retreats rather than formal classes, weekday rather than Sunday settings.

Single adult classes at church, especially when they seek to reach the post-college-age groups, usually include never-married, divorced, and single parents. Classes can include many different activities, according to the interests of the members. Some examples are:

—Bible studies, other adult curricula, guest speakers.
—Special topics of special interest to single parents, such as child development, life after divorce, etc.
—Activities, such as socials, volleyball, tennis, skiing, table games, tours, dinners, camping, retreats.
—Social work projects, such as painting homes of the elderly or poor.
—General church activities such as ceramics, bowling, all-church picnics for all households.
—Church-night dinners with a variety of activities, courses, and special-interest speakers and other presentations.
—Classes meeting with single parents and children.
—Intergenerational group activities focused around the church year, community needs, and common topics.
—Parents Without Partners and other groups organized for single parents. When well run, these groups can provide wholesome social contacts and very helpful information to single parents.[13]

Regardless of inner feelings, when we are loved by God and others we are then able to love ourselves again. Life is difficult at times for every individual, and many joint activities that include persons of different circumstances (single, married, with or without children, etc.) enable single parents to come to grips with being single in what often tends to be a couple's world, as well as enabling "non-single parents" to come to grips with issues and needs that single parents may have.

Conversation topics sometimes are awkward or difficult with single parents. Although no one intends harm, married and single persons will give different importance and emotional reactions to comments about "my wife/husband" or "ex-spouse." In subtle ways, both married persons and single parents may have some difficulty, at least initially, in knowing which topics are sensitive, or painful, or even boring. Nevertheless, with warm, caring efforts, all can participate jointly in many activities in the church.

In planning activities that involve single parents, there are several potential resources that we may overlook. First, friends are very valuable, as it is so much more fun to go with someone to a meeting, bowling, work, or about anything than it is to go alone. It usually requires more initiative to participate in activities when one is alone than when one has a friend who encourages participation. Some single parents may respond to a personal invitation from a friend to share a ride and go to a meeting together when they would not come alone.

Some teenagers and some adults without children in their homes may be especially delighted to assist in activities by helping to care for the children of single parents. A single parent with two young children at a church dinner may not ask for assistance but would welcome unobtrusive help from a warm and caring adult or teenager who genuinely enjoys children. Leaders can facilitate this by introducing potential "helpers" or informally suggesting ways that single parents and others can cooperate.

Titles of events may make a difference to some single parents who may think of themselves (incorrectly) as "not fully a family." For example, rather than the call it a "Family Night," a church may use the term, "Church Night," "Activities Night," or another name that encourages participation of all persons regardless of how they see themselves as "family."

Events that focus on a specific family relationship may need extra attention to the needs of single parents and their children. For example, "mother-daughter," "father-daughter," "mother-son," or "father-son" events may also need to provide substitute parents for some children and youth whose own parent has died, is not available, or refuses to come.

2. Ministries to Single Parents

Perhaps most obvious are the many adult religious education ministries "to" single parents. These may be available to single parents through church and/or community sponsored seminars, special topics speakers, printed resources, and other media. Discussion groups might also be formed around television programs, such as situations comedies involving single parents, serious educational programs, and other special programs of many kinds.

Ministry "to" single parents deals specifically with topics that single parents perceive themselves as needing. Not all single parents will need or want all of these topics, but at any one time in any community there probably are some single parents who are hungry for help in one or more of these areas. Among many possible topics aids to help single parents:

1) Coping with divorce and its aftermath—"single again."
2) Coping with death of one's spouse.
3) Financial aids and aspects of single parenting.
4) Improving skills for communicating with ex-mates.
5) Obtaining child care for children.
6) After-school care for children of working parents.
7) Job opportunities and increasing work skills.
8) Issues concerning dating and marriage.
9) Violence in the family, including spouse and/or child abuse, incest, neglect.
10) Helping children to develop faith, competence.
11) Coping with alcohol and other drug abuses.
12) Educational guidance for children.
13) Sexuality and sexual education with children.

Like two-parent families, some single parents have concerns about talking with children about sex. Parents may need help in learning to be comfortable in teaching their children correct terms for sexual anatomy and activities. In this process single parents can also assist their children of both sexes to develop positive attitudes toward sexuality as part of God's plan for us. In turn, these better informed children can share good information with other children, rather than having misinformed children to be the sex educators for children who have missed these opportunities with their own parent.

Single parents also need opportunities to share ways they affirm their children's sexuality, without punishing or making the child feel guilty about being a sexual person, masturbation, sexual development, or other facets of sexuality.[14] Parents can help their children to know that dreams, thoughts, and fantasies about sexual dimensions of life are normal. Behaviors can be either constructive or destructive, but not urges. Guilt is energy for repetition of unacceptable thoughts.

When children feel rejected or hurt, any behavior, including sexual activities, drug abuse, alcohol abuse, and eating, can become a compulsive but futile effort to gain love that they perceive as missing in their lives. Adolescents and adults need to realize that sexual activities, in and of themselves, are not reliable tests of genuine love.[15] Sex ranks far behind love, caring, sense of humor, sharing, and good communication as a sign of true love.

Finances are a major concern for most single parents. Divorce or death of a spouse drastically reduces the available money for a family, often when family financial needs are increasing. Budget planning, spending information, and stewardship education can be important ministries to single parents. Although the single parent with primary custody for the children may be awarded child support payments from the other parent, these necessary payments may not be paid on time and in full. Group seminars may be formed to help single parents in dealing with child support payments, budget planning, and other special financial and legal aspects of single parenting. Support from each other in a group may be reassuring as well as a more efficient way to assist single parents.

Being a single parent can be a lonely experience at times, whether this has been caused by divorce or death of the partner. Single parents who come from a happy marriage that was terminated by death usually experience the processes of grieving much differently than single parents coming from an unhappy marriage, whether voluntarily or involuntarily terminated. Although the grief process is similar, the death of a partner cuts off contact from the spouse and society provides much support for bereaved persons.

By contrast, in a divorce there can be constant aggravation when one or both ex-partners is unpleasant when visiting or working on arrangements for the children. Often there is more work to deal with the other person in divorce, especially when each partner continues to be affected by the ex-spouse in matters of children, finances, time scheduling, and property.

Helping single parents to deal constructively with death and divorce can be a very important phase of religious education ministry to them. Many of the books in the notes are helpful for individual reading. In addition, single parents can profit from participating in a group-led discussions in churches, schools, and other organizations.

Adequate, inexpensive child care can also be an important religious education ministry to single parents. While the single parent is at work it is reassuring to know that the children are receiving responsible care. In some work situations, single parents cannot respond to outside calls about their children. Having reliable and high-quality care for children helps both child and parent, whether the care giver is the church's day care center, a community day care program, or be grandparents, relatives, friends, or neighbors.

Grandparents are an important dimension of children's lives. In some divorces, children may be cut off from their grandparents who are the parents of the "ex-spouse but not ex-parent." Leaders and counselors may help open these channels for grandchildren. In other cases, grandparents may live far away and not be easily accessible. A rewarding religious education ministry in these situations is in programs that bring older adults who are either grandparents (whose children may also live far away) or "uncle/aunt" types to be available to children who have little or no contact with their own grandparents. These contacts with children can also be very rewarding to the adults involved.

Groups like the Big Brothers and Big Sisters organizations also offer single parents opportunities for their children to have contact with an older "sibling/aunt/uncle" friend. This can be especially helpful as a partial replacement of the other sex parent.

Single parents have their own emotional and sexual needs. How to care for the children and still be able to have their own personal needs met through time for activities with adult friends is often a struggle for many single parents. The church can facilitate child care availability for single parents through providing child care at church meetings and socials and by training responsible adolescents and others to do individual child care in homes. Names of these persons could then be made available to single parents as well as married parents.

Churches must clearly affirm that it is just as acceptable to remain single as to marry. For those who want to remarry, the church can be a fine opportunity to meet a potential spouse. However, many single parents do not want to be seen as coming to church in order to find a new mate and react negatively to any attempt to make a group into a dating bureau. Even so, many single parents will face the question of whether to marry again. Some may want to remarry but have children who do not want a new parent. Issues of blended families may require counseling and financial or legal consultation. Churches can help in these situations by making good counseling available to single parents.

There is no one way to live in our community or world. We are individuals and have self-worth as a person, and we are loved by God and others regardless. When we value ourself and others, they in turn value us. When we differ from others and we value them, that person is still valued even though the behavior may not be. We may see life differently from another, and that is fine, yet we can affirm each other and learn through our different life experience.

Sometimes when spouses are moving through a divorce and into new lifestyles, they may feel rejected and lose self-esteem. Recovering one's self-worth is especially important during the first two years after divorce. When things go badly at times, however, single parents may wonder, "What's wrong with me?" Here the church community and other friends can be present to help the new single parent pick up the pieces. It is especially comforting to experience love when one is feeling rejected by a partner who had previously vowed to stay until death intervened, or when work, children, or others seem to reject one. To feel valued and wanted, to know one is not alone, is so valuable to every person, especially in those times when everything else seems to be going badly.

Classes at church aid and encourage those who are lonely, often without realizing this need in some of the participants. It is each person's choice to stay single or to marry again and church classes and group activities need to meet the need of both of these decisions as far as interest, people, activities, and topics.

Most single parents face the question of whether or not to marry again. Some may give their children the deciding vote (which is not a good strategy), while others may completely ignore the wishes of the children involved. The ages of the children, who has primary custody, whether children are at home, or whether the potential spouse has children, or likes the children, are among many factors single parents face regarding another marriage. Some single parents face the dilemma of satisfying their own needs for social and sexual intimacy and satisfying the needs of their children. Through groups and individual counseling, leaders can help single parents deal with these decisions.[16]

Some single parents may be tempted to flee into another marriage that may be less satisfying than being a single parent. Previous experience with alcohol abuse, drug dependency, physical violence, incest, and other serious domestic problems may complicate the question of whether to marry again. In the general population, approximately one-fourth to one-third of women reported having been beaten or physically harmed by male partners. Although percentages are lower among active church women, still many have experienced physical violence in their homes. We need to help all persons cope more constructively with conflict, stress, and other causes of domestic violence and drug addiction. Some may need help in identifying early signs of these conditions before choosing to marry the potential spouse.

Mature (or healthy) love brings high energy, genuine enjoyment of the other person, and active caring. Immature "love" (or neurotic love) is, by contrast, exhausting, tiring, hostile, jealous, possessive, and demanding. An immature person demands and pressures to get his or her way, and if mature they would not put this kind of pressure on their partner. Some single parents may want to explore in greater depth the meanings of love and marriage.

Children's images of God are related to their images of their parents and other significant and powerful adults. In a one-parent family, children usually miss the other parent and cherish hope that eventually the parents will reunite. Even when both divorced parents consistently reassure the children that both parents love

them, from the child's perspective, the child may at times interpret the divorce as personal rejection. The child may then wonder
if God will also reject her or him, as the absent parent seems to
have done. Since parents are, knowingly or not, priests on behalf
of God, single parents may need to find meaningful ways to
enable their children to realize and interpret positively these
deeper losses so that the children can assimilate them into their
own growing theologies.

3. Ministries "from" Single Parents

Every person is in ministry to others, regardless of marital or
parental status. There are many religious education ministries
that single parents can provide as Christian adults, regardless of
their marriage or parental status. Becoming a single parent, in
and of itself, does not decrease one's competence in management,
music, sports, or other areas. The adult who happens to be a
single parent can certainly continue to be sensitive to others'
needs, to work for pay or voluntarily for any worthy cause or
goal, and be in ministry through one's employment, career, community agencies and groups, and church ministries.

Many single parents may welcome opportunities to work with
other adults in religious education ministries quite unrelated to
being "parent" or "single." Their work in these areas is as an
adult Christian, not as "single parent," as is the work of other
adults, whether married or childless. In the doing of ministries
with others, many single parents report that they also receive
ministry as an unanticipated by-product of giving.

The time and economic demands of being a single parent may
affect these adults' availability for religious education ministry,
yet this is really little different than time and economic concerns
that married or nonparent adults may also have. Perhaps the only
distinguishing factors are that some single parents have no one to
share home- and family-related work, and many single parents
have higher percentages of the family income going to child care
and other essential family expenditures.

In addition to the many ways each person can help others,
there are probably some unique ministries that single parents can
offer that may be overlooked. Many single parents who have
coped well with their own disappointments and losses can be in a

good position to offer encouragement, insights, and information to others who are just facing single parenthood. Single parents can testify that being a single parent can be done, and done well. Single parents may also help our society to look beyond outward appearances, such as whether a marriage is intact, to the deeper issues of marriage and parent relationships—how one deals with others, what steps lead to disappointments, how to change for the better, and how to express love in family relationships.

4. Ministries "on behalf of" Single Parents

Some adult religious education ministries can directly or indirectly aid single parents. Many of these are in the realm of influencing policies and interpreting the needs of single parents to policy makers and other groups.

As one step, leaders can identify resources to assist single parents. These may be printed materials, library acquisitions, films, and other media. More importantly, they include becoming acquainted with agencies and groups in the local community that seek to benefit single parents. In addition to Parents Without Partners and Big Sisters/Brothers, resources include mental health agencies, therapists, attorneys, and other professional persons in the community.

In the church, leaders can work to make current programs truly and warmly inclusive for single parents. These may be general church activities, classes, meetings of parents of children, and positions in the administrative structure of the church. Working to arrange special topic classes and ongoing groups for single parents is an adult religious education ministry on behalf of single parents.

In the community, church leaders can identify specific needs of single parents that may be met by modifications and/or new programs in the public schools, city-sponsored activities, and public agencies. In some areas, low-cost services for children after school, counseling, legal and medical services may be needed. Church leaders may also influence business and industry to permit more flex-time options for single parents and to establish policies that strengthen family relationships of single parents. Church leaders may also work with family courts, Family Guidance, Child Guidance, and other similar agencies in creating support groups for single parents outside of the church.

Some communities need programs to interpret to others what single parenthood is and is not. Some single parents are qualified and capable of presenting these interpretative programs to service clubs, school parent-teacher groups, and through television and newspapers.

Without prejudice to persons who now are single parents, in the longer run programs that help persons to learn how to build strong families with both parents present benefit individuals before divorce makes them into single parents. Other programs that teach persons to be self-sufficient, whether married or single, also aid single parents. While some single parents, for a wide variety of reasons, prefer to remain single parents, many others would prefer a two-parent family if they could find a suitable mate. Programs in interpersonal communication of love, conflict resolution, values clarification, goal setting, and other personal skills will assist single parents and their children.

SUMMARY

Religious education ministries, by, to, for, and on behalf of single parents originate in one's own empathy with single parents and in knowing the many, many dimensions of single parenthood. Ministries may be part of the general program of the congregation; they may be in cooperation with other local churches; and they may be individualized and through special groups for single parents. Single parents themselves must be centrally involved in these efforts in our religious education ministries with adults who are also single parents.

Some Dimensions along which Single Parents Can Be Categorized

This outline of categories and reactions can aid in considering ways that single parents may see themselves and in identifying what types of adult religious education ministries may be needed in a specific community.

One possible use would be to have a planning committee make estimates of the number or percentage of single parents in the church or in the community who are in each of the alternative categories in each dimension. This outline might also be modified into a community survey instrument or be the basis for discussing religious education ministry needs with single parents and with church leaders (some of whom may also be single parents).

A. Attitudes
   about self
   1. Positive, happy, satisfied
   2. Mixed, varied
   3. Negative, sad, anxious, dissatisfied

B. Skills and
   abilities
   1. Multitalented, competent
   2. Average abilities
   3. One talent, barely surviving

C. By experience
   with marriage:
   1. Divorced
   2. Widowed
   3. Separated
   4. Single never married

D. Relation to ex-
   spouse as spouse
   1. Cordial, cooperative
   2. Constant conflict
   3. Never see ex-spouse

E. Relation to ex-
   spouse as parent
   to children
   1. Work together for children
   2. Conflicted, difficult
   3. Child custody/support details

F. By anticipation
   of marriage
   1. Want to stay single permanently
   2. Planning/engaged to remarry
   3. Searching for a partner
   4. Bitter toward marriage
   5. Lonely without marriage

G. By own age
   1. Young adults
   2. Middle age
   3. Older adults
   4. Elderly

H. By age, sex, type
   and number of
   children
   1. Preschool, elementary, adolescent
   2. Same or other sex than parent
   3. Own, adopted

I. By health   1. Good health, high energy
                            2. Poorer health, lower energy
                            3. Chronic health, handicaps

J. Income level and   1. Stable, adequate, comfortable
   financial status   2. Must work to survive
                            3. Major debts, financial pressures
                            4. Subsistence, welfare

K. Vocational   1. Wage earner
   status   2. Professional career
                            3. Displaced homemaker
                            4. Hours to fit children's schedules
                            5. Income level, success vs. nonsuccess
                            6. Unable to find a job, no job skills

L. Friends and   1. Relatives nearby to help or distant
   family   2. Living with adult relatives/friends
                            3. Many vs. few friends
                            4. Friends of same sex and/or other sex
                            5. Isolated from children

M. Sexual dimensions   1. Celibate, not sexually involved
                            2. Committed to one sexual partner
                            3. Several sexual partners
                            4. Using sex for other purposes
                            5. Homosexual/gay/lesbian

N. Social and other   1. Many vs. few interests
   interests   2. Hobbies, volunteer involvements

O. Perspective on   1. Positive, comfortable, confident
   single parenthood   2. Mixed, varied, mood swings
                            3. Apologetic, embittered, angry

Some Questions for Reflection

The following questions are for personal reflection. After you answer these questions for yourself, you might add your own additional questions and use the list with groups of single and/or married parents to sample opinions and to generate discussion. Try to cite examples for each answer you give.

You may prefer to use gradations, such as always, usually, sometimes, seldom, or never.

1. Most single parents would rather be married to a desirable spouse.
2. The quality of parenting is much more important than whether a child has one or both parents in the home.
3. The only morally right setting for sexual intercourse is in marriage.
4. As compared with unmarried adults, married adults are better adjusted persons.
5. Single parents usually have been more deeply hurt by life events (death, divorce, career, etc.) than have parents in an intact marriage.
6. There are no major differences between married and unmarried adults, or between adults who are parents and adults who do not have any children.
7. Most single parents will marry again.
8. Single parents seldom receive all of the child custody payments awarded them at the time of divorce.
9. There is little difference between single parents whose spouse has died and single parents who are divorced.
10. The percentage of single parents in the general population (or in our community) will greatly increase in the next decade.
11. Lack of money is a much greater problem in homes with one parent.
12. Single parents are nearly always at a major disadvantage in raising a child of the sex other than the parent.

ANSWER WITH A WORD OR PHRASE TO EXPRESS
YOUR OWN VIEWPOINT.

13. The greatest problem most single parents face is _____.
14. A major advantage that many single parents have is _____ .
15. The best way for single parents to satisfy their sexual needs is _____ .
16. The most typical worry or concern that children of single parents have is _____ .
17. If my church made only one major change to minister with single parents better, it would be _____ .

NOTES

1. Among approaches to intimacy and adult development that offer ways to consider meanings of single parenthood are Leonard Cargan and Matthew Melco, *Singles: Myths and Realities* (Beverly Hills, Calif.: Sage Publications, 1982), Carole Klein, *The Single Parent Experience* (New York: Walker, 1973), Henri J. M. Nouwen, *Intimacy* (San Francisco: Harper & Row, 1969), Susan M. Campbell, *The Couple's Journey* (San Luis Obispo: Impact Publishers, 1980), James Fowler, *Life's Maps* (1980), W. Norman Pittenger, *Making Sexuality Human* (New York: The Pilgrim Press, 1979), and M. Scott Peck, *The Road Less Traveled* (New York: Simon and Schuster, 1978). For an extensive bibliography on single parents see Benjamin Schlesinger, *The One-Parent Family: Perspectives and Annotated Bibliography*, 4th rev. ed. (Toronto: University of Toronto Press, 1978). Studies of single parents in England are presented by Elsa Ferri and Hilary Robinson in *Coping Alone* and in *Growing Up in a One-Parent Family* (Windsor, England: NFER Publishing Co. 1976). Robert S. Weiss, in *Going It Alone: The Family Life and Social Situation of the Single Parent* (New York: Basic Books, 1979), provides a good summary of issues and meanings of single parenthood. Whether divorce is really a new freedom is explored by Esther O. Fisher in *Divorce: The New Freedom* (New York: Harper & Row, 1974).

2. Sources of statistics in this chapter are U.S. Bureau of the Census, "Marital Status and Living Arrangements: March 1980," in *Current Population Reports*, Series P-20, No. 365, (1981); Ira L. Reiss, *Family Systems in America*, 3rd ed. (New York: Holt, Rinehart & Winston, 1980), pp. 365-371; Hugh Carter and Paul C. Glick, *Marriage and Divorce: A Social and Economic Study* (Cambridge, Mass.: Harvard University Press, 1976); Byron Strong, Christine DeVault, Murray Suid, and Rebecca Reynolds, *The Marriage and Family Experience.* (St. Paul, Minn.: West Publishing Co., 1983); and David Mace, "Why Focus on Marriage?" ACME Marriage Enrichment 11(9) (October, 1983), p. 5 .

3. Betty Berson provides her viewpoint on many of these issues in "Sharing Your Lesbian Identity with Your Children," in *Our Right to Love; A Lesbian Resource Book,* ed. Ginny Vida (Englewood Cliffs, N.J.: Prentice-Hall, 1978), pp. 69-73. Also see Leon Smith, ed., *Homosexuality: In Search of a Christian Understanding* (Nashville: United Methodist Discipleship Resources, 1981).

4. Many articles in Marvin J. Taylor's 1976 collection, *Foundations for Christian Education in an Era of Change* (Nashville: Abingdon Press, 1976) and in the antecedent collections Marvin J. Taylor, ed., *Religious Education: A Comprehensive Survey* (Nashville: Abingdon Press, 1960), and *An Introduction to Christian Education* (Nashville: Abingdon Press, 1966) can still validly inform work with single parents. In addition, many of the research summaries in Merton P. Strommen,

ed., *Research on Religious Development* (New York: Hawthorn Books, 1971) are still quite informative for persons working with single parents.

5. See the chapter by Leon McKenzie in this volume.

6. For a brief summary of these perspectives, see James E. Loder, "Developmental Foundations for Christian Education," in *Foundations for Christian Education in an Era of Change,* ed. Marvin J. Taylor (Nashville: Abingdon Press, 1976), pp. 54-67.

7. Among many resources for appreciating the meanings of family experiences for individuals are Jerry Lewis et. al., *No Single Thread: Psychological Health in Family Systems* (New York: Brunner/Mazel, 1977); Paul Watzlawick, John Weakland, and Richard Fisch, *Change: Principles of Problem Formation and Problem Resolution* (New York: Norton, 1977); and John Narcisco and David Burkett, *Declare Yourself: Discovering the Me in Relationships* (Engelwood Cliffs, N.J.: Prentice-Hall, 1975). Robert S. Weiss, *Marital Separation* (New York: Basic Books, 1975) is one of several good resources on coping with life after separation and divorce. Developmental approaches such as James O. Lugo and Gerald L Hershey, *Human Development: A Multidisciplinary Approach to the Psychology of Individual Growth* (New York: Macmillan, 1974) also point to the multidimensional, rather than the time-oriented, approach to understanding adulthood and parenting, Kenneth Keniston, ed., *All Our Children: The American Family Under Pressure* (New York: Harcourt Brace Jovanovich, 1977) documents some of the factors in society that produce family disruption and divorce.

8. For more details see Charles V. Gerkin, *The Living Human Document: Re-visioning Counseling in a Hermeneutical Mode* (Nashville: Abingdon Press, 1983).

9. See H. Edward Everding, Jr. "A Hermeneutical Approach to Educational Theory," in *Foundations for Christian Education in an Era of Change,* ed. Marvin J. Taylor (Nashville: Abingdon Press, 1976).

10. Helpful discussions of family meanings in relation to parenting after divorce are in Kristine M. Rosenthal and Harry F. Keshet, *Fathers Without Partners* (Totowa, N.J.: Rowman and Littlefield, 1981); in Judith S. Wallerstein and Joan B. Kelley, *Surviving the Breakup* (New York: Basic Books, 1980); and in E. Mavis Hetherington, Martha Cox, and Roger Cox, "Stress and Coping in Divorce: A Focus on Women," in *Psychology in Transition,* ed. J. Gullahorn (New York: B. H. Winston and Sons, 1978); Maureen Green *Fathering* (New York: McGraw-Hill, 1976); and Michael E. Lamb, ed., *The Role of the Father in Child Development* (New York: Wiley, 1981). Theological interpretations of marriage and family may be found in J. B. Nelson, *Embodiment: An Approach to Sexuality and Christian Theology* (Minneapolis, Minn.: Augsburg, 1978) and in Walter Kasper, *Theology of Christian Marriage* (New York: Crossroad, 1981). See also the chapter by Sharan Merriam and Trenton Ferro in this volume for a discussion of some aspects of love. See Jeffrey Blustein, *Parents and Children: The Ethics of the*

Family (New York: Oxford University Press, 1982) for additional philosophical views of marriage and the family.

11. This chart outlined suggests many facets of an individual's relationships and statuses. The same individual will probably be described by one of the options in each item of the chart. For additional details on the divorce process see Morton and Bernice Hunt, *The Divorce Experience* (New York: McGraw-Hill, 1977); Paul Bohannan, ed., *Divorce and After* (Garden City, N.Y.: Anchor Books, 1971); and William V. Arnold et al. *Divorce: Prevention or Survival* (Philadelphia: Westminster Press, 1977). Additional issues are presented by Virginia Watts Smith in *The Single Parent* (Old Tappan, N.J.: F. H. Revell, 1976, 1983). For contrasts between single parents and never-married adults, see Peter J. Stein *Single Life: Unmarried Adults in Social Context* (New York: St. Martin's Press, 1981) and Alice Stolper Peppler, *Single Again: This Time With Children* (Minneapolis, Minn: Augsburg Publishing House, 1982).

12. See. E. Mavis Hetherington, Martha Cox, and Roger Cox, "Stress and Coping in Divorce: A Focus on Women," in *Psychology in Transition,* ed. J. Gullahorn (New York: B. H. Winston and Sons, 1978) and Kristine M. Rosenthal and Harry F. Keshet, *Fathers Without Partners* (Totowa, N. J.: Rowman and Littlefield, 1981) for detailed documentation of these two types of needs. For women's perceptions of the churches' responses to these needs, see Lee Coppernoll and Peggy Halsey *Crisis: Women's Experience and the Church's Response* (New York: Office of Ministries with Women in Crisis, General Board of Global Ministries, The United Methodist Church, 1982.)

13. For descriptions of religious education ministries with and to single parents, Russell Claussen, *The Church's Growing Edge: Single Adults, A Planning Guide* (New York: Pilgrim Press, 1980) offers excellent resources. This resource includes brief but very insightful statements about single lifestyles, perspectives on being single, including single parenthood, and provides many references on special topics. A list of selected books as a beginning library is also provided. Other program suggestions are available in Britton Wood, *Single Adults Want to Be the Church, Too* (Nashville: Broadman Press, 1977), which describes in detail the program in a large Southern Baptist Church. In some cases, aids to divorce mediation may be an effective religious education ministry of the church. See John M. Haynes, *Divorce Mediation: A Practical Guide for Therapists and Counselors* (New York: Springer Publishing Co., 1981). Elizabeth Ogg, *One Parent Families* (New York: Public Affairs Committee, 1976) is a helpful inexpensive booklet that churches could make available to divorcing parents. For single parents whose spouse has died, Elizabeth Kubler-Ross, *Questions and Answers on Death and Dying* (New York: Collier, 1974) can be a helpful resource.

14. Some denominations have very helpful materials and programs on human sexuality for children, adolescents, and adults. For example,

see Joan and Richard Hunt, *Affirming Sexuality in Christian Adulthood* (Nashville: Graded Press, 1982).

15. See Nora Stirling, *You Would If You Loved Me* (New York: Batan, 1978) suggests that friendship, intimacy, communication, and *other* relationship dynamics are much more important than sexual activities in keeping a marriage together.

16. Among many helpful resources for single parents who consider another marriage are Joan and Richard Hunt, *Preparing for Christian Marriage* (Nashville: Abingdon, 1981), and June and William Noble, *How to Live with Other People's Children* (New York: Hawthorne Books, 1977). Tom McGinnis, *More than Just a Friend* (Englewood Cliffs; Prentice-Hall, 1981), may be especially helpful to persons for whom a romantic affair is (or has been) a part of the question of remarriage. Unmarried single parents who live together may benefit from Joseph Simons, *Living Together: Communication in the Unmarried Relationship* (Chicago: Nelson-Hall, 1978).

Chapter 8

Working with Adults in Separation and Divorce

NEIL R. PAYLOR

Divorce is an experience we will all go through at some time in our lives. It may be our own divorce or the divorce of someone close to us, but these days we can expect divorce to touch and change all of our lives.

How can we understand it? What does it mean? One thing is sure: Divorce has profound significance for teaching and learning in the church.

Let's begin with a story of a family whose names are fictional but whose experiences are collected from the lives of real people.

THE ANDERSON FAMILY

The first phone call Monday morning was from Ted asking John, his minister, for an appointment. "Barbara wants a divorce," he said almost choking on the words. John arranged a time for them to meet that morning wondering what had gone wrong in what seemed to him like a sound marriage.

The couple had been members of this parish since John came seven years ago. He had come to know them and their two daughters as one of the more active families in the congregation. Rachel was 15 and Kathleen 17.

John remembered Barbara saying at a Lenten dinner that they were celebrating eighteen years of marriage in March. "That was just last month," John thought. "Come to think of it, I haven't seen either one at church since then."

When Ted arrived he looked like he hadn't slept in two or three days. Dark circles rimmed his eyes. His face lacked color. He had prided himself on his work as a district supervisor of the water company in Pittsburgh. The neatness of his dress always seemed to reflect his self-confidence. Not this day. He was loosely put together. He walked as if it took a great deal of energy to put one foot in front of the other. He collapsed his six-foot frame into a chair at the corner of John's desk.

"It seems sudden to me, but to hear Barbara tell it, it's been building for a long time, John," he began. "I thought we had a good marriage. Good kids. I've advanced in my work. But she says she's been aware of her unhappiness ever since she had the miscarriage two years ago. She was 37 at that time and we had decided not to have more children. Barbara wanted to go back and finish her college degree. She quit when we got married. The pregnancy came along by accident. I thought we had resolved that losing the child was for the best. She began taking courses last fall. Everything seemed good. Three weeks ago she tells me she wants a divorce. I don't know how I can make it without her." Tears began to rise in Ted's eyes as he looked out the window and thought of the future alone. His deep sadness was apparent.

After a moment, John inquired, "What made her decide on a divorce?"

"You'll have to ask her. She thought it would be better if we talked to you separately," Ted replied. "She tells me she cares for me, but she doesn't love me. She said last night she's not sure she ever really did."

John wanted to find out what Ted thought the causes for her decision were.

"I'm struggling with that question. I think it goes way back. Barbara's father was an alcoholic," Ted continued. She was so close with my family even before we dated. I wondered if she was marrying me or them when the wedding day came. We've stayed close to them throughout our marriage. Mother's death was real hard on Barb last year. It seems like a lot of things are changing."

"How did you decide to call me, Ted?" John asked.

"I tried handling this whole thing on my own, but I feel so depressed. Barbara says there's no way she'll change her mind. I guess I want you to help me survive. I'm not sure I can make it."

John talked with Ted about his struggle and after an hour or so the two men made plans to continue their conversation on Friday. In the meantime John would talk with Barbara.

It was the next afternoon that John drove to the Anderson's home. "Twenty-five years in the ministry and I never have been able to guess the other person's side of the story," John thought to himself as he got out of the car and moved up the front walk.

Barbara opened the door before he could reach for the bell. "Come in, John. I've been wanting to talk to you for a long time," Barbara greeted. "Let's sit in the family room" she said over her shoulder as she led the way.

"Coffee?"

"That would give me a boost," John answered as he settled into an easy chair.

"You'll probably need one," Barbara said with an edge to her voice.

John let himself reflect on the situation while Barbara was in the kitchen. She seemed her usual easy self to him. "Soft" was the word that always came to his mind when he saw her. She didn't look 39 and on the verge of leaving her marriage. More like early 30s. Barbara returned with the coffee.

"I don't know how much Ted told you, but I want out of our marriage, John," she said removing her shoes and drawing her legs up beside her on the sofa across from him. "I feel quite sure about it. Ted has been good to me, but after the abortion I realized how much I've leaned on him and how little really we've shared."

"Ted didn't mention an abortion," John interrupted. "He said something about a miscarriage."

"That was the story we told people. Everyone seemed to believe it. In some way, we did too. We hid it from ourselves. Ted is still doing that. I can't any longer. I feel just too sad to go on pretending.

An old clock ticked in the corner accentuating the silence which closed them both in their thoughts as Barbara's face darkened.

"It's like it happened a long time ago, John," she continued, "and we weren't aware of it. I don't know really how it happened. That's part of the sadness. We closed each other out somehow. I was raising kids. He was working. I wanted to get back to finishing my schooling. He seemed resentful of that. I think I married Ted so he could take care of me the way my father never did. Yet I ended up feeling just as alone and loveless as I had as a child.

John found himself intrigued by the persistence into adulthood of experiences which had occurred so long ago. "How did your mother fit into your growing up?"

"She worked hard to keep the family together. I remember her as always smiling and saying things would work out fine. I used to ask her why she didn't leave or throw Dad out. She'd smile and tell me not to worry. I can't go on smiling any longer, John."

"No, I suppose not," he responded. "Sounds as though the problems you and Ted have began before the abortion."

"Oh my, yes," Barbara went on. "The abortion served to bring things into focus for me. I may have given up a child, but I certainly gained a new image of myself. In a way, I was born instead of the baby. Some people will say I'm selfish. That's what Ted thinks. He even says it. It's more than going back to school. It's more like changing my life and the way I live it. Ted wants me to depend on him. He can take care of me that way, and he doesn't have to take me seriously."

The pitch of Barbara's voice was rising. The tone was anger. Red blotches were appearing on her neck and face.

"I have to get out of here," she exclaimed "before what's left of my life dies unborn."

Her intensity convinced John that Barbara could not, would not hear any talk of reconciliation. At least, not yet. He had to admit that his own hopes were diminished from what they had been when he arrived.

The antique clock chimed the hour and John was surprised how long he had been there and how quickly the time had passed. He had two other calls to make that afternoon, so he got to the edge of his chair ready to leave.

"I can tell how strongly you feel about your decision. You've obviously given it a lot of thought. You know my affection for you has not changed. I'm glad you could tell me about something as important as this. I'll stop back or give you a call in the days ahead to find out how things are going."

"I wanted to tell you sooner, John," Barbara said as they both got to their feet. "Some days I have more courage about it than others. Yesterday it was hard just to get out of bed. Now I don't have to live with this secret around you and Anne. Tell her for me, will you? The deception is wearing me out."

"I will," John replied. "I'm going to see Ted again on Friday."

"Good. He needs your support right now."

"I want to talk with you, too, about Kathleen and Rachel. I'll be back in touch," John said. "There's more than we can cover in one time."

"You'll probably see them around the church tomorrow. They'll be at the youth meeting. See what you think about how they're doing," Barbara added.

"How much have you told them about your decision?"

"Nothing yet. I dread that," said Barbara.

"None of this is easy," said John as he went out the door.

The next afternoon John was watching the young people come into the church basement for dinner and a program. Most of them had come directly from school for a class followed by a period of recreation and a meal of sloppy joes. The kids were junior and senior high-school age. Most of them attached themselves to a group of others their age, sometimes hanging on to a friend, talking, laughing, walking fast, sometimes striding backward so as not to miss any of the conversation or break the ties of their circle. A few drifted in alone or in pairs. John soon spotted Kathleen with a group of seniors and then Rachel with her usual girlfriend. Appearance gave no hint of the turmoil at home.

"How easy it would be to overlook these two," John thought. "How many more are there in this group we don't know about whose families are coming apart?" He wondered.

That thought reminded him of the idea he'd had the day before when he was leaving Barbara. The young people were settling into dinner. John was scanning the room for Carole when she came through the door with her tote bag and an arm full of books. She had taught one of the afternoon classes.

Carole was in her mid-40s and solid as a rock. She was an active lay person who volunteered her time to the church. John valued her common sense and her sensitivity to people and their situations. They had worked together for six of his seven years there. The kids along with the adults trusted her. Once again John sought her insights.

"I could use your counsel for a few minutes now," he called to her.

"Sure," she replied. "Why don't we go to the church office where we can hear each other. Get us two plates and I'll meet you there."

John returned with the food and they began to talk. At first, about the day's program, then about Carole's graduate study in public health adminstration, her family, and finally about John's concern.

"I've been wondering if you know when a family in the church is considering a divorce. Can you tell from the kids or do parents say something or teachers comment?" he asked. "I usually find out after the separation occurs."

"And there's a fight over who gets custody of the church," Carole added.

"Something like that," John laughed. "Usually one spouse leaves and the other stays. But so much happens before the break-up," he continued. "If we were aware of it we could care for those children and adults just at a time when they feel so isolated in their families and from their friends."

"Sounds to me like you've someone particular in mind," Carole said.

"I do," John acknowledged. "Can you tell me right now whose parents might be having difficulty from among our junior and senior highs?"

"That's a good question. Parents seldom tell me. A teacher will occasionally pick something up in a church school class, under-stand what it means, and mention it to me. More often it's when I'm with a group of kids who start talking about one of their friends who's having a difficult time because of family conflicts. They wonder how to help. It's unusual for a child or a young person to come to me directly about a situation at home. There are some pretty good clues that something's bothering a kid from her behavior and her emotional tone, but it's hard to know what's causing those changes. Right now I know of two families who are having serious marital problems and two others that I suspect something like that is in process just from the way the children are acting. It's with the Andersons and Crawleys where I have a hunch something is brewing."

"You're right on the mark with the Andersons," John confirmed. I talked with Ted and Barbara earlier this week."

Carole elaborated. "Kathleen has seemed very angry to me lately. She's belligerent with her friends. Testy in class. Her best friend said she was bragging about getting drunk last weekend. Rachel is more withdrawn and quiet. Not her usual good-natured bossy self. As a rule she wants to answer all the questions. I had to call on her in class today. When I did, she said she didn't know anything. That's pretty strong stuff from this 15-year-old."

Carole called time because she had to get back to the young people. She'd planned a film for the evening's program, and she wanted to make sure it was ready before they arrived.

"What you've been telling me has so many interesting implications, Carole," John said, gathering up the paper plates and cups as she got her materials together. "The awareness you have of these girls' needs is foremost in my mind. Do you think we could help our teachers who work with children and adults be more sensitive to the signs of a family's deterioration? More than ever these four Andersons are bringing their individual needs to us because they are not available to each other in the usual ways."

"I don't see why not," Carole said turning out the light and closing the door to the office. "Let's talk more about it."

John turned toward his office as Carole continued down the hall. He felt convinced that religious educators were a frontline ministry to the people of divorce. He wanted to hold onto that thought and see where it took him as he talked with Ted and Barbara in the days ahead. "I've never before put those things together," he said half out loud and with a sense of discovery. "Separation, divorce, and the religious education program of the church. Fascinating to explore where that idea will lead us."

John did make an important discovery. The needs of people at the time of divorce are often expressed in the educational program of a church. It happened with the Andersons' daughters. It happens with younger children as well as adults. The teaching and learning process may be used by these people to work on their family conflicts. Those of us in that process, friends, adult religious educators, and ministers, become involved with them in that work. How well we understand that process and what they are working on will likely shape how helpful we can be to them at such a time.

Ted and Barbara did get a divorce in September. Six months later Barbara remarried and has not returned to the church. Ted is currently considering a job change and moving to another city. Kathleen started college but dropped out after one term because of lack of motivation. She's working and, together with Rachel, living with Barbara. The girls come to church regularly with their father. It's impossible to assess the impact of this experience on these people. Their lives have certainly been changed by it. So have the lives of John, Carole, and many other members of that church community.

DIVORCE IS ABOUT MARRIAGE

When persons get a divorce or separate they are leaving not only a person but the relationship of marriage. What is it in marriage that adults are divorcing? Certain themes are repeated in the history of marriage which suggest answers to that question.

Augustine, the African bishop of Hippo from A.D. 396 to 430, expressed three of these themes in his life and writing. His place is central in the history of the theology of marriage and his views continue to represent powerful tensions in marriage today.

The primary goal of marriage for Augustine was the bearing of children. "Marriage itself among all races is for the one purpose of procreating children."[1] This proposition has been at the heart of the church's teaching about marriage for roughly nineteen hundred years. The Episcopal Lambeth Conference as recently as 1958 reported, in part, "No marriage would be according to God's will which did not bear fruit in children."[2] One year later the General Assembly of the United Presbyterian Church was struggling with Augustine's influences when it said, in part:

Marriage is a relationship of love and fidelity which involves both companionship and parenthood, and believing that the sexual life within this relationship is given by God . . . and is neither an ethically neutral aspect of human existence nor an evil which needs to be justified by something else, as for example the procreation of children, the 171st General Assembly approves the principle of voluntary family planning and responsible parenthood.[3]

This statement elevates companionship to a place of importance equal to parenthood. It goes so far as to mention it first as if to alter the Augustinian priority. Barbara Anderson said her life had been busy raising children. Parenthood is often the centerpiece of a marriage. It may be the primary means a husband and wife have to relating to one another. Marriages sometimes come apart when children leave home. Marriage and parenthood are frequently confused with parenthood being a substitute for marriage.

A second theme in Augustine comes from his life. His own marriage was arranged by his family, a usual practice in his day. Children lived their youth as well as their adulthood under the authority of parents. Perhaps marriage is always an attempt to deal with our past in terms of the future. A woman marries to get away from a dreadful home life only to find her past repeated in her new relationship. The same experience holds true for men. Husbands and wives often wonder whether they married by their own choice or whether they were compelled by social tradition, family experiences, and their own needs at the time. Feeling trapped in marriage by your own childhood often provides the energy for a separation and divorce.

Augustine describes marriage as a sacrament, a sacred bond.[4] He does not use the word "sacrament" in a formal sense, but to suggest a sign or symbol of the union between Jesus Christ and his church. The essential characteristic of this union is its indissolubility. This is a third very important theme. Augustine could acknowledge divorce but not as we know it. "When divorce intervenes, that nuptial contract is not destroyed, so that the parties of the compact are wedded persons even though separated."[5] Our understanding of divorce did not exist in A.D. 401. It is this ancient tradition of the permanence of the marriage vows which troubles so many adult religious educators in the contemporary Christian community when they encounter divorce. Divorce as it is currently understood is a relatively recent option.

It is the interplay of these three themes with one another and

the way they are curiously compounded with human experiences, social custom, medical science, theological doctrine, the
common sense and uncommon chicanery of politicans which
compose the history of marriage. It is this history which informs
the personal story of every divorce and the manner in which it
touches and changes our lives.

The Middle Ages made important modification in the Augustinian positions. Especially the twelfth century. Why? No one
really knows.

In the year 1175, a council presided over by the archbishop of
Canterbury and held in the presence of King Henry II firmly laid
down:

> Where both partners do not consent there is no marriage. Therefore
> those who give maidens in marriage when they are in their babyhood
> do nothing, unless both the children give their consent when they
> reach the age of discretion. By the authority of this decree we very
> strictly forbid that henceforth any couples be married of which one
> partner or the other has not reached the age determined by civil and
> canon law, save that perchance on occasion such a union may be
> tolerated where there is very urgent necessity for the sake of peace.[6]

The last clause reminds us of the facts of life in medieval England. Young Henry had been married by the older king when he
was three-and-a-half. Henry II reckoned to have a firm grip on
the marriage of his children by the time they were four. In spite of
those realities, there it is. *Where there is no consent there is no
marriage.* The idea of consent and the kernel of choice it contains
were planted there and grew in quiet ways for centuries breaking
through the social, ethical, and religious patterns to provide opportunities to express personal preference in our own age. Contemporary couples sometimes change that part of the customary
wedding vow which says "as long as we both shall live." In this
way, they express their autonomy from the past by what they
substitute in its place and by the very act of altering tradition.

It was in the twelfth century, too, that marriage became a
formal part of the Roman Catholic sacramental system. The
inclusion arose more from political than theological grounds.
What had been only symbolic for Augustine became a literal

representation. The new reality gave the church the key to control the succession of lands and power. Marriage was now under the jurisdiction of the church. As marriage began to move out from under the control of the family, it began to take shelter in the church, began to attach itself more firmly to a religious ideology. No one dreamed that would strengthen the foundation for the freedom children would have from their parents in choosing a marriage partner. The Protestant Reformation, in removing marriage from the sacramental system altogether, built upon that groundwork emancipating it further from the regulation of the past. The impact of what we do is often greater than we know or even imagine.

Philippe Aries dates the discovery of childhood in art in the twelfth century.[7] Children began to be seen for themselves and not just as little adults. Their status as *homunculi* had been, in part, due to the high mortality of childhood. If a child survived the first five years of life, he or she was accorded the designation of an adult. Once again this modification was only a faint beginning, but nonetheless a beginning. It would take several centuries before children would emerge as having distinctive periods of development and unique personalities apart from adults. The process of this recognition was nothing less than the erosion of Augustine's basic tenet that children were the highest aim, the sole purpose of marriage.

Children and their discipline preoccupied the New England Calvinists who drew upon Augustine and the belief in the perversity of the human will. The infant was looked upon as a repository of disobedience and sin. Evangelical parents were at war with their children. "Break their wills," John Wesley urged, "that you may save their souls."[8] Child rearing was a process through which the impulses of self-expression and independence were conquered.

Marriage may have taken place only upon the consent of the couple in the eighteenth century, but the young man and woman raised in a Christian evangelical household had their parents within them. The capability of choosing had been limited long before the age of marriage. Wesley reminds us of those strictures when he wrote, "Not even marriage cancels or lessens the general obligation of filial duty."[9]

He might just as well have said that, in fact, marriage should reinforce the parent-child relationship. There were striking parallels between the submission of children to parents and wives to husbands. Wesley insisted that a wife must

> know herself the inferior, and behave as such. When the woman counts herself equal with the husband the root of all good carriage is withered, the foundation thereof dried up. Whoever therefore would be a good wife, let this sink into her inmost soul, "My husband is my superior, my better: he has the right to rule over me, God has given it him and I will not strive against God. He is my superior, my better."[10]

"This pattern of dominance and submission, of authority in the male and subjection in the female, of superiority as the perogative of masculinity and inferiority as the badge of femininity, continued to characterize marriages for many generations."[11]

The model for the relationship of parents with children and husbands with wives was a theological one. Wesley, striving to define the nature of a true Christian and the essence of genuine Christianity, noted that the ruling temper of a Christian's heart was

> the most absolute submission, and the tenderest gratitude to his Sovereign Benifactor. And this grateful love creates filial fear: an awful reverence toward him, and an earnest care not to . . . displease that indulgent Power.[12]

Augustine had been revised. His emphasis had been altered. Bearing children was no longer the primary goal of marriage. In eighteenth-century America the highest aim of marriage was to be "as children." Breaking the wills of children could only serve to remind the mother of her wifely duty to her husband and the father of his obligation to God. Marriage was the means of having children and being children. No one ever grew out of their childhood. Divorce was unthinkable. It would have meant breaking the relationship between parent and child between God and his offspring. In concentrating its attention on the perversity of children and the need to make them submissive, evangelical theology had succeeded in unwittingly giving the child a central place. It had made extravagant claims for the piety of childhood as a religious ideal. "Except ye be converted, and become as little children, ye shall not enter into the kingdom of heaven."[13] Marriage had become identified with parenthood beyond Augustine's wildest dreams. The stage was set for an increased interest in and a different interpretation of childhood.

The middle of the nineteenth century produced just such changes and found a culture in America which was receptive to them. These new views did not displace the view of the child as perverse. In a curious way they seemed to have grown out of that very view which began by subjugating the child and ended by holding up the child as a model of religious piety. Freud would have called such an alteration a reaction formation. The anger we feel toward an object is so threatening to our own sense of well-being we transpose the emotion into love even reverence. Evangelicals must have known a considerable amount of anger at being children all their lives.

The new view of children took many forms. One expression of it was a genre of literature on child development unlike earlier works which dealt mostly with child etiquette.[14] A modern and natural image of childhood was emerging in the Sunday School movement in England and America. It presumed a lower rate of mortality. "There was time to spare, time to enjoy the pleasures of a prelude to adulthood. The modern child had breathing space, a freedom from the onslaught of maturity and the distant rumor of death. For a few years . . . the American youngster should enjoy the temporary grace of childhood."[15] This view picked up the idealization of children affirming their innocence. It literally broke into songs about sunbeam children. "Jesus wants me for a sunbeam. To shine for him each day." The theme of these songs was

the carefree, playful, trusting and dependent sunbeam casts the momentary light of innocence upon an otherwise soiled and troubled world. Sunbeam children may have been created as much to provide momentary escape for Sunday school workers raised under the symbols of hard faith as they were to explain childhood to children.[16]

The last sentence aptly describes the dynamics of a reaction formation. Whatever the motive, children were being appreciated for who they were and not for what they could contribute to the adult world. The separation of childhood from adulthood was firmly in place. The significance of this development was considerable in the erosion of Augustine's formulation of the purpose for marriage.

Augustine's proposition that the chief end of marriage was the procreation of children had created a dependency of marriage on the bearing and proper raising of children. Marriage was not an end in itself but the means to parenthood. It came to be thought that marriage was incomplete without the issue of children. The identification of marriage with parenthood prevailed until children began to be seen as separate from adults. As children came to be recognized for themselves, marriage began to be emancipated from childhood. Adults were not children nor children little adults. Children had their own realm. Adults had to find theirs. It was this divergence which set adults free to explore and discover who they were apart from their own parents. There was more time for such investigation as children were given the latitude to develop and grow from within themselves and parents were less obsessed with imposing upon them the mold for their lives.

The first adults to recognize this freedom and to express it were women. Women in American culture had come to bear more and more the responsibility for child rearing as the society shifted from agriculture to industry in the nineteenth century. Husbands went off to work leaving the domestic realm to the wives.

> The literature of the time shows a consistent preoccupation with the career of the well-meaning but sorely pressed male, deeply involved in the work of the world, yet holding ever before his eyes the saintly image of the lady in his life. "It was she" to quote from a popular sermon "who like a guardian angel, watches over his interests, warns him against danger, comforts him under trial; and by her pious, assiduous, and attractive deportment, constantly endeavors to render him more virtuous, more useful, more honorable, and more happy." Such a creature was "a pearl beyond price."[17]

Women were the custodians not only of the children but the marriage. Their economic contribution to society was less visible and tangible than their colonial grandmothers. Marriage and successful parenthood were the keys to their social recognition and security. The separation of children from adults and parenthood from marriage marked a step forward for women. Their lives would no longer be so identified with and consumed by children. This struggle is obviously continuing in our own day. It is intensified by the alternatives of birth controls and the recognition of women's rights in the workplace. The choices are complex and very difficult for women. Many wonder and with good cause just how much substantial progress has been made in their behalf. The history of marriage is in some sense a history of the domination of women by men: a good reason to pay attention to that history, what we as women and men can learn from it, and the changes which have taken place in it.

The separation of childhood from adulthood in the nineteenth century gave husbands and wives the occasion to be married for other reasons than the procreation of children. Marriage could be considered for marriage's sake. It was a new mode of partnership, formal and self-conscious at first. Many of the new alliances did not survive. Divorce rates rose steadily after the mid-nineteenth century.[18] Despite the casualties, marriage was developing into a relationship between adults. It could be thought of as dissoluble without breaking the ties with God, Christ, the church, family, or children.

The twentieth century has elaborated these changes and contributed some of its own. Marriage is the choice of adults in our day. It is less the dictates of parents and society. Young people live together as a statement that marriage is not a prerequisite for sexual intimacy or personal commitment. The need to make such a statement is itself a confirmation of the constraints they feel from the social tradition of the past. Perhaps what they are saying is more of hope. Divorce seems like a similar statement that marriage does not in itself always bring any kind of closeness or have any lasting bond for the people in it. The imperative character of marriage is breaking up and being replaced in this century by categories of adult development, such as young adult, mid-life crisis, empty-nest syndrome, the two career worker, married, and divorced. These terms describe the adult's search for an identity. Divorce is likely to be viewed as part of this search, a transition state on the journey to maturity.

A theological shift has contributed to this revision of marriage.

The parent-child theology of earlier American piety does not hold the position it once did. Helplessness, submission, dominance, and dependency are no longer major motifs. Theologians from such diverse times and experiences as Dietrich Bonhoeffer and J. A. T. Robinson began to urge that Christian faith respond to the political powers in society and the critical reason of human inquiry. Their writings along with the voices of Third World theologians have prompted some observers to call our day the "post-Christian era." The model now is much more one of God's being involved at the center of life. Mutuality, participation, and respect are the themes used to describe relationships between men and women, wives and husbands because these are the characteristics of Yahweh's relationship with his children.

Summary

Wives and husbands for centuries found the justification for their marriage and the satisfaction of their lives in the children they bore with one another. Separating marriage first from the control of the family and next from the jurisdiction of the church weakened that Augustinian connection. It was the recognition of children as separate from adults which finally collapsed it. Children didn't need parents to break their wills. A couple could no longer derive from parenthood their sole purpose for being married. They were forced to look for other grounds. Marriage began to be examined for itself. When that occurred divorce became a reality and marriage was seen as having new possibilities. Society cannot go back. Marriage is no longer defined by parenthood. Marriage seems to have created a divorce between childhood and adulthood where before it was a link between them. How do we live with a sense of continuity and constancy and dependency as adults separated from our past?

MARRIAGE IS ABOUT LOVE

Love is the name of our common journey. That's why divorce touches all of us. Divorce is about marriage and marriage is about love.

Love is the centerpiece of our Christian faith.

I may be able to speak the languages of men and even of angels, but if I have no love, my speech is no more than a noisy gong or a clanging bell. I may have the gift of inspired preaching; I may have all knowledge and understand all secrets; I may have all faith to move mountains—but if I have no love, I am nothing. I may give away everything I have, and even give up my body to be burned—but if I have no love, this does me no good.[19]

No wonder Jesus asks: "Simon, son of John, do you love me?"[20] Being open to love means being open to suffering. Jesus said, "Follow me."[21] We are made for love. That is why divorce touches all of us. We have all loved someone who has left us.

Everyone who has ever been married has been angry at the person they love, angry enough to leave. This anger can be so intense it seems like the marriage was a mistake, as if there was never any love there.

Children sometimes wish their parents would get a divorce so that the hostile silences and the loud fights between them would stop. They often feel responsible for the conflict and that is a very heavy burden for children to carry.

"I'm so sorry," a woman said to her friend, as they talked following the Sunday morning church service. The friend had just told her she and her husband were getting a divorce. Both women had worked together in the church. In fact, the friend had been president of the church council just the previous year.

As the friend was about to leave the sanctuary, this same woman caught up with her. "What I said a moment ago was thoughtless. I've always admired you and your husband. I took it for granted you two were happy. I haven't been aware of you and your pain. I'll try to be more sensitive in the future."

The friend thanked her and left feeling a new measure of understanding between them.

It is hard to know what to say when someone you know tells you they are divorcing. We are not always aware of how much we invest in other people's marriages or just how much we mean to them. When friends divorce we are saddened and even angry that they have disturbed our ideal of love. We may feel our own disappointment so keenly it is difficult for us to be in touch with their pain.

When a daughter told her mother that her husband had left for another woman, her mother inquired, "Are you sure you did all you could?" The question seemed like an accusation to the daughter. Parents often experience the divorce of a son or daughter as their own failure. They are moved to defend or accuse, taking sides when what is needed is support and trust and love.

Jesus took divorce as a sign of how hardened we are at the center of ourselves.

> And Pharisees came up and in order to test him asked,"Is it lawful for a man to divorce his wife?" He answered them, "What did Moses command you?" They said, "Moses allowed a man to write a certificate of divorce, and to put her away." But Jesus said to them, "For your hardness of heart he wrote you this commandment. But from the beginning of creation, 'God made them male and female.' 'For this reason a man shall leave his father and his mother and be joined to his wife, and the two shall become one flesh.' So they are no longer two but one. What therefore God has joined together, let not man put asunder."[22]

The Jewish law regarding divorce had been set down in Deuteronomy 24. There was debate about the interpretation of that law between the two leading rabbinic schools. It is probable that the Pharisees wanted to know where Jesus stood in that debate.

Jesus began to talk to them about the human heart. Divorce was not a matter of law for him. He spoke of it as an inward condition. The Greek word is *sclarocardiúm*. It means hardness of heart, coldness, obstinacy, stubbornness. Our words sclerosis and cardiac are cognate terms. The root word for the Greek *sclaros* meant skeleton, the age-old symbol of death.

Jesus came inviting people to accept the rule of God in their lives—even in their most intimate relationship of marriage. The rule is not a rule of the law, but one of love. It bids a woman and a man not to be afraid of one another, but to become "one flesh"— a new person, a corporate personality, a joint life. Such a life is not the loss of individuality. It is the creation of a new being as it was in the beginning when God used the bone of man to make a new creature, woman. He takes the hard parts of us, the *sclaros,* and creates new life with them.

We sometimes live in ways that mock love. We make coarse our most tender parts. We turn Jesus' invitation into a set of jokes about women trapping men so that marriage is stereotyped as a jail, not a joint life. Becoming one flesh has been translated by the church into the narrow-minded physiology of sexual intercourse. No wonder Augustine had to justify marriage with the procreation of children. It is no surprise that young people do not want to save sex until marriage. They hope there will be more to marriage than sex and more to sex than biology. Do you suppose some of these same young people were, at an earlier age, the children whose parents told themselves, and in some way the children, too, that they were the reasons the parents were staying married? Children can be a substitute for love, for the procreation of a new being between a man and a woman in marriage. It is the divorce within us which separates us from God, and, in turn, from one another that Jesus had in mind. Divorce is about all of us when it comes right down to it.

LOVE IS ABOUT TEACHING

Divorce is not just about marriage. It is about the struggle all of us have to let God's love rule our lives. That struggle gets into the process of teaching and learning. "And Jesus said to them, 'Moses wrote this law for you because you are so hard to teach.' "[23] *Sclarocardiúm* is translated in the *Good News Bible* as "hard to teach." Divorce is a sign that we are "learning disabled."

Students and teachers are capable, at times, of composing an intimate relationship. I have always learned more when a strong bond existed between me and a teacher. I mastered the subject by means of the person of the teacher. What I really learned was the teacher.

Adult religious education can have a sclerotic quality to it. Some teachers seem bent on breaking the wills and hardening the minds of their pupils. I suppose that's how they have been taught. That can kill creativity. Students harden themselves against such a teaching and their learning becomes a set of rules. A piece in a student publication of a theological seminary humorously caught this mood. It was titled "Every Answer You'll Ever Need!"

When you are given an objective test:
"It doesn't let you express yourself."

When you are given an essay test: "It's
so vague; you don't know what is expected."

When you are given minor tests: "Why not
have a few big ones? They keep you on
edge all the time."

When you are given no tests: "It's
not fair! How can he possibly judge
what we know?"

When every part of the subject is taken
up in class: "Oh, he just follows
the book."

When you are asked to study part of the
book by yourself: "Why, she never even
discussed it."

When the course is in lecture form:
"We never got a chance to say anything."

When the course consists of informal lectures
and discussions: "He just sits there!
Who wants to hear the students? They
don't know how to teach the class!"[24]

Many ministers find themselves resistant to reading for their
work because their graduate study made learning such an ordeal
that they want to avoid anything which resembles a return to it.

Who are the divorced among us, the ones who are hard to
teach, the learning disabled in the religious education program of
a church? How can you, as an adult religious educator, help them
recover their creation?

They are the people of divorce who come feeling they have
failed at love and that love has failed them. Children, parents,
divorced men and women like the Anderson family are in our
churches and communities. Search them out. Find out if teachers
like Carole and pastors such as John can identify them. Once you
know who some of them are, pray for them. Listen to what they
say. Their presence may be defined by their absence in many

churches. What makes it hard for these people to learn about love? What are their needs?

Richard Hunt in chapter 7 and Mary Louise Mueller in chapter 8 describe the needs of single parents and the work of mourning a loss. Divorce is a death, the death of a dream. The notes at the end of this chapter include additional resources which will be useful to persons in times of separation and divorce as well as to their teachers.[25]

A common problem for separated and divorced adults is their sense of isolation. They feel alone and often ashamed of what has happened. A church may be able to bring them together with other persons who are having or have recently had similar experiences. Discovering they are not the only ones who have been through the breakup of a family and had the thoughts and feelings they are having can often be an enormous relief. These support groups also enable men and women to explore and find directions they want to go with the perplexing problems they face.

Groups are an important asset for teachers who have questions about helpful ways of relating to the children and adults of divorce. One teacher told of a four-year-old girl, of recently divorced parents who held a coin tightly in her hand and refused to put it in the Sunday School offering plate. The teacher scolded her. This sequence of events repeated itself for several weeks until the frustrated woman mentioned it during a teacher training workshop. The leader pointed out that the coin might be an important link with the only remaining parent this child has. The coin was the last thing her mother gave her before they parted that morning for what was another and very frightening separation for the child.

A lot of divorced people and their children are uncomfortable at a church's "family night dinner." They do not feel like a family in the traditional sense.

One young woman goes to a different church in town than her parents because she is divorced. She doesn't want to embarrass them. These are the people of divorce among us.

Teaching to love is essential for loving to teach. As religious educators in the church are available to love their students, they will love their teaching and themselves for doing it. The task of loving the student is not always an easy one. Teachers can get lost in what they are teaching and become hardened to the ones they are teaching. Their own needs can blind them to the needs of students. The possibilities for a new creation are brought to life when teachers are invited to accept the rule of God's love into their lives.

These possibilities are brought to life by you. The nurture you give to the educators in your parish bestows a recognition on them that they are loved for who they are. The job covets the person, not the person the job. You can express that through your relationship with these teachers. When you do, a teacher can become a student learning of God's love from you. As teachers become students, then students may be seen as teachers. The two have the potential for creating a new being. Think of the teachers you carry within you now. It is their constant influence in your life which is enabling you to become a teacher.

And of course the people of divorce are sometimes found among the ministers of the church for whom the work of love has become a lonely, frightening, disappointing, sometimes overwhelming task for which they feel ill-prepared, depleted, and angry.

Ministers are set apart as "ideals" by persons in the parish. People bring to them the experiences they have had with other idealized individuals in their lives. It is out of these experiences that the expectations of ministers develop. If a man or woman has been disappointed by any important person, he or she may *expect* the pastor to be a disappointment and ask so much of her that eventually she does seem to fail the test.

It is difficult at times for a minister to understand these expectations and the needs they represent. He may take them more personally than they are intended and feel he should live up to them. When he cannot, the failure seems personal, too. Ministers have expectations of themselves from within which exert enormous demands on them.

Adult religious educators can help ministers when they understand the character of these expectations and the pressure pastors feel from them. They can enable clergy to understand more about people and their needs. The way Carole helped John with the Anderson family is an example of how an educator enables a pastor to see beyond the surface and into the struggles people are having. When the minister gets in touch with the needs of the people he cares for he can be a better pastor to them and to himself.

You have a ministry to these ministers. There are women and men who may be considering a divorce from the church or in their personal relationships with a spouse and family or who may feel divorced within themselves and be living in a hardened condition with church and home. Invite them to accept the rule of God's love once again in their lives. You won't use those words, but do it through your own way of considering their needs. You've come about people, God's people and his love for them. The minister needs to be included in that community. She too often feels set apart from it.

Divorced adults and their children, teachers, ministers: These are among the people of divorce. There are divorces that end marriages. There are divorces within marriages. There are divorces within people that separate them from God. Divorce is an experience we all go through at some time in our lives.

Summary

Jesus spoke of divorce in the relationship we have with our Creator. He invited people to accept the rule of God in their lives. The rule is not a law but a love. The name of our life journey is love.

Divorce is part of a person's struggle to leave the past and to become a mature adult. It also expresses a longing to be loved. It marks an ending and perhaps a beginning for that original love which created us and which beckons us into the future.

Our work is to help adults find within themselves this love that has come from beyond themselves so they can express it between themselves in marriage as well as in all their other relationships.

NOTES

1. Roy J. Deferrai, ed., *The Fathers of the Church,* 71 vols. (New York: Fathers of the Church, Inc.), Vol. 27: *The Good Marriage,* by St. Augustine, p. 33.

2. "The Report of Committee Five," *The Lambeth Conference: 1958,* (New York: The National Council of the Episcopal Church, 1958), p. 2.145.

3. "Planned Parenthood," *Social Progress* XLIX, no. 9 (July, 1959), p. 28.

4. St. Augustine, *The Good Marriage,* p. 31.

5. Ibid., p. 19.

6. Christopher N. L. Brooke, *Marriage in Christian History* (Cambridge: Cambridge University Press, 1978), p. 15.

7. Philippe Aries, *Centuries of Childhood* (New York: Alred A. Knopf, 1962), p. 43.

8. Quoted in Philip Greven, *The Protestant Temperament* (New York: Alfred A. Knopf, 1977), p. 35.

9. Ibid., p. 29.

10. John Wesley, "The Duties of Husbands and Wives," *The Works of Rev. John Wesley,* 16 vols. (London: 1809-1812), Vol. 9, pp. 74-75.

11. Greven, *The Protestant Temperament,* p. 127.

12. Ibid., p. 21.

13. Matthew 18:3 [King James Version].

14. John Demos, "The American Family in Past Time," *The American Scholar* 43, no. 3 (Summer, 1974), p. 430.

15. Robert W. Lynn and Elliott Wright, *The Big Little School* (Birmingham and Nashville: Religious Education Press and Abingdon Press, 1980), p. 83.

16. Ibid., p. 86.

17. John Demos, "The American Family in Past Time," *The American Scholar,* p. 433.

18. Ibid., p. 438.

19. 1 Corinthians 13:1-3 [Good News Bible].

20. John 21:16 [Good News Bible].

21. Luke 5:27 [Good News Bible].

22. Mark 10:2-9 [Revised Standard Version]. I am indebted to William F. Orr, professor emeritus of New Testament, Pittsburgh Theological Seminary, for his valuable assistance in understanding this passage.

23. Mark 10:5 [Good News Bible].

24. Lisa Lancaster, "Every Answer You'll Ever Need," *Logos* (Pittsburgh Theological Seminary, January, 1984), p. 16.

25. Additional Resources:

FOR CHILDREN.

—Richard Gardner, *The Boys and Girls Book About Divorce.* New York: Bantam Books, 1970.

—Lauthi Thomas, *Eliza's Daddy.* New York: Harcourt Brace Jovanovich, 1976.

—Eda LeShan, *What's Going to Happen to Me?* New York: Four Winds Press, 1978.

FOR ADULTS.

—Charles Cerling, *The Divorced Christian.* Minneapolis, Minn.: Baker Books, 1984.

—Earl Grollman, *Explaining Divorce to Children.* Boston: Beacon Press, 1969.

—Mel Krautzler, *Creative Divorce.* New York: The New American Library, 1975.

—Jim Smoke, *Suddenly Single.* Old Tappan, N.J.: Fleming Revell, 1982.

For family members and friends.

—Neil Paylor and Barry Head. *Scenes from a Divorce.* Minneapolis, Minn.: Winston Press, 1983.

The authors of these books interpret the emotional, social, and spiritual impact of divorce on children, adults, family members, and friends. Their approach is to make the experience less frightening and more manageable.

Chapter 9

Working with Adults in
Death-Related Circumstances

MARY LOUISE MUELLER

Working with adults following separation and divorce demands among other things some understanding of research findings in the area of grief and bereavement. However, the finality of the separation due to death adds factors which the religious educator cannot neglect. It is, above all, in circumstances related to death that human beings seek transcendent meanings. Death education falls under all three of the New Testament concepts delineated in chapter 1. It is obvious that anything associated with death pertains to the message (kerygma) of the Christian tradition. Under the rubric of koinonia, adults come together to join in a collaborative process to share and to strengthen the values implicitly present in the community faith. This explication and deepening of beliefs which span the barrier of death can serve the real needs of both adult learners and adult religious educators (diakonia.) In terms of both content and intent, education in areas related to death is, for believers, religious and holds the potential, when properly explored, of being a redemptive process for all concerned.

Certainly the religious educator needs cognitive knowledge of the various dimensions of death education, including research findings and theological reevaluations. But this personal understanding is only a beginning. A truly effective religious education program for adults must address the topics of bereavement, grief, and mourning as well as those of dying, death, and eternal life. To facilitate the twofold purpose of aiding individual growth and program planning, the body of this chapter is organized into two major areas each with appropriate subsections. In each section, basic information and relevant research findings as well as reflective and somewhat more speculative discourses are included. Notes are kept to a minimum; educational activities are suggested when these flow naturally from the text.

BEREAVEMENT—GRIEF—MOURNING

Death has always been and, despite some pseudo-scientific claims, it will always be. God is God of life and of death. This has long been affirmed by the adage: "The Lord gives and the Lord takes away"; not in a morbid nor individualized sense that God wills, causes, or permits an individual's death, but that life on planet earth cannot be without death. Some must die that others may live. Indeed, that life itself may be meaningful there must be a built-in ending. This was recognized by the Hebrew theologian almost a thousand years before the birth of Jesus. In his story of the man, the woman, and the snake (Genesis 2-3), each, in turn, is given a curse or a punishment for defying the will of the Creator. And in the end it says, "Thus shall it be until you return to the ground," or, as we might say, for one's whole life.

When a death occurs, when universal death is particularized and someone we know and care for dies, we are bereaved. This state of bereavement is greeted, as in any loss, with the natural emotional response of grief. While this grief varies in intensity due to many factors, it can be, and frequently is, powerful enough to engulf the bereaved, at least temporarily. As Edgar Jackson points out, it is important to know how grief works for it has been discovered to be a major source of stress to mind, body, and spirit, precipitating illness, crisis, and even suicide.[1] Certainly adult religious education can be a vehicle for promoting the understanding Jackson and others advocate and for experiencing what Granger Westberg describes as good grief.[2] The chart below visualizes the general lines along which grief will be treated in the text.

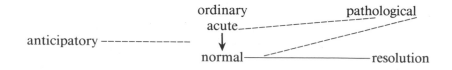

Ordinary Grief

To speak of grief as ordinary is not to negate the extraordinary emotional toll bereavement extracts but to distinguish it from the abnormal or pathological which will be discussed later. Ordinary grief can be described as normal or acute. The difference lies chiefly, but not solely, in the intensity, which is usually determined by a variety of factors.

Factors Affecting Grief

Group preparation of a comprehensive list of the factors which affect grief is an activity that can highlight the individuality of each person's grief. Such a listing would include: 1) nature and closeness of the relationship between deceased and bereaved, 2) circumstances of the death, 3) age, sex, status, birth order of the deceased, 4) coping skills of the bereaved, 5) religious and/or philosophical perspective of the bereaved, 6) physical and mental health of the bereaved, 7) financial status of the bereaved, 8) age and current family structure and degree of community support. A sensitivity to the effect on grief as these factors interact in a multitude of combinations is beneficial. It can aid the religious educator in understanding one's own experiences of grief. It can sensitize the educator to the limitations the grieving process imposes on the learner, and it can prevent the tendency to say another, "I know how you must feel."

Acute Grief

The period immediately following the death of someone very dear to us and/or a death which was sudden, senseless, or violent, is usually a time of acute grief. It is essentially a crisis period in which a person's resources are minimal or nonexistent.

According to Erich Lindemann's now classic study,[3] the picture of persons in acute grief is remarkably uniform. Common to all are the following symptoms: 1) various sensations of somatic distress which last from twenty to sixty minutes at a time; 2) an emotional strain which pulls the bereaved away from other people while drawing the energy into an intense preoccupation with the image and/or perceived presence of the deceased; 3) increasing and disproportionate displays of hostile reactions, particularly anger and irritability; 4) replacement of familiar patterns of conduct with frenzied but aimless activities alternating with listless, disinterested accomplishment of routine tasks.

The final symptom, and, perhaps the most devastating to the

bereaved person's hold on stability, is the strong, often over-whelming and debilitating sense of guilt. During this time the bereaved accuses himself of negligence, constantly reviews the circumstances prior to the death to pinpoint real or imagined failures for which he then berates himself. Often the religious educator can direct the griever to a deeper understanding of the meaning of divine forgiveness by learning to forgive oneself.

When the death is unexpected and results from a situation in which there was equal chance of dying or surviving, those who do survive are particularly prone to guilt feelings. Over time this has come to be called survivor's guilt. A role-playing activity in which someone portrays a person suffering from survivor's guilt could highlight the professional or paraprofessional help needed to set-tle this form of grieving into undistorted grief reaction.

Normal Grief

For the process of grief work to be successful, acute grief needs to be settled into normal, uncomplicated grief reaction. Once this is accomplished, the grieving process, more or less unaided, will follow a fairly identifiable three-phase pattern. Once a person passes the initial reaction of shock and disbelief (usually one to three days) the process of emancipation from the deceased be-gins. Initial denial is a protective mechanism that permits the newly bereaved time to regroup his resources as reality sets in and the feelings of loss become acute. During this phase, emotions are quite close to surface and come and go with little external provo-cation. There is crying for oneself, anger at the deceased for perceived desertion, loneliness, and reminiscences. The time an individual needs to remain in this stage of grieving varies enor-mously and is greatly determined by the factors discussed above. The greatest need at this time is to have a good listener. This need can be most effectively met by someone who has experienced a similar loss, hence the success of programs like Widow-to-Widow or Compassionate Friends.

Resolution of grief comes gradually and not without relapses. One learns to recognize the signs of abating sadness: memories of the deceased are being truer to the reality; revived interest in domestic, professional, social, and volunteer activities; lessened dependence on medication; and an overall adjustment to one's environment without the deceased.

Pathological Grief

Acute grief which is not resolved or normal grief which is delayed or which fails to progress toward resolution is likely to become pathological. Generally speaking, pathological grief does not differ in kind from ordinary grief but rather in duration and intensity. The bereaved can be described as being stuck in grief, fixated in one phase (e.g., denial), one aspect of a phase (e.g., anger) or lacking any externalization of grief.

Some of the symptoms that when *present in combination* indicate that grief is pathological are: 1) prolonged depression accompanied by feelings of worthlessness, bitter self-accusation and need for self-punishment; 2) escape into drugs, including excessive daytime medication, alcohol, casual sex; 3) worsening of symptoms of previous illness or acquiring symptoms previously exhibited by the deceased; 4) continuing to speak regularly of the deceased in the present tense; 5) obsessive clinging to objects, even nonfunctioning ones, which belonged to the deceased; 6) radical behavior changes, e.g., from overly religious to nonreligious, from cooperative to obstructionist behavior. This listing is not complete and is usually accompanied by an overall attitude in which life becomes frozen at the time of the death and which is marked by its lack of any real desire to go beyond the present. While the religious educator cannot be expected to provide the therapy frequently required by someone in pathological grief, he/she needs to recognize that little learning can take place for such a griever.

Anticipatory Grief

When any tragedy is expected or viewed within the realm of possible outcomes, anticipatory grief is triggered, perhaps as nature's way of helping one to handle the actual experience. From our first anticipated spanking to each anticipation of a loved one's death we have all known this form of grief. It is, in a sense, almost a constant in human life, especially for the older adult. As with other forms of grief, anticipatory grief is not a matter of choice, it is a given. The option is will it be functional or nonfunctional. Anticipatory grief is functional in that it provides the time for adjusting to the inevitable, for taking care of unfinished business, personal and legal, a time for, as Henri Nouwen says, a gentle letting go which allows one to break through the illusion of human immortality.[4]

However, it can happen that grieving begins too long before the anticipated event, or that one is led, by the circumstances, to expect a very brief time to elapse before the death. In these cases, anticipatory grief can become dysfunctional; the grieving is completed before the event or death, and the yet-to-be is treated as a *fait accompli*. This is equally damaging whether it prevents a person from attempting an examination which he has convinced himself he will fail or from remaining with a loved one through the final stages of dying. In some small measure this possibly may be a reason some physicians delay apprising a patient and/or family members of a terminal condition. It is not difficult for those in Christian religious education to relate the often paralyzing effect of anticipatory grief to the various accounts of the agony of Jesus in the Garden and/or the account of Peter's denial.

Role of Rituals

Human grieving is expressed through a variety of mourning rituals. Some of these are dictated by culture; many of these are inspired by faith, and all are intended to affirm the value of life. Edgar Jackson points out that rites and ceremonies at the time of death serve to verify beliefs for the grieving individual(s) and for the supporting community which needs to reassert its viability.[5]

At minimum, our culture demands that a death be acknowledged (in some formal way), that the body be disposed of (in some suitable manner), and that a period of mourning be observed. These minimal requirements are specified and enlarged upon by the status, class, ethnicity, and religion of the deceased and of the bereaved.

While major religions, and sometimes denominations or rites within a religion, differ on the specifications of the mourning rituals, all affirm in some way the spiritual nature of man and God's love for him. Religious rituals dictated by faith can often be the single greatest source of comfort in bereavement. Whatever form the religious rituals at death take they provide solace in that they affirm, for the believer, the right to grieve; and they do this in a manner that is familiar, community-based, and affirming of the transcendent. This is not to suggest that religious beliefs are a substitute for grieving but rather to assert that they can be viable instruments for its healthy expression.

Prayer in the time of grief is an acknowledgment that God does exist and that the bereaved can be comforted. William McCullough discusses four specific areas in which conflicts between beliefs and emotions can arise in persons of faith as the full impact of a death is realized.[6] Because of their nearly universal occurrence, these areas of loneliness, guilt, questioning, and the future need to be meditated on in light of one's faith. Resolution of grief demands that conflicts be faced so that the strength needed for healthy grieving is not diverted or used for repression.

Panels can be highly informative and nonthreatening means of death education. Two areas easily adapted to panel presentations are body disposal and religious rituals as death. A panel presentation by a funeral director, an officer of a Memorial Society and, if such exists in the community, representative(s) of alternate forms of body disposal can make people more conscious of their choices. It could even generate some intrafamilial discussion and preplanning. A panel of representatives from major religions or major variations within a religion can engender more knowledgeable participation in the services of one's own and other's religion. This is especially necessary in Judaic-Christian relations.

Grief Following a Suicide

There are a number of factors which complicate the ordinary grieving process after a death of a significant other by suicide. First of all, it has the effect of a sudden, unexpected death, despite the numerous clues which may have preceded it. A death by suicide gives the family and close friends no time to anticipate the death or what it will be like not to have the person around. There is a far greater guilt on the part of the bereaved because of the many "if only's" such an action evokes; and, often as not, there were opportunities missed or expectations that just could not be met although they were recognized. Grief is more likely to remain acute when the bereaved feels he might have been able to prevent the death.

Moreover, because of the ambivalent feelings in our culture about suicide, the bereaved often do not get the same kind of support which other grievers are given. The community, if not consciously, then unconsciously, tends to blame the survivors and, consequently restrains its support. Many still operate out of the framework that sane people just do not kill themselves; therefore, the deceased was either insane or in sin. This thinking translates into action or nonaction that says, "I don't want to be too involved with a family that has that kind of character in it." This attitude often prevents the funeral from being all that it could be and almost always causes the family to omit the needed gathering after the service to begin the journey to normal grief and its resolution. The key to successful mourning after a death by suicide is for all concerned, especially the community, to shift the focus from the suicidal nature of the death to the loss that the survivors are attempting to put into perspective.

Some efforts at suicide education could help in changing this focus. However, it is not easily done, as suicide touches a usually well-protected area in most people: that life is frequently unsatisfying because it never completely fulfills our deepest aspirations. Louis Evely holds that when a person ends his own life it is because he refuses to surrender to a life that is so far from true living.[7] Perhaps our inability to sympathetically view an act of self-destruction reflects more our love of self than our love of neighbor. The adult religious educator and all others who are in Christian ministry positions need to have examined their attitudes on suicide, not only to prevent any action which violates the Lord's command to judge not, but also to exemplify the command to comfort those who mourn.

While the depth of grief in one bereaved by a suicide is fairly evident to all, there are other cases in which, at first glance, the mourning seems out of proportion to the loss. This can be the case, for example, when an alcoholic husband dies or a partner from whom one is long divorced commits suicide. Somehow we find intense grieving inappropriate until we remember that even alcoholics have their good days and that young love is seldom totally eradicated from the heart's memory. The inconsolate old person who grieves his adult son's death and the young executive who becomes depressed over a neighboring teenager's loss to leukemia strike us as out of proportion. But a closer look brings to light that in both cases some of the depth of grief comes from disappointment. For the elderly parent it is not only his child's, but in some sense his own dreams that have been cut short. For the young executive it may be a mourning for personal disappointments, areas of unfulfillment, things that she knows it is too late to do or directions that cannot now be reversed.

Two quite disparate deaths are very often not recognized by the community despite the deep grief they can bring to those involved. One of these is the miscarriage or stillbirth of an expected child or grandchild. The other is the death of a pet. In both cases the grief occasioned is in proportion to degree of emotional investment the potential parent/grandparent or pet owner has made in the expectation or possession of the now absent source of happiness and joy.

End of Mourning

The behaviors, both internal and external, associated with mourning gradually decrease over time as the most painful phase ends. One feels less empty, less like crying at every reminder of the deceased, more like getting dressed up for a social event, more like initiating projects. One begins to nourish the memory of a shared life and can admit that although this new life was not consciously wished for, it, too, can be enjoyable. While the former relationship is now a memory, there often remains a familiar and very real sense of presence, sometimes more real than when both parties were earthbound.

Most people do not wish to be grief-bound despite Francis Kane's attempt to discredit the idea of one's being encouraged to "work through grief."[8] To desire the resolution of a painful state may be, as Kane indicates, an attempt to overcome our vulnerability, at least in the short run, but it is also a testimony of the human spirit to the value of life, though not in an absolute sense.

Learning about grief and mourning gives one a touchstone, a comfort that what one feels and does is normal. It reinforces our hope that, although life will truly never be the same again, bereavement can be survived. Sometimes the bereaved need our permission, so to speak, and encouragement, but not pushing, to reach a resolution of their grieving. Our understanding of the process can guide us in this role.

Finally, bereavement may lead one to a lesson he would, perhaps, have preferred left unlearned. Confronted with the death of a loved one, almost every believer asks, at least inwardly, why God allowed it at this time and/or in this manner. Believers seldom question the universality of death nor even the inevitability of a particular death. What they do struggle with and become angry about is the timing and/or the mode. What some come to is a belief that God is good but not interfering, is merciful but not all-powerful. In his best-selling book, *When Bad Things Happen to Good People,*[9] Harold Kushner described how the serious illness and death of their son brought him and his wife from the image of God as an all-powerful parent to one of God as loving but limited by our human condition. This image may not be as initially comforting as that of the wish-fulfilling God but, upon further acquaintance, we recognize it as the God of Jesus who suffered and who died.

Conclusion

Education in bereavement, grief, and mourning supplies the theory which when integrated with personal beliefs, feelings, and experiences provides a basic orientation to understanding the grieving process as well as the personal and societal responsibilities to the bereaved.

A means of aiding this integration as well as providing a social event is the well-planned series of book or movie reviews. Today's adults were, for the most part, raised when leisure reading was a value and a part of life. Movies and plays in theater, on television, or on videotape are probably one of the few common elements in today's society. The sharing of a book's story and some of its appealing incidents by a skilled reviewer followed by a question-answer or dicussion period often gives the insights that bring theory into focus. The same format can be used for movie reviews or even for plays, for example, American Playhouse offerings on educational television.

The growing accessibility of the video recorder opens another avenue of education. Episodes of weekly programs, movies, plays (or parts therof), documentaries, and other specials can be taped and shown to a small group (once) without violating the present interpretation of copyright law, provided no fee is charged. Because of the condensed time frame in most programs there is often a variety of illustrations of theory and practice in each one.

This or other means of vicarious experience can unify an otherwise diverse group and enable the religious educator to proceed sooner into content material of the lesson or series. In death education as in all religious education, the learner needs to be led to the understanding that when one is the most vulnerable one is also the most open to the healing power of faith.

DYING—DEATH—ETERNAL LIFE

Man has always lived knowing he would die. People have, in fact, lived with this knowledge quite well, taking death, for the most part, as a matter of course, praying usually only to be spared "a sudden and unprovided death."

This remains the attitude today in societies less influenced by science and technology than is the United States. With increasing speed, ever since the Industrial Revolution, we have become more and more fascinated by and dependent on technological advances. In doing so, we have unconsciously perhaps, transferred some areas of life from the realm of religion to the kingdom of science.

Implicit in this transfer is the hope that, if God and/or the rituals of religion cannot prevent universal death or a particular death, perhaps the discoveries of science and increased technology can. So here we are in a culture which suffers from the twin afflictions of anxiety about old age and death and boredom with life.[10]

Our society has been so shaped by frontierism—the American determination to conquer the frontier be it on land, in the air, or in space—that the ever-declining number of such frontiers has engendered a natural *ennui* and the habit of referring to fear of aging and of death. Somehow our language and our thinking has identified aging and death as two new frontiers to be conquered or, at least, averted for an indeterminate time.

All major institutions in our society cooperate in this interpretation of death. Most textbooks omit death from the human life cycle. We hide our elderly and our terminally ill in out-of-the-way institutions or wards. We take our children to amusement parks that offer death-defying rides, and we flick on our televisions to watch, "That's Incredible." We speak in euphemisms, such as 'she lost her mother' or 'Uncle Harry croaked.' Most sympathy cards rarely use the word dead, and it is next to impossible to find an appropriate card to send to a terminally ill friend or family member. Even religion with its frequently heavy emphasis on life after death has avoided death. There is life and there is death, and there is, we believe, life after death; however, no one of them should eclipse the other two.

In a recent survey[11] of fifteen hundred persons chosen to represent our nation demographically, 60 percent acknowledged distress about the shortness of life and fear about the pain of dying. Although at least 50 percent of the respondents feared death and were anxious about death related topics, less than 3 percent had discussed the topic recently with friends. Whatever the reason or combination of reasons the discussion of death and death anxieties is avoided and, therefore, adult religious education in this field can be a great service. The chart below visualizes the general lines along which dying will be treated in the text.

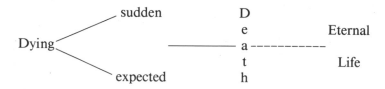

Process of Dying

In our century and in our culture we have witnessed and are, to a great extent, the product of a radical shift from the God of heaven and earth to the god of the machine. The abundance of studies conducted in the areas of dying and death, including clinical death, seem to be saying that we are no longer willing to leave dying and death to either of these exclusively. There is a growing conviction that God does not will individual deaths nor can machines insure individual lives. Consequently, we are reaffirming death as the natural conclusion of the human form of existence and we are returning the process of dying to our shared human experience.

To achieve this reorientation the adult religious educator needs a knowledge of contributions that aid our understanding of the dying process. Primarily these would include the work of Avery Weisman, Elizabeth Kubler-Ross, B. G. Glaser, A. L. Strauss and

Jeanne Quint, E. Pattison, and Cicely Saunders. For obvious reasons the ensuing discussion will be related to the expected death. This is the only situation that allows for the dying process; sudden, unexpected death catapults those remaining into the acute grieving phase of bereavement.

Fallacies About Dying

Borrowing from Avery Weisman and others,[12] one could construct a list of some fairly common fallacies about dying and dying persons. Probably the most often repeated is the least often true: An individual cannot conceive of his/her own death. Yet as symbol maker, man can conceptualize, albeit with some inaccuracies, anything for which he can create symbols. That we do not want to think of our own death is probably true; that we cannot possibly do so is false.

The second fallacy, heard from childhood, is that no one wants to die. Even a cursory look at our rising suicide rate and the growing right to die movement should put this untruth to rest. Likewise, a serious look at life belies the companion myth that there is a biologically rooted instinct for physical self-preservation. In the study on American attitudes referred to above, less than 10 percent agreed "that a person, seriously ill, should be kept alive by all possible means."[13]

Self-protection often causes one to cling to the half truths that since reconciliation with death is impossible, dying people really do not want to know what the future holds. Yet any scientifically conducted study always reveals that up to 89 percent of those asked would want to be informed of impending death. The question today is not *should* a person be told, but *when* and *how.* Contrary to common practice it is advocated that the dying person be told first and that he/she decide what and when to tell significant others, including any children involved.

A fifth fallacy that fear of death is the most natural and basic fear of man is, perhaps, in danger of becoming true of our culture. Research supports that at some level (conscious, fantasy, or subconscious) all persons, even the elderly and the very religious, fear death. This is healthy and complements an equally healthy love for life. However, when either life is absolutized as all good or death is separated and seen as all bad, society is polarized and greater values such as love of God and concern for neighbor are minimized and lesser cults and causes flourish.

Fear of death itself is paralyzing "because it seems to regard death as an embodiment of every form of human evil, failure, disgrace, disaster, and corruption."[14] It is, likewise, fundamentally opposed to our Christian faith which assures us that the life begun in Jesus' radiance will not be interrupted by biological death. Despite its clear relationship with death, religion and religious education have not been shown empirically to have made any significant difference in the way people face the inevitable. This may be due in varying degrees to our society's attitude toward death, to the superficiality of our faith, and to the success-achievement orientation of our lives.

Adult religious education can be structured to seriously address these factors and, hopefully, to make a difference. Listing the various misconceptions (fallacies) in true-false format can be a productive springboard exercise. It enables the educator to address areas which otherwise might not surface. If the listing is purposely nonexhaustive, the exercise can also allow participants to add some insights of their own. The device of the open-ended sentence seems ideally suited to highlight our cultural worship of success. The following or similar sentences can be used: "We in North America worship success. This can be seen clearly in _____ ." After allowing some time for this exercise using the increasing dyad approach described by Leon McKenzie in his *Adult Religious Education,*[15] the educator can illustrate how death can easily become in our minds the supreme enemy.

It is at this point that the traditional role of religious education comes sharply into focus. If our faith does not address this issue then our religion will truly be the opium of the people. It is the challenge of religious education to solve, at least for participating individuals, the conflict between the cultural view of death (and old age as well) as the enemy and the religious belief in eternal (not a future) life. As Louis Evely points out, there is only one preparation for death: "to be so alive that one can live forever." He urges us to have recourse to the gospel for an account of "human experience of inexhaustible richness" in which it is revealed to us "how we ought to live in order that our being will know a hereafter."[16] Authentic bible education is always, but particularly so in the New Testament, education for life which takes the sting out of death. Such an adult religious education will allow the last stage of adulthood (old age) to be, as Robert Havighurst described, "partly a test of one's previous personal religious growth and partly a challenge to the religious community to help people reach the end of earthly life with serenity and satisfaction."[17]

A Healthy Death

For the most part the focus of our educational efforts should not be with death which we can only assimilate but rather with the process of dying which we can enhance. A final fallacy narrows the dying person's only means of support to the attending physician whose chief role, once hope for recovery is no longer realistic, is to keep the patient pain free. Yet never more than near the end of physical life is one's need for emotional, psychological, and spiritual support greater. An understanding of death as a crisis allows one to aid the dying patient (and eventually oneself) to deal with the various parts of the dying process. It is within the framework of crisis intervention theory that E. Mansell Pattison analyzes the fears which the knowledge of one's dying evoke and suggests ways in which the dying person can be helped to resolve these part problems. When this resolution enhances self-esteem, dignity, and integrity one can be said to have a healthy death.[18] The seven fears discussed by Pattison are 1) fear of the unknown, 2) fear of loneliness, 3) fear of loss of family and friends, 4) fear of loss of body, 5) fear of loss of self-control, 6) fear of the loss of identity, and 7) fear of regression. Generally, Pattison sees these fears as sequentially faced. Through this crisis management, given supportive interest and guidance by others, the dying person may use his dwindling capacities to do what he can and to gracefully relinquish those tasks he can no longer accomplish.

This interplay is touchingly shown in the movie "Arthur." When the beloved manservant is dying, he says, "Arthur, I'm frightened." Acknowledging the fear, Arthur responds, "I know you're frightened, and I'm going to take care of you." The special attention and companionship he receives allows the servant to say to Arthur, "It's not so bad. You don't have to be so frightened about it." Any death education efforts need to be short on horror stories and long on examples of peaceful dying.

Stages of Dying

Dying peacefully, however, is often the end of a long process which has been studied by various persons interested in assisting the patient, attending physician(s), staff, family, and friends to understand better its dynamics. Without a doubt, the modern pioneer in this field is Elisabeth Kubler-Ross. Her seminars of the 1960s at the University of Chicago Billings Hospital and the presentation of her findings in the form of the five stages which terminally ill patients go through are fairly well known.[19] While Kubler-Ross emphasizes that the stages do not necessarily follow one another and are often overlapping and frequently repeated, it is difficult to learn about them except in a sequential manner. For purposes of instruction, her stages can be pictured as below.

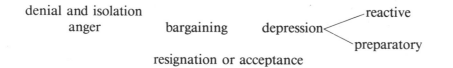

Usually a person's reaction to any life-changing announcement is denial. This reaction permits one time, often alone, to collect himself and gradually to take in the news. When the news is that of one's impending death, the period of denial allows one to absorb the seriousness of the situation and to gather strength for the time to follow.

In most cases denial lessens, frequently in response to mounting physical evidence. In its place come a variety of emotions, principally anger as the implications of the dawning truth become clearer. The object of this anger is the universality of death and/or at the timing of its occurrence. Since neither of these can be dealt with directly, the anger usually focuses on circumstances or on anyone who is, even remotely, involved in the life of the patient. Even God is not exempt from tirades or the complaining. If one can remember that helplessness is the source of much of the anger the behavior can be tolerated and, with empathy, dissipated.

Many persons acknowledge the seriousness of their condition by bargaining. This in a sense says that death is a distinct possibility but asks that it be delayed. Religious persons most frequently bargain with God; others most frequently with themselves or with hospital personnel. In a way, bargaining is modified denial of a truth that is hard to embrace.

Everyone who truly believes that his death is imminent will have times of depression, times of grieving over things which can, even now, no longer be done. This Kubler-Ross calls reactive depression. She also describes preparatory depression in which the patient mourns those things which, for him, never will be, for example, an awaited grandchild, a retirement, a dreamed-of trip. Like denial, this is a time alone in which one prepares to accept loss, this time the loss of everything and everyone he loves.

Sometimes depression levels out into a state of resignation, a giving up, almost in defeat. For others who have had the understanding person or persons who were willing to listen, the final stage is that of acceptance. This is a quiet, peaceful state marked by diminution of interests and seeming to need only the supportive presence of one person. Often it is the time when the family needs more support than the dying patient. Ruth Kopp, in *Encounter with Terminal Illness,*[20] offers some very concrete guidelines for responding within the context of Christian faith to the patient in the various stages as described by Kubler-Ross.

A lesser-known contribution to the understanding of the dying process by Kubler-Ross is her classification of language as threefold: straightforward, symbolic verbal, and symbolic nonverbal. The symbolic nonverbal attempts to communicate through art and acting-out are generally restricted to the very young, the retarded, or the senile. However, adults will often symbolically acknowledge the seriousness of their condition by the giving away of treasured objects, by letting subscriptions to favorite magazines lapse, or in other nonverbal ways. Symbolic verbal communication usually employs a rather obvious analogy for it (death), such as dreams of train wrecks, worries about nuclear destruction, premonitions about long, cold winters, or the sensation that a dark cloud hangs overhead. It is a middle ground in which denial is no longer possible and before which one is sure that it is safe to talk plainly about dying. When one can speak openly about one's dying then there is the opportunity which sudden unexpected death steals from us. This is the chance to finish unfinished business and to die in union with the Johannine Jesus who says, "It is finished," before he gives back the spirit to the Father. (John 19:30)

A session or sessions to increase familiarity with the Kubler-Ross material could be approached by creating with the group, on chalk or poster board, a triptych for each of the stages. This would include sample verbal and nonverbal behaviors and some appropriate responses. A model is given below in the chart for denial and isolation.

Stage: Denial and Isolation

Verbal Behaviors	Nonverbal Behaviors	Some Appropriate Responses
"There is a mistake. You have me mixed up with another patient."	Noncompliance to dietary restrictions and other health regulations.	Gently challenge the logic of the behavior.
"When do I get out? I need to get back to work; the office, etc."	"Shopping around"; undergoing more and more tests.	Suggest "we wait and see" how this medicine, this operation works out.
"You can cut it out, can't you?"	False cheerfulness, evasiveness.	Search for any area of acceptance (seriousness of the doctor's tone, amount of pain, etc.)
"You can't keep a good guy down. I'll be out of here before you can grow a beard."	Withdrawal and/or behavior changes to prove virility, stamina.	Don't push Be hopeful, but do not lie.

Attempt to include hope in some form in the appropriate response column for each stage.

Awareness of Dying

The work of Glaser, Strauss, and Quint provide a context in which fears of dying are or are not faced and stages of dying are experienced. Their observation of dying patients led to the construction of a typology of four awareness contexts. Essentially an awareness context is the knowledge each of the principals (patient, physician, family, staff, close friends) has about the patient's possible death plus the effect this information has on interaction with the patient.

The first context, which they label "closed awareness," is one in which the patient is unaware of his possible death while most of the other principals have varying degrees of knowledge of the diagnosis. Usually occurring in the early stages of the disease, this context supports a pose of false optimism. At first this is quite comfortable. However, as physical discomfort and medical procedures increase tension mounts and interaction is marked by increasing uneasiness.

As the patient becomes more familiar with his disease and with hospital procedures, he begins to doubt that his prognosis is as favorable as he has been led to believe, and the suspicion context becomes the framework for interaction. In this context the patient makes various efforts to obtain "the truth." This is a very uncomfortable time for all concerned and frequently results in the trivializing of interaction. Moreover, the strain is likely to cause others to reduce the frequency and the length of time spent with the patient.

If the situation persists long enough and if the patient has the physical and psychic energy, he will deduce from verbal and nonverbal cues sufficient information to confirm his suspicion. At this point the patient has three options: 1) he can give up, choose isolation and despair, and submit to a premature death; 2) he can deny the seriousness of his condition and move into the pretense context; or 3) he can attempt to talk about his impending death, his fears, and his anger, to some or all of the other principals. Glaser and Strauss call this latter option the "open awareness" context.

It is truly only within this context of openness to possible (or probable) death that one can deal with the various parts of the dying process and can reach the stage of acceptance. This does not mean, however, that this is necessarily a comfortable context for the principals. Rather it is draining; for facing death, one's own or that of someone with whom we are involved, requires a fairly high degree of stamina. It is important to note that the open awareness context can be arrived at suddenly or can gradually emerge as the dominant framework. Likewise it can be a temporary situation, reserved perhaps for interaction with only a few of the other principals; or once having been established it can characterize all (or almost all) the remaining time with all other principals. Dying is a part of the life given to us by God. As believers we make an effort to live for God; the open awareness context allows us to make an equivalent effort to die for God. This demands in death as it does in life that a person be permitted freedom of choice, even when his choices are inconvenient to us or are, in our opinion, mistakes.

An effective means to highlight the role of the awareness contexts on interaction with the dying patient is some form of the exercise "Visiting Hours." The scenes, which could be enacted for the entire group or done in several smaller groups, require a "patient" and four successive "visitors." Each visit occurs within a different awareness context, beginning with the patient's being in closed awareness. The sample dialog below reflects the effort to maintain mutual pretense. The role of the adult religious educator here is twofold: to assist the participants in recognizing the various contexts in which the dying interact with others and to lead them to compare these contexts with that which we see modeled by Jesus when his death was imminent.

DIALOGUE: MUTUAL PRETENSE CONTEXT

V = VISITOR; P = PATIENT.

V: You certainly are looking good today. Is that a new bed jacket? I don't remember your wearing it the last time I was here.

P: Yes, my daughter brought it. It's a great color—nice and cheery! These hospital robes are so ugly.

V: What have you been up to since last week?

P: I've been visiting the other patients. I met a really nice woman who's in a room at the end of the hall. She's just as bored as I am, but she's not as lucky as me. She's really very ill and has to stay in bed, poor thing. So I've been keeping her company.

V: That's great! Must make the time go by faster for you both. I can see you're champing at the bit to go home.

P: I can't understand why the doctor won't tell me when I'm going to be released. I'm obviously well enough—no more pains and I can get around just fine.

V: When was the last time you asked him?

P: Day before yesterday.

V: I guess doctors just don't like to make promises. But I'm sure he will be letting you know in the next day or so. Did John say anything more about your going to Florida on vacation?

P: We talked about it yesterday. I think I have almost got him convinced.

V: Well, in case you don't talk him into it, just remember that I would be more than willing to take his place and keep you company. I see that you finally got started reading *War and Peace*.

P: Oh, right! With all this time on my hands, I don't have an excuse for putting it off any longer.

V: By the way, if you are still planning to put rose bushes in front of the living room window I've found a terrific nursery over in _____. They have every kind of shrub you could think of. You'll have to remind me to take you there before you get ready to plant.

Oh, it's getting late; I've got to get back to the office. I'll drop by again in a few days. I'll call before I come in case you've been released. Take care.

Factors Affecting Dying

As with grieving, there are several factors which affect one's chances of dying a healthy or appropriate death. Among those which need to be recognized for each person are 1) the age of the dying patient, 2) the extent to which the person's goals have been achieved, 3) the self-image/self-esteem which the dying person has (whether or not it matches reality), 4) the responsibilities one's dying causes one to neglect or forfeit, 5) the amount of unfinished business and/or guilt which burden the dying patient, 6) economic circumstances, 7) time factors, 8) the depth of personal (and, often, family) faith, 9) the amount of psychosocial support one is given in one's dying, and, finally, 10) the degree of physical stamina and mental alertness the dying patient has at his command. With practice one becomes increasingly sensitive to the effect these and other factors have on all the interaction which occurs during the dying process.

The Hospice

For those who can operate consistently within the open-awareness context, the hospice movement provides an alternative to dying in a hospital. In all of its various forms, the hospice attempts to enhance the remaining days of life for terminally ill persons. The philosophy of the modern-day hospice movement, which can be traced to the work of England's Cicely Saunders, begins by redefining success from getting better to dying well. To allow a person to achieve this success, the hospice staff and patient's family cooperate to keep the patient pain-free and alert, to offer emotional and spiritual support, and to reduce the financial burden of dying. Because of the relative newness of the hospice movement and the corresponding ignorance of its theory and its actual operation within a given locality, this topic needs to be included in detail within any adult religious education program. Moreover, the position of the hospice that the care of the spirit is just as important as the care of the body makes it a welcome topic in today's highly technological world in which the socio-emotional and spiritual are nonaccountable components of care in most hospitals. For a study of the hospice movement, as well as other death related topics, as they exist in the state of Texas, Robert Connelly's work provides the most comprehensive work currently available.[21]

Death

The end of the dying process is called death. For believers death is also seen as the beginning of life in a new and better mode. Ladislaus Boros, a philosophical theologian, sees man as constantly striving to go beyond himself. Each time he does so, he leaves his former, less-mature self behind. In this context, death, even sudden death or suicide, becomes the final thrust forward through which we experience life no longer encumbered by temporal restrictions.[22]

Research, beginning with the interview and case-study type[23] but also including scientifically rigorous investigations,[24] regularly offers to modern man a comforting picture of the moment of death experience. Probably the word most consistently used to describe death is peaceful. Recalling how often we have prayed for a peaceful death, one can take solace in this research and focus one's energies on fully living a truly Christian life. According to Louis Evely, Jesus reveals that a life of faith and love is of itself eternal.[25] To bring this comforting message can be one of the most rewarding aspects of adult religious education.

Eternal Life

Adult religious education can address the twofold anxiety of mature persons who wish to face death. There are, on one hand, the fears which attend the knowledge that one is dying. These and other related areas have been addressed in the preceding pages. On the other hand, there is the confidence which belief in God and the promise, variously worded in the New Testament, of everlasting life can give. This is the point at which death education and spiritual education most profitably merge.

The Pauline epistles make sense only in the light of belief in the resurrection which we have already begun to experience through our baptism. The Fourth Gospel is replete with quotations in which the author has Jesus affirm that our faith in him is our entry into the eternal life of the Godhead. (See particularly John 5:24.) Matthew's account of the gospel builds to a minor climax just before the passion narrative. In this frequently quoted judgment scene (25:31-46) the only factor that seems to distinguish the sheep and the goats after death is the practice of love shown before death. Eternal life is clearly not something that begins after death. Rather it is that which makes it possible for man to transcend death. If the love of God is in you, and to the degree that it is in you, you are immortal.

It is this conviction which should allow adult Christians to confront the pervasive pessimism learned from daily frustrations. It is with the strength from this belief that while acknowledging the pain of death, we can be grateful for life and hopeful for the resurrection. Ignace Lepp says that he does not "think it can be disputed that man is more than his material body, that a part of him transcends the empirical order even in this life, that he is destined to survive the dissolution of the body."[26]

For most, the difficulty lies less in being convinced of life after death[27] than in being able to clarify the nature of this continued existence. This is an opportunity for the religious educator to lead believing adults to understand how our present idea of afterlife, in the majority of cases, reflects a syncretism of Hebrew thought regarding an earthly kingdom plus Platonic ideas of the world of spirits. Somehow this has produced the concept of a Christian kingdom in the next world in which the souls of the just continue to live, often while awaiting a bodily resurrection.

In our eagerness to describe that which eye has not seen nor ear
heard we have concretized metaphors and symbols and substitut-
ed them for hope. Granted, this is not an easy area for the
religious educator to approach, and care should be taken in
choosing the person to attempt it. However, its inclusion is necessary if the death education is to be in keeping with the maturity
level of adult learners. Adults need both continuity with the past
and critical involvement in the examination of their faith.

Conclusion

Death education fulfills the purpose of adult religious education as described by Leon McKenzie[28] when, because of it little
by little persons come to recognize normal grieving patterns in a
variety of circumstances, when they can talk about freely or be
comfortably quiet in its presence. Death education is successful
religious education when the participants draw more support
from their faith and when they live life more fully in an increasingly unselfish and loving way, knowing that this is the only way
to be assured of eternal life. Modern man does not need a new
ideology or a reformulation about life after death. He does need
to know that the most lasting comfort in the face of death, whether one's own or someone else's, is the realization that the love of
God was the guiding force in life and that, in this sense, his death
is the will of God allowing him to experience the fullness of that
relationship begun in this life.

NOTES

1. Edgar N. Jackson, "The Importance of Understanding Grief," in
Religion and Bereavement, eds. Austin H. Kutscher and Lillian G.
Kutscher (New York: Health Sciences Publishing Corporation, 1972), p.
3. See also David K. Switzer, *The Dynamics of Grief* (Nashville: Abingdon Press, 1970).

2. Granger E. Westberg, *Good Grief* (Philadelphia: Fortress Press,
1971), p. 11. See also Lily Pincus, *Death and the Family: The Importance of Mourning* (New York: Vintage Books, 1976).

3. Erich Lindemann, "Symptomotology and Management of Acute
Grief," in *Death and Identity,* ed. Robert Fulton (New York: John Wiley
and Sons, Inc., 1965), pp. 187-190.

4. Henri J. M. Nouwen and Walter J. Gaffney, *Aging: The Fulfillment of Life* (Garden City, N.Y.: Doubleday, 1974), p. 74. See also

Nouwen's account of his dealing with the death of his mother in Henri Nouwen, *In Memoriam* (Notre Dame, Ind.: Ave Maria Press, 1980).

5. Jackson, "The Importance of Understanding Grief," p. 4. See also Robert J. Kastenbaum, *Death, Society and Human Experience* (St. Louis: C. V. Mosby Company, 1981).

6. William B. McCullough, "Counsel from a Doctor Who Is a Minister," in *Religion and Bereavement,* ed. Austin H. Kutscher and Lillian G. Kutscher (New York: Health Sciences Publishing Corporation, 1972), p. 3. See also Harold S. Kushner, *When Bad Things Happen to Good People* (New York: Schocken Books, 1981).

7. Louis Evely, *In the Face of Death* (New York: Seabury Press, 1979), p. 99.

8. Francis Kane, "Therapeutic Death: Trivializing the Inevitable," *Commonweal* 109(February 24, 1984), p. 110. See also Sara and Richard Reichert, *In Wisdom and in Spirit: A Religious Education Program for Those Over Sixty-five* (New York: Paulist Press, 1976).

9. Harold S. Kushner, *When Bad Things Happen to Good People* (New York: Schocken Books, 1981).

10. Louis Evely, *In the Face of Death* (New York: Seabury Press, 1979), p. 82.

11. Roger D. Blackwell and W. Wayne Talarzyk, *American Attitudes toward Death and Funerals* (Columbus: Management Horizons, 1974), pp. 6-9, 14-15.

12. Avery Weisman, *On Dying and Denying: A Psychiatric Study of Terminality* (New York: Behavioral Publications, 1972), pp. 23-41; Glenn M. Vernon and William D. Payne, "Myth-Conceptions about Death," *Journal of Religion and Health* 12 (January, 1973), pp. 63-76. See also Elisabeth Kubler-Ross, *To Live until We Say Goodbye* (Englewood Cliffs, N.J.: Prentice-Hall, 1978).

13. Blackwell and Talarzyk, *American Attitudes toward Death and Funerals,* p. 17.

14. Weisman, *On Dying and Denying,* p. 16.

15. Leon McKenzie, *Adult Religious Education: The Twentieth Century Challenge* (Mystic, Conn.: Twenty-Third Publications, 1975).

16. Evely, *In the Face of Death,* pp. 5, 25, 49.

17. Robert J. Havighurst, "The Teaching of Religion," *Notre Dame Journal of Education* 5(Fall, 1974), p. 205. See also Monika K. Hellwig, *What Are They Saying about Death and Christian Hope?* (New York: Paulist Press, 1978).

18. E. Mansell Pattison, "Help in the Dying Process," *Voices* 5(Spring, 1969), pp. 6-14; reprinted in Sandra Galdieri Wilcox and Marilyn Sutton, *Understanding Death and Dying* (Sherman Oaks, Calif.: Alfred Publishing Company, Inc., 1981), pp. 90-99.

19. Elisabeth Kubler-Ross, *On Death and Dying* (New York: Macmillan, 1969), pp. 38-137.

20. Ruth Lewshenia, *Encounter with Terminal Illness* (Grand Rapids, Mich.: Zondervan, 1980).

21. Robert J. Connelly, *Last Rights: Death and Dying in Texas Law and Experience* (San Antonio: Corona Publishing Company, 1983), pp. 80-141, 156-164. See also Anne Manley, *The Hospice Alternative: A New Concept for Death and Dying* (New York: Basic Books, 1983).

22. Ladislaus Boros, *The Mystery of Death* (New York: Herder and Herder, 1965).

23. Raymond Moody, *Life after Life* (St. Simons Island, Ga.: Mockingbird Books, 1975) and Richard Kalish, "Experiences of Persons Reprieved from Death," in *Death and Bereavement,* ed. Austin H. Kutscher (Springfield, Ill.: Charles C. Thomas Publisher, 1969), pp. 84-96.

24. Michael Sabom, *Recollections of Death: A Medical Investigation* (New York: Harper & Row, 1982).

25. Evely, *In the Face of Death,* p. 52. On p. 89, Evely asks: "How can you believe in a future resurrection if you have never felt immediate resurrections? How can you believe that love is stronger than death if it has not made you alive?"

26. Ignace Lepp, *Death and Its Mysteries* (New York: Macmillan, 1968), p. 170.

27. Blackwell and Talarzyk, *American Attitudes,* p. 11, reports that less than 10 percent of those surveyed do not believe in an afterlife.

28. McKenzie, *Adult Religious Education,* p. 11.

Chapter 10

The Future of Adult Religious Education

NANCY T. FOLTZ

It is possible to examine the written word, observe the work of practitioners and suggest both trends and a trend schematic for the future. The trend schematic, Figure A represents a way of looking to the future. It offers a way of integrating basic contributions which are essential in the reconceptualizing process.

Several statements can be made about the schematic. First, adult religious education is being affected constantly by strong outside forces. John Elias suggests that: "A sound adult religious education must be based upon an understanding of the developmental stages of adulthood, the social contexts in which adults develop, and the processes of socialization in adult life."[1] If this is one of the many filters needed for a sound perspective of adult education then we have some corrective capability in our viewing for the future.

The second force at work in looking to the future is to incorporate the four content areas of: cognitive, affective, psychomotor, and lifestyle. James Michael Lee reminds religious educators that to concentrate on a single content area may present a disjointed view. The task of adult religious education is that of integration, of bringing into harmony what we think, feel, act, and live. These together with the three forces named by Elias offered a way to view the future.

A third dimension suggests observable trends which may guide our work. The five trends suggest the importance of recovering the historical dimension, continually examining the present and determining the trends. The five trends are: LEADERS: Exclusive-

Inclusive; 2. COMMUNITY: Dependent-Interdependent; 3. MOD-
ELS: Schooling Model-New Paradigms; 4. DISCIPLINES; Isolation-
Intergration, and; 5. COMMUNICATION: Hierarchy-Network.

Figure 1: A Trend Schematic

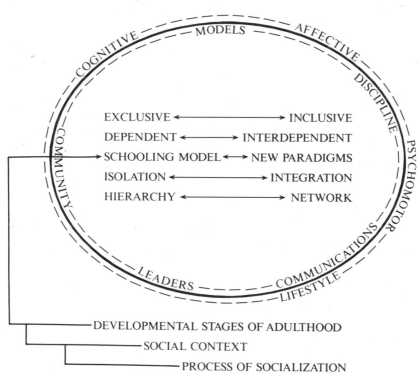

EXCLUSIVE ⟷ INCLUSIVE
DEPENDENT ⟷ INTERDEPENDENT
SCHOOLING MODEL ⟷ NEW PARADIGMS
ISOLATION ⟷ INTEGRATION
HIERARCHY ⟷ NETWORK

DEVELOPMENTAL STAGES OF ADULTHOOD
SOCIAL CONTEXT
PROCESS OF SOCIALIZATION

1. LEADERS: Exclusive-Inclusive

Who are the leaders in adult religious education? Who deter-
mines who the leaders are? If the leadership is a "learned behavioral skill which includes the ability to help others achieve their
potential as individuals and team members,"[2] then who are the
leaders? Are adult education leaders in churches and synagogues
identifying themselves or are they chosen by others? Who and
how are the professionals and the practitioners being informed,
introduced, encouraged to go beyond the present boundaries in
adult religious education?

Leaders are symbolic or operational or both. Symbolic leaders are those who hold positions of power and are expected to have influence due to their role. The symbolic leader is the chair of the department, the pastor or priest of the church, the rabbi of the synagogue, or the director of adult education. The operational leader helps to shape the learning environment, to assist the group to function, to be a decision maker, and to carry out the goals. Some leaders are both symbolic and operational.[3]

Adult religious education needs strong leaders. The professional and the practitioner, the symbolic and the operational leader are essential pieces when putting together this giant jigsaw puzzle of adult religious education. Putting the border pieces in first sometimes clarifies the framework. The reconstruction of adult religious education includes strong leaders. I suspect that many individuals engaged in the "doing" of adult religious education are unaware of their contribution. Persons who are teaching adults in seminaries, instructing leaders in children or youth ministry, individuals designing seminars, or counseling adults are all engaged in adult education. An exclusive rather than an inclusive naming of adult religious educators will narrow and dilute the potential strength of the work.

The "educated apologist" of early Christian times as discussed by Elias was to defend the Christian way of life and to interpret it for the educated persons.[4] Seminaries were established to educate the apologists. The apologist is still among us, known today as the adult religious educator. The role of the interpretation of the Christian life has not changed.

The most distinctive difference between early Christian times and the present is best described by Gabriel Moran in his account of the position of the professional in relation to the community. Moran compares the premodern and modern notion of professionalism: In the premodern form, he writes,

> the professional lived in the community and served it on a permanent basis. In the modern meaning there is a "professional community" which supplies individuals to local communities on a temporary basis. . . . In premodern times the professional accepted his/her knowledge as a grace to be shared: the community granted "license" to this person's challenging the community. In its modern form the professional's knowledge and status give a protected status: the community is not allowed to intrude.[5]

The adult religious educator as a leader of the community is just one of the problems to be addressed. The relation of the educator/leader within the community is equally significant. The leadership role becomes complicated by competing expectations from the community. A leader cannot assume more than a symbolic role in the beginning. The operational leadership role is born out of careful nuturing from within the community. A leader from one community may not enjoy the same privileges in challenging the community as will a leader from within.[6]

The identification of leaders, the recognition of their position and their challenging privileges within the community is a start in the reconceptualization of adult religious education.

Adult educators are experiencing new problems, such as job obsolescence. The average well-informed professional, according to S.S. Dubin, should spend 20 percent of work time learning about recent developments.[7]

The future calls for flexible leaders who demand from themselves constant study. Preparation for adult religious education work is never completed; it is a dynamic process. The well-informed professional will make a difference in our future.

We have a rich heritage with a central place in the religious community for the role of the apologist, the adult religious educator. The reality of job obsolescence can awaken us to new possibilities for adult religious education. Constant updating, rigorous study, and examination of theory and practice will serve us well in shaping the future. Flexible adult leaders who anticipate and who have the ability to see between the cracks, to envision and to look beyond the obvious are a part of the future.

What kind of adult educator do we need? John Elias calls for a vision of moral leadership that can be seen above all the details of programing. We need persons who, with faith and morality and skills to inspire, can lead others to transform their organizations into communities of understanding, love, and action.[8]

Competencies in any profession are necessary to set standards and to maintain levels of credibility. Perhaps the future will engage us in a closer look at the competencies needed for adult religious educators.

Malcolm Knowles' "Core Competency Diagnostic and Planning Guide" describes competency areas for adult educators as learning facilitator, designer and conductor of learning experiences, program developer, administrator, and consultant. Each area is evaluated from low awareness to a high expert level.[9]

Most adult educators are on their own to determine their level of competency. The core of knowledge needed is so diverse that no common standard exists. Looseness in setting standards for competency poses a threat to our future.

Merriam and Elias suggest,

> True professionals know not only what they are to do but are also aware of the principles and the reasons for so acting. Experience alone does not make a person a professional adult educator. The person must also be able to reflect deeply upon the experience he or she has had. In this manner the professional adult educator is more like the person of art who creatively combines experience and theory in the activity of teaching.[10]

Developing professionals who integrate theory and practice is a step in the right direction. Knowledge of our historical role as adult educators is another giant step. Acknowledging the need for both the professional and the practitioner is essential to future progress.

One danger looming over adult religious education is the possibility of becoming exclusive. Are adult religious educators theoreticians, practitioners, or both? Exclusiveness often brings a narrowness of vision, a provincialness that threatens to isolate professionals from the marketplace. Inclusiveness brings a diversity often hard to reconcile. Finding the unity within the diversity is the struggle. Often seeing the richness in the composition of adult religious educators is overlooked. There are territorial problems in either a too exclusive or a too inclusive naming of adult religious educators. For the future our perceptions, our naming of who we are is more likely to be enriched by an inclusive naming, a broadening, a bringing together of those who have a common vision.

The future is calling for moral leaders. Adult educators are needed who are more than symbolic members of a community. Operational leaders are needed who are practicing professionals. Leaders are being called to build credibility within the community, to defend and interpret the faith, to reflect and lead out of their knowledge and experience. The future is calling for leaders with vision.

Mortimer Adler suggests the need is for leaders who 1) manifest competence as learners, 2) who show interest in their own education, and 3) who are motivated to learn as they teach.[11] Adler goes on to describe the kind of leader needed as being resourceful and innovative.[12] Leaders are needed who understand the Socratic mode of teaching, by asking questions and by leading discussions.[13] These words about leaders conjure up images of openness and eagerness for new information and experiences. This kind of adult leader is able to view the learner as potential teacher.

Leadership is about motivating and knowing what encourages a person to learn. Leadership is more than being an able leader; it is also identifying and encouraging others. It is stepping aside to let someone else lead. P. Burgess studied the reasons adults learn. The 1,046 adults surveyed gave multiple reasons for their interest in learning, The study presented seven dominant factors that motivated the learners: (1) desire to know; (2) to reach a personal goal; (3) to reach a social goal; (4) to reach a religious goal; (5) to escape; (6) to take part in a social activity; and (7) to comply with formal requirements.[14] Examining motivational forces may help to guide educators. Often adults are not able to describe a program or an experience that will appeal to them. A more accurate assumption is that adults will recognize what they need when they see it offered.[15] Who would have guessed that in 1975 older adults who were slow to travel and hesitant to spend money and unsure about their learning potential would gravitate to the idea of elderhostels which involve travel, money, and learning. There is a need for educators with imagination and knowledge of what motivates adults.[16]

Spiritual directors are needed as leaders. What you know, feel, do, and live are all important. Leaders who strive to live the scriptures, who understand prayer as a way of life are in great demand. If the purpose of adult religious education is to assist persons to find meaning in life, then the leaders must understand what meaning in life is. Adults cannot "become spiritual companions unless their leaders are spiritual companions to them."[17] The spiritual life of leaders is most important.

What is effective leadership? The best way to understand a play is to read it. The best way to understand a game is to play it. So it is in adult religious education. The most effective leader is one who examines his/her lifestyle and motivation and tries to live it.[18]

Adult religious educators must assume a strong position of leadership. The leader role needs to be a facilitating role. Naming who adult religious educators are is not a simple task. Every sector of the society is growing in adult learning opportunities, more adults than ever before are gravitating toward them. Educators have the opportunity to lead rather than to follow this parade. It is time to risk for new learning.

At times our exclusive discriminating capabilities will serve us well and at other times we will need to use the inclusive role. Whatever the position, both are needed to define and redefine the leaders and the work of adult religious education.

2. COMMUNITY: Dependent—Interdependent

There would be no need for adult religious educators without the community. The place to serve, the locus for the work, the people are the community. Much can be learned from the community. Adult religious educators can examine the dependent and interdependent roles of the communities. As a child struggles to move from a dependent role in early life to interdependency, we applaud their growth and development. So it is with communities. There is a need to consciously encourage communities to grow, to become interdependent, to truly rely and depend on one another. Adult religious education needs others, other faiths, other communities to trust, to exchange ideas and experiences in order to be stimulated for the future.

Educators can examine the dependent and interdependent patterns existing in and within communities. Religious communities, like individuals, said Elias, have personalities, specific pecularities that make them different from one another. Communities, like leaders, do not live in isolation but are interdependent in their relationships. The singular notion to be retained is the need to examine how communities are dependent upon one another. It is this mutual reliance that will strengthen adult religious education.

Each community is unique; observe the acts of the community

and listen for the ways the community speaks. Through these observations adult educators can view the dependent and/or interdependent nature of the community. This is not a simple task. The workplace may differ, but the sense of community will exist. To know the community is first. Gabriel Moran reminded us of the centrality of community life when he wrote: "(Gandhi's and King's) great contribution was not to talk about ideal community. Their greatness was in being true to their personal roots and struggling with real limited communities."[19]

Identifying the reference groups, or communities, helps to narrow the scope. Elias says in this regard, "I recognize that all religious educators have as reference groups all three publics of academy, church or synagogue, and society. What is important to emphasize is the effects that these reference groups have on the stance and writings of religious educators."[20] Elias goes on to clarify the three publics. The academy includes "types of institutions of learning: seminaries for training ministers, departments of religion or theology in church related colleges or universities, divinity schools, departments of religion in private or state colleges and universities, and departments of education in colleges and universities."[21] The public of the church includes those identified with "catechesis, nurturing theories of religious education, religious socialization or enculturation."[22] The public of society refers to "the socio-economic realm, the realm of politics, and the realm of culture."[23] If our communities are a part of a learning society, and if the communities which are our reference groups can be identified, what other information can assist the educator in naming the community? Another way to raise the question is to ask how much information is enough?

Elias reminds us that there are six types of religious bodies, based on the type of community they serve. The communities range from the 1) neighborhood church or synagogue, 2) the metropolitan or regional body, 3) the downtown, 4) the special-purpose community defined by theology rather than geography, 5) The small-town organization, and 6) the open-country church or rural parish.[24] There are many ways to describe a community. *Reference groups* or the *types of communities* served are two of the ways. The future will offer increasingly sophisticated use of demographic studies, population trends, and mobility patterns for our transient society. Educators can use identifying procedures to describe communities in which they function.

Observing the acts of the community can be useful to the adult educator. How does the community gather? When the community comes together, what does it do? Elliot Dorff tells about the *havurot* groups in many synagogues which invite about "twenty people who learn together, celebrate together, mourn together, and simply socialize together on a whole variety of levels. . . . It gives people a sense of the living reality that Judiasm can be."[25] This description is similar to other small groups.

The lifestyle of a community reflects the incorporation of what the people think, feel, and do. Tasks, meetings, agendas are preparation for the act of doing. The act of "doing" is the living reality of what Judaism or Christianity can be. Whether the small groups are called *koinonia* or *havurot* matters not; what those communities "do" is of utmost importance.

Communities may be Leon McKenzie's "bringers of meaning to the world" or John Westerhoff's "stewards of God." Whatever the metaphor, it is a way of describing the community. This naming through the metaphor is a creative way of recovering the history of community life and projecting into the future. This clue of listening for the metaphor is another way of understanding the community. Perhaps adult religious educators can hear communities naming themselves.

Paying attention to the community's life is a way of acknowledging the worth of the community. "The insistence that religious educational theorizing attend to the communal is a call for respect; it is based upon the premise that there is a wisdom in historical religious communities of people, that their prereflective way of being together contains a revelation."[26]

Listening for the ways the community speaks is another vehicle to gain insight into the dependent and interdependent patterns of the community. Each community has spiritual power, a residue of strength which comes from the corporate body. Often the spiritual strength is diluted because our language is muddled.

Avery Dulles' research study examined five models of the church, or five ways of valuing the church. The orientations described the church as: 1) institution, 2) communion, 3) sacrament, 4) herald, and 5) servant.[27] Each of the five orientations used descriptive phrases which offered a value orientation to the term church. McKenzie stated that "when religious educators and adult learners discuss the church, it is probable they are misinterpreting one another's messages."[28] If the community is struggling to speak a common language, how far removed are we from direction setting for the future.

There is a language in each community; many times it is confusing and misleading. The value orientation also exists within the community. What we mean by certain words and how many interpretations we have are both important considerations. The future will find adult educators working to decode the language in and within communities.

Religious communities have the potential of being learning communities. C. Ellis Nelson suggests:

> We must begin to think in more radical terms of how the whole congregation can function as a learning community. I hope in the near future we can turn our attention to the dynamics of congregational life and explore the natural communication processes going on there, with a view to generating ways of making spiritual growth a more conscious goal of congregational living. . . . The issue is how to use the enormous spiritual power of the congregation's common life for enlightenment and service and not just for fellowship and guilt reduction.[29]

Often the spiritual life and power of the community has been a latent source of revitalization.

Imagine the effect on religious communities if energy was seriously directed to the spiritual needs of both the adult educator and the community. Acknowledging the spiritual dimension of the community and giving attention to the way congregations speak about and through their spiritual life are important cornerstones in our future. The inner life, the spiritual journey, the corporate response to the spiritual life can be powerful forces in shaping tomorrow.

Knowing how to balance life within a community, how to describe and how the community names itself, and how to observe the language are important directions for the future. There is wisdom in the educator who observes, participates, and gently directs. Knowing how and what to do is learned as one observes.

Being able to guide a community in their faith sharing, spiritual growing, and other acts demonstrating the living reality of Judaism or Christianity is the work for today and for tomorrow. Moving toward an interdependence pattern that encourages communities to depend upon one another is a positive directional trend.

Educators such as C. Ellis Nelson and John Westerhoff call our attention to the strong influences of the cultural milieu in the faith community. These influences should not be ignored for they are often more influential than the educational efforts of the congregation.[30] James Fowler clearly states that "if we regard the future of mankind as requiring our learning to live in an inclusive, global community, then, in a sense, radical monotheistic faith depicts from the form of our universal 'coming faith,'" which must transcend and transform our more parochial faith orientations."[31]

3. MODELS: Schooling Model-New Paradigms

There is no single effective way to model adult religious education. That is not to say that some ways are not preferable to others. The selecting of the model is based upon the theory, philosophy, and understanding of basic principles which guide adult religious education. Models are not selected at random but rather are carefully developed. A variety of models is needed in any one educational effort.

The schooling model, as John Westerhoff points out, is not synomonous with religious education. In many places it is strongly rejected by adults. If adults do not want the Sunday School then what new creative learning experiences can be offered? New paradigms are needed. The imagination, the creativity of the adult educator is needed to envision adults in active learning places doing their faith.

Old patterns for the new adult learner will not work. We need new paradigms, new patterns, new examples of how the adult can learn. Patricia Cross says, "The need, as I perceive it, is for conceptual models capable of accommodating new knowledge and shifting questions."[32]

A paradigm offers "an outstandingly clear or typical example."[33] A paradigm offers a place to study adult religious education in action, a place where theory and practice mesh. Paradigms are not necessarily easily transfered from one setting to another, so the development of the new paradigm and the examination of the model in action are both needed. For our purposes we will state briefly three paradigms which may be a part of tomorrow. Each has enjoyed a central place in the history of religious education. Each is valid and useful.

The first paradigm is the example of Jesus, who not only exemplified the model teacher but the model leader, educator, instructor. Examining Jesus in times of conflict, celebration, and envisioning for the future is an important piece in constructing the paradigm of model teacher. The ministry of Jesus was a ministry to adults. He preached and taught adults. Jesus challenged the adult faith and put difficult problems before his listeners. Jesus challenged adults to conversion. The examples Jesus used were from adult life. James Michael Lee says, "It is clear that the way of life of a Christian, a follower of Jesus, demanded an adult decision to live a life that was different in many ways from the lives of those outside the group."[34] Jesus as model teacher, leader, educator, instructor offers one historical biblical paradigm for adult religious educators.

Lee goes a step further and suggests the examination of Jesus the Christ as a performance-based educator: "Jesus the Christ exhibited a marked penchant for performance-based learning. . . . Jesus tells the apostles that their religious education ministry consists of, among other things, the following kinds of performances: preaching the gospel, healing the sick, cleansing lepers, casting out devils, and so forth."[35]

The second paradigm is the adult educator as storyteller. Westerhoff suggests that the challenge to the storyteller is threefold:

First we need to provide a learning environment which nurtures our God-given ability to dream, imagine, fantasize, create, and envision. Second, we need to find the means to sustain and transmit the biblical vision of God's SHALOM kingdom within a learning and witnessing community of faith. And last, we need to devise ways to help persons and the church to use God's vision as they prepare for and engage in Christian social action.[36]

The adult religious educator can be the storyteller. Through storytelling adult educators can encourage the envisioning and creativity called for in the future.

The third paradigm for instructing the adult educator is termed the laboratory for Christian living. This paradigm suggested by Lee is "a structured pedagogical situation in which a learner is enabled to existentially experiment with and actually perform one or another desired lifestyle activity or lifestyle behavior."[37] Lee's laboratory for Christian living contains seven major elements: 1) concrete here-and-how performance, 2) first-hand experience 3) holistic integration of all the major domains of human functioning, 5) experimentation, 6) ongoing performance-based validation of Christian lifestyle activities and behaviors, 7) intertwines theory and practice in a mutually expansive and corrective fashion.[38] For Lee, instruction for the educator is the laboratory for Christian living. Nelson suggests a center where professional and lay teachers can be trained. "The institutions sponsoring these centers should fund and support the work for at least twenty years so that there would be a culumative effect going beyond the personal interests of an individual professor."[39]

Adult religious educators need a commonality, a place for integration of theory and practice. The future can no longer sustain adult educators who literally "practice" on the faith community. The practice needs a new home. The schooling model, as Westerhoff warns, is not sufficient and certainly is not synonymous with the church education paradigm needed for tomorrow.[40]

Paradigms, outstanding examples of adult religious education in action, are needed. The central question in the search for excellence in developing adult educators is how and where can the educator test the theories in practice with supervision and guidance.

4. DISCIPLINES: Isolation-Integration

Adult religious education needs "integrators." An integrator is one who can bridge the gap between the professional and the practitioner. The integrator is willing to stretch both ways to embrace the knowledge of the professionals and the experience of the practitioner.

The integrator incorporates new disciplines, looks for the connecting bit of knowledge, searches for the bridge to new information. The role of the integrator is to converse with the researchers and the practitioners in order to bring communities together for open conversation about adult religious education.

To live in isolation from the political, economic, and social world is to deny the existence of major forces which impinge upon the shaping and the future of adult religious education.

The most critical problem that faces Christian education is that of self-understanding, says Harold Burgess.[41] This problem of self-understanding is due to a lack of theory. Christian education needs to know "how it is related to the cultural situation, to the church's life and thought, and to the educational process."[42] There are other questions, such as: "What is the role and function of religious education," "Does theology subsume religious education?" "Is the field of religious education to be subservient to practical theology?" Mary C. Boys states that neither theology or religious studies subsumes religious education, but both make different and necessary contributions.[43]

"Religious educationists tend to be characterized . . . by 'bias toward the practical' but also by their typical use of impressionistic evidence as a basis for selecting and evaluating religious education practices."[44] The use of such "soft" evidence, Burgess suggests, contributes to the lack of advancement of the field.

Confusion in a discipline, such as adult religious education is further evidenced in the lack of agreed upon philosophy and theory. What is it adult religious educators do, and what is their needed source of knowledge? Not only will the future require further thought on theory and philosophy but the field of adult religious education can be enriched by other disciplines such as anthropology, psychology, and sociology.

To isolate adult religious education would be foolish. As a discipline, religious education can benefit from numerous supporting disciplines. The ramifications of a future which draws knowledge and experience from numerous supporting disciplines are extensive.

Isolation in the sense of staking the territory marked adult religious education is important. Isolation for the purpose of determining the boundaries is valid and useful as a process. Integration can then be done. Maturation and change are as much a part of organizations and disciplines as they are of individuals. At this juncture in history, reconceptualizing is clarifying and staking the borders, it is also dipping into the deep wells of supporting disciplines that can refresh the work of adult religious education. The encouraging trend in adult religious education to integrate approaches and disciplines is illustrated in books such as *An Invitation to Religious Education, Generation to Generation,* and *Contemporary Approaches to Christian Education.*

In the first book Harold Burgess identifies four distinct approaches to religious education: "the traditional theological approach, the socio-cultural approach, the contemporary theological approach, and the social-science approach." John Westerhoff III and Gwen Neville, in *Generation to Generation,* yoke a socialization/enculturation view with a perspective from anthropology.[45] In *Contemporary Approaches to Christian Education* Jack Seymour presents a chart with five approaches: 1) religious instruction, 2) faith community, 3) spiritual development, 4) liberation, and 5) interpretation. In the first approach, religious instruction, James Michael Lee is discussed with his social science/religious instruction approach. John Westerhoff and the faith community with the supporting discipline of anthropology is a second contemporary approach. The spiritual development approach names James Fowler, with developmental psychology as his supporting discipline. The notion presented in Seymour's chart is the use of supporting disciplines.[46] Each has brought a freshness, a newness, a richness that has made us fuller and wiser. Whatever the future trend in relation to adult education, surely there will be an increasing use of strong supporting disciplines.

Integration of supporting disciplines is one direction. The implications of such integration for colleges, seminaries, synagogues, and local communities is quite another matter. Perhaps the courses listed for adult religious education will show the incorporation of a larger number of texts from other disciplines.

To join minds with colleagues from other professions is a challenge. Perhaps integration is most needed in the ecumenical community. Joining as equals in a society could mean conversation about the faith, about adult religious education practice, and about how our adult communities could be strengthened.

The questioning of theology and its place in religious education, the relying on other disciplines for knowledge, the interchange that can strengthen the work is a bright star in the future. Isolation for times of reconceptualizing is helpful and those times will serve us well. They are our professional times in the wilderness, they are times when we look at the model and struggle to integrate, to reconstruct, to readjust our perceptions, our images about adult religious education. Just as the wilderness time is needed so the time to get out into the villages and integrate, to call for the lifestyle examination, to question and constructively criticize the work is needed.

5. Communication: Hierarchy-Network

An organization may have a most important message; but if there is not a system of communication, a way to tell the story, an intentional delivery route, the message may be lost. We know from the advertising world that to tell the story only one way is not enough. Effective communication is central in the telling of the story.

Churches, synagogues, colleges and universities have systems that organize their bodies into ranks with some being subordinate to others. This connectional linking or hierarchy is the organizations' system of authority, the chain of command, the means of communication. Adult religious education will find an increasing need to use these complicated hierarchical patterns.

Another direction is the use of a matrix system where tasks are identified and the working force is periodically regrouped to accomplish the completion of the task. Although this notion of a matrix system may not exist in many religious bodies it is a possibility for the future.

The knowledge explosion and mass communication efforts of the last decade have forced educators to process large bodies of knowledge at accelerated speeds. One clue to the future about our networking in a highly technological age comes from John Naisbitt: "whenever new technology is introduced into society, there must be a counterbalancing human response—that is, HIGH TOUCH—or the technology is rejected. The more high tech, the more high touch."[47] With the high technological decade ahead, where the masses use the technology of the past decade, adult educators can be advised to remember the need for communication that includes high touch. That may mean more human hours personalizing what we have mass produced, making human the acts of the church, reintroducing one another in new ways. The use of high technology for mass communication is one trend; but the balancing need for the personal, the human touch, the meeting of individual need is another. Organizational structures must not forget people. This challenge will intensify as the technological era increases. The danger in both a hierarchy and a network as organizational communication patterns is the loss and neglect of human potential.

Both the hierarchy, which is a part of most organizational structures and the network which is both formal and informal are necessary in the future work of adult religious education. The question becomes whether we can be effective and intentionally human in the use of our internal structures of communication.

It is not possible to work in any discipline free from either hierarchical organization patterning or networking. Both are structurally glued to the foundation of adult religious education. Denominational hierarchy and networks exist; the challenge is to productively use them. It is impossible to ignore the structural patterns of an institution; it is far wiser to creatively use them.

Conclusion

The play, "Fiddler on the Roof" best epitomizes my thoughts for the future. First, *adult religious educators are called to "be" the tradition.* In the opening scene Tevye, the lead, looks to the Fiddler on the roof and says: "in our little village of Anatevka, you might say every one of us is a fiddler on the roof. You may ask, why do we stay up here if it's so dangerous? And how do we keep our balance? That I can tell you in a word . . . TRADITION."[48] From the adult religious educators' perspective, a sound way of viewing, a reconceptualizing of adult religious education will be done perched on the roof of tradition. Each educator lives in the historical light of their own tradition, whatever that is. To deny, or ignore the tradition is to rob the future of the richness and wealth of history. Tevye goes on to say, "Because of our traditions, everyone knows who he is and what God expects him to do."[49] Tradition without reflective, examination and reassessment is worthless. Educators must examine who they are and what God expects. The traditions must also be tested.

Second, *adult educators are the "questioners."* Tevye's three daughters were the questioners of "tradition," the ones who knew the tradition well but who dared to ask the new questions that tested the old traditions. When Tevye's daughter came to him asking permission to marry she challenged tradition. Tevye's words to his daughter Tzeitel were: "Unthinkable. This isn't the way it's done. This should never be changed."[50]

Many fear changes in adult religious education. To change the tradition, to dare to ask questions which shake the traditional timbers is frightening. Tevye gave the traditional response of resistance to change. But in hearing the argument, while he was defending the tradition with every ounce of passion, his heart was crying to find a way to change what had always been. Adult religious educators need to know the traditions and be willing to hear new questions, new ways of reconceptualizing, new ways of responding, new ways of being the tradition shapers.

Adult religious educators are change agents. The powerful scene at the end of the play comes after Tevye has succumbed to the changes in tradition, his daughters have selected their own mates, and now Tevye is left with a new set of questions. Not only has Tevye changed tradition in his life but that change has presented a new set of questions. The old answers no longer fit. One touching scene finds Tevye asking his wife: "Golda, do you love me?"[51] Once tradition was changed, the new questions could be asked. In changing the traditional pattern for marrying, Tevye was open to a new way of seeing old relationships. Adult religious education is about relationships. It is about understanding how we relate, work with, share the faith, and are in community with one another. At times tradition stands in the way of people and relationships. It blocks the doorway to the future. The task of adult religious education is assisting persons to find meaning in life, to establish relationship with God. Relationships rather than accomplishments must be held in creative tension, not ignoring one another or refusing to admit they both exist.

Adult religious educators are a transient people. When it came time for Tevye and his family to pack their cart and leave their beloved Anatevka, Tevye said: "Soon I'll be a stranger in a strange new place, searching for an old familiar face from Anate-vak."[52]

Adult religious educators are transient in ideas, in ways of viewing, often they are called to move on, to new places, new traditions, new ways of viewing.

Each adult educator has an Anatevak. In many ways we are each members of the cast, at one time or another. We are the fiddler, precariously perched, sounding out the familiar tunes. At other times we are Tevye, holding tenaciously to the traditions we love, trying hard not to change. We are from time to time Tzeitel, the one who asks the tough questions, the unimaginable, outrageous questions.

We are the potential change agents for the future—the ones who are slow to adapt to new changes, who lead ahead into the new future, who dream the dreams and build the castles for tomorrow. We each live in our own Anatevak, our world of work, and the forces that impinge upon us are not much different from the ones Tevye experienced. Adult religious educators are the traditionists, the questioners, the change agents, the transients who are looking for new places, new thoughts, new directions. Adult religious educators are the trend setters for the future, each one knowing who he or she is and what God expects each to do!

NOTES

1. John L. Elias, *The Foundations* and *Practice of Adult Religious Education* (Malabar, Fla.: Robert E. Krieger Publishing Company, 1982), p. 122. This comprehensive work sets the historical background and present interdisciplinary approach to adult religious education.

2. Jerry W. Robinson, Jr., and Roy A. Clifford, *Leadership Roles in Community Groups* (University of Illinois: North-Central Regional Extension Publication No. 36-3, 1975), p. 2.

3. Ibid., pp. 2-3.

4. Elias, *The Foundations and Practice of Adult Religious Education*, p. 122.

5. Gabriel Moran, "The Ambiguities of Professionalism," *PACE* 9 (1978), p. 2.

6. R. M. Stogdill, "Personal Factors Associated with Leadership: A Survey of the Literature," *Journal of Psychology* 25 (1948), pp. 37-71. Matthew B. Miles, *Learning to Work in Groups* (Columbia University, New York, 1959), p. 16.

7. J. L. George, and S. S. Dubin, *Continuing Education Needs of Natural Resource Managers and Scientists* (University Park, Pa.: Pennsylvania State University), 1972. K. Patricia Cross, *Adults As Learners* (Jossey-Bass Publishers, San Francisco, 1982), pp. 29-30.

8. Elias, *The Foundations and Practice of Adult Religious Education,* p. 202.

9. Malcolm Knowles, *The Adult Learner: A Neglected Species,* 2nd ed. (Houston: Gulf Publishing Company, 1978), pp. 204-212.

10. John L. Elias and Sharan Merriam, *Philosophical Foundations of Adult Education,* (Huntington, N.Y.: Robert E. Kreiger Publishing Company, 1980), p. 9.

11. Mortimer J. Adler, *The Paideia Proposal: An Educational Manifesto* (New York: Macmillan, 1982), pp. 58-59.

12. Ibid., p. 75.

13. Ibid., p. 29.

14. Quoted in Cross, *Adults As Learners,* pp. 89-90. See also P. Burgess, "Reasons for Adult Participation in Group Educational Activities," *Adult Education* 22 (1971), pp. 3-29.

15. Ibid., p. 148.

16. Ibid.

17. Morton T. Kelsey, *Companions on the Inner Way* (New York: Crossroad, 1984), pp. 194-195.

18. Adler, *The Paideia Proposal,* p. 31.

19. Gabriel Moran, *Interplay: A Theory of Religion and Education* (Winona, Minn.: Saint Mary's Press, 1982), p. 55.

20. John L. Elias, "Three Publics of Religious Education," *Religious Education* 77, no. 6 (November-December, 1982), p. 624.

21. Ibid., pp. 616-617.

22. Ibid., p. 620.

23. Ibid., p. 622.

24. Quoted in J. D. Anderson and E. E. Jones, *The Management of Ministry: Leadership, Purpose, Structure and Community* (San Francisco: Harper & Row), 1978.

25. Elliot N. Dorff, "Mission and Method in Jewish Education," *Religious Education* 79, no. 1 (Winter, 1984), p. 82.

26. Padraic O'Hare, "Contribution of Gabriel Moran," *Religious Education* 79, no. 1 (Winter, 1984), p. 113.

27. Avery Dulles, *Models of the Church* (New York: Doubleday Image Book, 1978), pp. 197-198.

28. Leon McKenzie, *The Religious Education of Adults* (Birmingham, Ala.: Religious Education Press, 1982), p. 235.

29. C. Ellis Nelson, "Toward the Year 2003," *Religious Education* 79, no. 1 (Winter, 1984), p. 107.

30. Quoted in Jack L. Seymour and Donald E. Miller, *Contemporary Approaches to Christian Education* (Nashville: Abingdon, 1982), p. 58.

31. James W. Fowler, *Stages of Faith* (San Francisco: Harper & Row, 1981), p. 23.

32. Cross, *Adults As Learners,* p. 249.

33. Webster's New Collegiate Dictionary, p. 823.

34. Elias, *The Foundations and Practice of Adult Religious Education,* p. 121.

35. Lee, *The Content of Religious Instruction,* pp. 616-617.

36. John H. Westerhoff III, *Tomorrow's Church* (Waco, Tex.: Word Books, 1976), p. 40.

37. Lee, *The Content of Religious Instruction,* p. 619.

38. Ibid., pp. 619-23.

39. C. Ellis Nelson, "Toward the Year 2003," *Religious Education* 79, no. 1 (Winter, 1984), p. 107.

40. John H. Westerhoff III, *A Colloquy on Christian Education* (Philadelphia: Pilgrim Press, 1972), p. 62.

41. Harold William Burgess, *An Invitation to Religious Education,* (Birmingham, Ala.: Religious Education Press, 1975), p. 9.

42. Ibid., p. 2.

43. Mary C. Boys, "The Role of Theology in Religious Education," *Horizons* 11, no. 1 (1984), pp. 61-85.

44. Burgess, *An Invitation to Religious Education,* p. 7; John H. Westerhoff III and Gwen Kennedy Neville, *Generation to Generation* (Philadelphia: Pilgrim Press, 1974), pp. 15-17.

45. Ibid., p. ix.

46. Seymour and Miller, *Contemporary Approaches to Christian Education,* pp. 11-34.

47. John Naisbitt, *Megatrends* (New York: Warner Books, 1982), pp. 39-53.

48. Joseph Stein, Jerry Bock, and Sheldon Harnick, "Fiddler on the Roof" (New York: Crown Publishers, 1964).

49. Ibid.

50. Ibid.

51. Ibid.

52. Ibid.

Biographical Profiles of Contributing Authors

Chapter 1: LEON MCKENZIE

Is a professor at Indiana University. His contributions to the fields of adult education and adult religious education are well known. Dr. McKenzie is a member of the Commission of Professors of Adult Education. Five of his recent books include: *The Religious Education of Adults* (1982); *Decision Making in Your Parish,* (1980), *Adult Education and the Burden of the Future* (1978), *Creative Learning for Adults* (1977), and *Adult Religious Education* (1976). Dr. McKenzie's writings are foundational to the understanding of adult religious education.

Chapter 2: NANCY T. FOLTZ

Is the Leadership Development Director for the Western Pennsylvania Conference of the United Methodist Church. Dr. Foltz has lectured at Wesley Theological Seminary, Iliff School of Theology and Pittsburgh Theological Seminary. She is the author of numerous articles, workbooks, and guidebooks. Dr. Foltz is a certified director of religious education and a diaconal minister in the United Methodist Church. Her doctorate comes from the University of Pittsburgh in Foundations of Education with an interdisciplinary specialization in adult education.

Chapter 3: SHARAN B. MERRIAM

Is an associate professor of Adult and Continuing Education at the College of Education, Northern Illinois University. Dr. Merriam has authored and co-authored several books, including *A*

Guide to Research for Educators and Trainers of Adults (1984), *Adult Education: Foundations of Practice* (1984), and *Philosophical Foundations of Adult Education,* (1980) which she co-authored with John L. Elias. She is a researcher, guest lecturer, and author of over twenty articles and book reviews. When Dr. Merriam was invited to participate in the project she suggested Trenton R. Ferro to share the writing project.

TRENTON R. FERRO has studied with Dr. Merriam. He is a doctoral candidate at Northern Illinois University. At present he is teaching at the center for Christian Growth and Lutheran High School in Rockford, Illinois. He has published articles such as "References to Apocrypha, Pseudoepigrapha, and Extrabiblical literature as Noted in the Outer Margins of the Nestle Aland Greek New Testament," *Concordia Theological Monthly* XXXIX (May, 1968). In chapter one of this book Leon McKenzie refers to Ferro's review article on *The Religious Education of Adults,* which appeared in *Adult Education Quarterly* 34, no. 3 (Spring, 1984), pp. 179-182.

Chapter 4: R. E. Y. WICKETT

Teaches at the University of Saskatchewan and holds a doctorate from Toronto. Dr. Wickett has numerous published works and has lectured in Sweden, Britain, United States, Canada, and at the Open University in Wales.

Chapter 5: LINDA JANE VOGEL

Is a professor at Westmar College in LeMars, Iowa. Dr. Vogel received her doctorate from the University of Iowa. She is a diaconal minister in the United Methodist Church. Her published books include *The Religious Education of Older Adults* (1984), and *Helping a Child Understand Death* (1975). Dr. Vogel has lectured at Claremont School of Theology and Scarritt College.

Chapter 6: R. MICHAEL HARTON

Is an associate professor of Administration and Adult Education at The Southern Baptist Theological Seminary in Louisville, Kentucky. He received his doctorate at Indiana University where he studied with Dr. Leon McKenzie. Dr. Harton has published numerous articles for denominational periodicals including

Adult Leadership, Mature Living, and *Church Administration.* The article, "How Adults Define Faith," was written with Dr. McKenzie. Dr. Harton was the co-recipient of the Association of Theological Schools grant to develop multimedia approaches to teaching social gerontology. He has been the recipient of awards through the Kentuckian Metroversity Consortium for innovative instructional development in adult education.

Chapter 7: Richard A. Hunt

Is a professor of psychology at Southern Methodist University. His doctorate was awarded by Texas Christian University. Dr. Hunt has authored and co-authored numerous books such as *Creative Marriage* (1979), *Affirming Sexuality in Christian Adulthood* (1982) and *Preparing for Christian Marriage* (1981) which was co-authored by Joan A. Hunt. Dr. Hunt is a consultant to Dallas Pastoral Counseling and Education Center.

Chapter 8: Neil R. Paylor

Is a producer of "Mister Rogers" television program and is in the private practice of pastoral counseling, primarily with clergy and their families. He received his doctorate at Harvard University. Dr. Paylor is lecturer at St. Vincent Seminary and Pittsburgh Theological Seminary and a consultant to Family Communication, Inc. Dr. Paylor has written articles such as "The Preacher Game," *Princeton Theological Review* (1981) and has co-authored a book with Barry Head, *Scenes from a Divorce* (1983).

Chapter 9: Mary Louise Mueller

Is professor at Incarnate Word College in San Antonio, Texas. Dr. Mueller was the first in the southwest to offer a college course for credit on Death and Dying, in the summer of 1973. Her doctorate comes from the University of Notre Dame. Her many published works include: *Regarding Religious Education* (1977), co-authored with Mary K. Cove, and "The Funeral Family and the Special Needs of Those Bereaved by Suicide." She presented a demonstration-lecture on "Death Education and Religious Education." Dr. Mueller's areas of specialization in teaching include Old and New Testament, Introduction to Religion, Death in America, and Teaching Religion.

Index of Names

Index of Subjects